The Politics of Truth and Other Untimely Essays

The Politics
of Truth
and Other
Untimely
Essays

The Crisis of Civic
Consciousness

Ellis Sandoz

University of Missouri Press
Columbia and London

Library of Congress Cataloging-in-Publication Data

Sandoz, Ellis, 1931–

    The politics of truth and other untimely essays : the crisis of
civic consciousness / Ellis Sandoz.

      p. cm.

    Includes index.

    ISBN 0-8262-1213-1 (alk. paper)

    1. Political science.   2. Civics.   3. Liberty.   I. Title.

JA66.S26   1999

320'.01'1—dc21   98-45474

                                                CIP

Designer: Stephanie Foley

Typesetter: Bookcomp, Inc.

Printer and binder: Thomson-Shore, Inc.

Typefaces: Diotima and Palatino

For those who know the price of liberty, especially my friends among the former Czech and Polish dissidents

It shall never be recorded of me that either tears or prayers could ever dissuade me from performing the duty of knight; and therefore, good Sancho, hold thy peace; for God, who hath inspired me to attempt this unseen and fearful adventure, will have an eye to my weal, and also to comfort thy sorrow.

I would have thee know, friend Sancho, that I was born, by the disposition of Heaven, in this age of iron, to renew in it that of gold. . . .

Miguel de Cervantes
(Thomas Shelton translation)

Contents

Preface

THE PRESENT VOLUME COLLECTS occasional pieces written during the decade of the 1990s. Half of them are new to this book, and half have appeared previously elsewhere, as detailed in the acknowledgments. Some of these essays (all revised for publication here) originated as informal talks, others as lectures, still others as technical studies with a full complement of annotation.

The central themes of these essays are those that have most concerned me over these several years, with an emphasis on the most dramatic events of the time: namely, the collapse of the Soviet Russian empire and the struggle toward independence and democracy of the formerly enslaved countries of east central Europe. At the center of the book are the abiding questions of the common elements of human nature, the dignity of personality shared by all human beings, and the mystery of their historical embodiment in such ethnic, political, and religious diversity; of whether liberty and the quest for justice in political regimes is a common possession of all human societies at least potentially, or forever reserved for a fortunate few; and of whether these universal aspirations can be better understood, and may even be more likely to be realized in time, after the long nightmare of our own oppressive century.

While each essay stands alone, the various key elements in the puzzle of identifying the preconditions of liberty for individuals, societies, and the institutional order are addressed. The root is found in the philosophical anthropology of classical philosophy and Christianity as the generic heritage of liberty that has emerged in Western constitutionalism. Specific attention is given to the terms of institutionalization in the American founding as the leading historical instance. The central place of the life of the mind and spirit is stressed, of philosophy and religion, in the emergence of modern democratic government. The place of a civic consciousness is emphasized, one formed concretely by a legal and constitutional tradition both safe-guarded and articulated by the common law and its spokesmen, the great jurists and lawyers of England and America. The specifics are illustrated in an essay on the greatest fifteenth-century political thinker, Sir John Fortescue, the chief justice and lord chancellor of England, and in another essay on higher law.

In essays more directly on the American founding, that singular alliance of philosophers, statesmen, and evangelists is explored as the force fostering communities of persons bound together by their faith and a derivative mutual regard of individual persons for one another on the basis of a shared vision of individual worth under God, of public good *(salus populi),* and of implied profound con-victions about the ineluctable limits of institutional claims. Religion and natural law, thus, are shown to texture the underlying bedrock of civic consciousness in our traditions. The fact powerfully argues both for the essential importance of a tension toward transcendent divine Being—"the Laws of Nature and Nature's God"—in a stable regime dedicated to liberty and for the potential adaptability of some Anglo-American solutions to widely different ethnic, social, and historical settings. Arguably, at least, we must believe that there are indeed generic implications of particular experiences because of the universality of human nature and of the aspirations of all people everywhere to liberty and justice, aspirations now heightened by decades-long experiences of crushing tyranny and mass murder. What are they and to what degree can they usefully be applied elsewhere? These are more than merely academic questions.

That the preservation of our fragile liberty under law is no easy thing is constantly considered. It is addressed in many ways, most directly by reflecting upon the deepening nihilist crisis of American society itself, a crisis of which Nietzsche was both supreme diag-nostician and evident proponent. The concluding essays are studies of the recovery of reality heroically conducted by Eric Voegelin, the most trenchant thinker of our century.

The drift of the argument throughout—and its novelty—is to em-phasize the civilizational depth of the modern constitutional politics that came to memorable fruition in the American founding, considered as the rearticulation of Western civilization. Its lineage is traced to distant antiquity in Israel and Hellas, as enriched by the experience and learning of medieval scholasticism and Reformation Christian civilization, and finally fashioned in the American Common Sense Enlightenment's remarkable celebration of the worth and dignity of every human being for whom, consequently, government based upon consent is an imperative. Such a coherent vision of personal and public order is thus rightly to be prized as a treasure beyond calculation. As our grim century ends, it sometimes seems to be more of a prize to those who have only aspired to it than to those who have been its principal historical beneficiaries. Government exists for man, not man for the government, whatever the contextual demands and institutional forms. Thus an invitation to adaptation, augmentation, and renewal of human beings' open quest for freedom under justice forms the persuasive gist of the volume, a hope to be nurtured through every means at our disposal.

Acknowledgments

S OME OF THE ESSAYS included herein have been published
in earlier versions, and I wish to thank the several copyright
holders for their kind permissions to reprint, as follows:

"The Politics of Poetry," in *Modern Age* 34 (fall 1991): 16–32, Copyright © 1991 Intercollegiate Studies Institute; "Religious Liberty and Religion in the American Founding Revisited," in *Religious Liberty in Western Thought*, ed. Noel B. Reynolds and W. Cole Durham Jr. (Atlanta: Scholars Press, 1996), 245–89, Copyright © 1996 Emory University; "Philosophical and Religious Dimensions of the American Founding," in *Intercollegiate Review* 30 (spring 1995): 7–21, Copyright © 1995 Intercollegiate Studies Institute; "The Crisis of Civic Consciousness: Nihilism and Political Science as Resistance," in *Political Science Reviewer* 25 (1996): 22–42, Copyright © 1996 Intercollegiate Studies Institute; "Voegelin's Philosophy of History and Human Affairs: The Systematic Importance of *Israel and Revelation*," in *Canadian Journal of Political Science* 31:1 (March 1998): 61–90, Copyright © 1998 Canadian Political Science Association; "The Politics of Truth," which appears here in English for the first time after publication as "Politika Pravky," *Žurnál UP* 26 (May 1995): 1–6, reprinted with the kind permission of Palacky University Olomouc.

Last, it is a pleasure to acknowledge with thanks the fine editorial guidance of Beverly Jarrett, director and editor-in-chief, and the expert copyediting and gentle persuasiveness of Jane Lago, managing editor, of the University of Missouri Press, in preparing the manuscript for publication.

The Politics of Truth and Other Untimely Essays

1

The Politics of Poetry

Where there is no vision, the people perish: but he that keepeth the law, happy is he.

—*Prov. 29:18*

Man shall not live by bread alone, but by every word that proceedeth out of the mouth of God.

—*Matt. 4:4; Deut. 8:3*

There are some things worth suffering for.

—*Jan Patočka*

L ET US BE DONE with muddling explanations for the collapse of socialism and admit that it fell because the poetry of personal liberty makes a sweeter, truer song. It is, indeed, spirit and not only bread that counts in the long run, and thus the future of socialism fades away into deserved oblivion. Better poetry wins the hearts of men—always did, always will. In other words, Dostoevsky and Solzhenitsyn have been proved right—or, at least half right. I leave it to others to recount details of the merely social, economic, military, and political dimensions of the collapse and what it portends. Allow me to reflect on the human essentials for a few pages.

I

There is no doubt that the Soviet and East Bloc economies were (and are) stagnant, verging on disintegration along with the political units composing these several countries, which are spinning out of control toward secession and independence propelled by highly complex centrifugal forces, with the Red Army being the not-so-loving tie that binds. (Unremarkably, it remains firmly in place in central and eastern Europe in November 1990, despite all the truly remarkable changes in that region since 1989, with a 10 percent reduction promised by 1991.)[1] The political economy of Marx-Lenin was wrong from the start, so why be surprised that it did not and does not work? With a focus on the USSR, the secular prospects appeared this way to the experts in the summer of 1989:

> The central, most fateful aspect of Soviet political life to-day is a desperate race between two parallel developments: the disintegration of the Soviet economy (and the concomitant delegitimation and demise of the current political regime) on the one hand and the emergence of new political structures enjoying popular support and consent on the other. If the former trend outpaces the latter, . . . this giant land . . . is likely to plunge into violent political chaos, a Lebanon-like war of all against all.[2]

In October 1990, another Sovietologist assessed the situation in equally dire accents. Dimitri Simes, of the Carnegie Endowment for International Peace, spoke of "the unprecedented specter of a nuclear superpower sliding into bloody chaos," of "the Soviet Union . . . falling into the abyss."[3]

To the poets and philosophers of politics, the surprise may only be that this system, with its defective ideological foundation and ethnic antagonisms, has lasted as long as it has, anchored in a palpable second reality, in a dreamworld in the mode of modern gnosticism.[4] Why didn't the experts know sooner? Reality, including the reality of human nature, is finally asserting itself—as the original craftsmen of the so-called containment policy more than forty years ago commonsensically assumed it would. What is collapsing before our eyes, then (with unforeseeable attendant horrors perhaps yet to come) is more than merely a command economy and an apolitical totalitarian regime. Rather, it is the socioeconomic superstructure of the Soviet imperial orthodoxy that, considered altogether, President Ronald Reagan in 1983 characterized as an Evil Empire. In recalling that episode, can any reader of Solzhenitsyn's *Gulag Archipelago*, for instance, or any otherwise informed person doubt that Reagan spoke truly? Why then the outrage at the time and the derision intermittently since then? Mikhail Gorbachev's tenure as Soviet leader began only in March 1985, and he did not gain real credibility with most observers as committed to genuine change until after concluding the Intermediate Nuclear Forces (INF) Treaty in December 1987 at his third summit with Reagan. Moreover, despite proclamations of glasnost and perestroika and a vociferous peace offensive, the nine-year Soviet intervention in Afghanistan actually concluded only in 1989. The most recent assessment of Gorbachev's policies by Solzhenitsyn, who is not one to be easily taken in, is worth quoting:

> What have five or six years of much-touted *perestroika* brought us? Pathetic reshuffling in the Central Committee. Slapping together an ugly, artificial electoral system with a view solely to the Communist Party's clinging to power. Slipshod, confused, indecisive laws. . . . Towering high above us is the granite monolith of the KGB, blocking our access to the future. . . . There is no longer any justification for this Cheka-KGB with its 70 years of bloody and malevolent history, nor does it have the right to exist.[5]

It will be observed that, even in 1990, Solzhenitsyn did not believe that recent reforms had washed the Soviet secret police organizations white as snow. Why, then, does *Evil Empire* so offend the intellectuals? Perhaps because things were better in 1983 than they had been under Stalin? Symptomatic of the modern and widely prevalent deformed consciousness fecund with second realities that still haunt mankind's dreamlike existence, the real answer to the question is: precisely because what Reagan said was true, of course!

With this paradox we near the heart of our subject. Jack F. Matlock Jr., the United States ambassador to the Soviet Union, in discussing Dostoevsky's "Grand Inquisitor," wrote as follows:

> The similarity of the basic features of the Grand Inquisitor's society with that created by twentieth-century totalitarian

political movements is overwhelming. Some of the most obvious features which come to mind are the following: the goal of creating a paradise ("The Kingdom of God") on earth; adoption of a "truth" as the exclusive possession of a few initiates (the ruling party elite); imposition of the adopted ideology on all, and forcible suppression of questioning, not only of the ideology itself but of the political decisions made in its name by the rulers; development of a quasi-religious cult around the founders and often around the current leaders of the political movement.

Dostoevsky would lead us to expect from this an eventual spiritual bankruptcy. And, in fact, evidence is rapidly accumulating that this process is far advanced in those societies where totalitarian political movements have been in power for an extended period of time. In the Soviet Union, for example, ideology has become a mere instrument of state policy, used to delude political innocents abroad who have not experienced it in practice and to provide an increasingly hollow pretext for the status quo at home, rather than a vital motivating and mobilizing force. [Such] observations on this point are paralleled by those of virtually all close observers of the current Soviet scene.

What strikes today's reader of *The Brothers Karamazov* with particular force [in 1979] is Dostoevsky's insight into the ultimate implications of some of the ideologies of his day long before these theories were applied in ruling societies. We must agree . . . that Dostoevsky's diagnosis of the dangers implicit in the socialism of his day can be read as prophetic of the human and spiritual devastation caused by the twentieth-century totalitarian regimes which trace their ideological lineage to that tradition.[6]

Now the *truth* and *truth sayers* of interest here, obviously, are not the pettifogging compilers of statistical tables, the analysts of economic indicators or of voter turnout and coattails in presidential elections, the weather forecasters, or the like. Rather they are those who provide us with moral, philosophical, and religious truth— hence often *Truth* with a capital *T* as opposed to *Lie* with a capital *L*. Their pronouncements have a strange resemblance to common sense, too. Such people tell the truth about the Emperor's New Clothes ("'But he has nothing on,' a little child cried out at last"), for instance; or they speak of Evil Empires where millions of human beings are treated like animals and some even butchered for fun, to the contemptuous indignation of intellectuals with ready access to the media who can't bear to hear a word said against the left, and most especially not a demonstrably *true* word. Such a word as this one, from 1973, for instance: "The ethnic-cultural diversity of mankind is still an important factor in spite of the assiduous work of social and cultural destruction perpetrated by empires in the course of their expansion and self-preservation. It is unimaginable that, for instance, a Soviet empire can permanently maintain itself in its present form against the ethnic cultures of the non-Russian people who make up more than 50 percent of its population."[7]

II

To speak of the politics of poetry is to notice, most obviously, the striking oddity that poets, novelists, and playwrights have suddenly come center stage from a persecuted underground existence as "dissidents" and assumed positions of power and authority in the newly liberated countries of central and eastern Europe: Premier Tadeusz Mazowiecki in Poland, President Václav Havel in Czechoslovakia, President Arpád Göncz in Hungary. Perhaps because of the palpable facts before us, this development makes as dramatic a statement as history affords of the spiritual bankruptcy of Marxism-Leninism and of Marxist intellectuals whose toadying propped up the communist regimes of the region. It is profoundly convincing evidence to everyone except for some holdout Western academics for whom the emperor must remain fully clad and who, therefore, continue to play the only game they know, the "para-Marxist buffoonery" derided by the distinguished French scholar Raymond Aron. The true artists and scholars were not taken in, but the entire philosophy department at Charles University in Prague was promptly sacked after the liberation as sycophants of the communist regime.

The central claim of the poets of politics is given by that prince among them, Aleksandr I. Solzhenitsyn, in a famous passage in *The First Circle:*

> But then why have literature at all? After all, the writer is a teacher of the people; surely that's what we've always understood? And a greater writer—forgive me, perhaps I shouldn't say this, I'll lower my voice—a greater writer is, so to speak, a

second government. That's why no regime anywhere has ever loved its great writers, only its minor ones.[8]

To be sure, there is the official authority vested in institutions and bureaucracies. But there is also the superior authority beyond party and all convention called nature and God that is accessible to humans by virtue of their very being. This abiding authority of mind, heart, and spirit confides the Truth before which all lesser truths must inexorably be judged. It is the solemn duty of the artist, scholar, philosopher, and every other truth sayer to serve this higher truth. Indeed, to do so is the very price of one's human vocation under God. Not to do so is to commit a blacker treason than can be done to any earthly power.[9] That there is a superintending reality that transcends temporal authority and is the source of justice and goodness in men and their institutions is an insight that breaks the crust of party dogma and dissolves the hold of even the most repressive state on its most abject victims—such as the *zeks* of the labor camps, those citizens reduced to mere human material for the building of socialism in the old Soviet phrase.

Here is the fountainhead for the core ideas of the "parallel *polis*" of the Czech and other dissidents that have crept from under the rubble in the curious events of 1989 and 1990 as the "second government" has been unveiled to become the official government. Václav Havel writes, in a related context, of the "ideological pseudo-reality" and of ideology itself as "that instrument of internal communication which assures the power structure of inner cohesion. . . . It is one of the pillars of the system's external stability. This pillar, however, is built on a very unstable foundation. It is built on lies. It works only as long as people are willing to live within the lie."[10] The revolution we are witnessing, like the American Revolution two centuries ago, claims the high ground of Justice and Truth for its own. President Havel drove home the points in his address to the U.S. Congress in February 1990 when he said:

> [W]e still don't know how to put morality ahead of politics, science and economics. We are still incapable of understanding that the only genuine backbone of all our actions, if they are to be moral, is responsibility.

Responsibility to something higher than my family, my country, my company, my success—responsibility to the order of being where all our actions are indelibly recorded and where and only where they will be properly judged.

The interpreter or mediator between us and this higher authority is what is traditionally referred to as human conscience. . . . If the hope of the world lies in human consciousness, then it is obvious that intellectuals cannot go on forever avoiding their share of responsibility for the world and hiding their distaste for politics under an alleged need to be independent. . . . I think that you Americans should understand this way of thinking. Wasn't it the best minds of your country, people you could call intellectuals, who wrote your famous Declaration of Independence, your bill of human rights and your Constitution and who, above all, took upon themselves practical responsibility for putting them into practice?. . . . They inspire us all; they inspire us despite the fact that they are over 200 years old. They inspire us to be citizens.

When Thomas Jefferson wrote that "governments are instituted among men, deriving their just powers from the consent of the governed," it was a simple and important act of the human spirit. What gave meaning to the act, however, was the fact that the author backed it up with his life. It was not just his words; it was his deeds as well.[11]

III

To a great degree, a recovery of Truth in the modes of classical philosophy and Christian faith undergirds the repudiation of Marxist socialism in eastern Europe. This is most evident in the role of the Roman Catholic Church in the rise of Solidarity in Poland, of course, where the counter to communism is plainly rooted in the refusal of the Poles to abandon the faith. Behind Walesa and Solidarity looms a long tradition of underground education, which includes Cracow's and Lublin's philosopher priest Karol Wojtyla, known to the world as Pope John Paul II, whose scholarly point of departure was a reworking of the phenomenology of Max Scheler, a starting point shared with Eric Voegelin. According to Lech Walesa, instead of force meeting countervailing force, the logic of action in Poland is infused by the consciousness of a third way: "the rebirth of man himself" through "conversion" with the promise not of violence but of hope for reconciliation and community.[12] The broad range of *samizdat* activities sustained a veritable underground "evening" or "flying" university through an elaborate network of clandestine communications and publications fostered by a number of individuals, notably George Soros, the millionaire financier and Hungarian expatriate in New York, and Roger Scruton, with his Jan Hus Foundation in London and (now) Brno. As the latter wrote: "In fact, the 'dissidents' were the only normal people in a society of Gadarene madness: the only ones who had refused to follow their countrymen to the trough of corruption into which the Party poured their daily feed. This is why they are now entrusted with the highest offices of State." This "catacomb culture" constituted the core of the parallel polis previously mentioned, with smuggled books and tapes, full-scale university programs and publishing endeavors, activities ranging from visits by a cosmopolitan stream of lecturers including Richard Rorty, Jacques Derrida (who was arrested and briefly detained), and Oxford's John Gray, to "translating forbidden authors like Hayek and Voegelin and . . . providing information to their colleagues in the West."[13]

Ivan Havel, the president's brother, and Martin Palouš of Civic Forum in personal conversations have attested to the influence on Czech leaders of Eric Voegelin's reconstitution of political theory on the basis of Greek and Christian philosophy and his analysis of modernity (especially in *The New Science of Politics* and the first volumes of *Order and History*), as well as F. A. Hayek's emphases on rule of law and personal initiative (especially in *The Road to Serfdom*). In Poland, whose philosophical richness is legendary, translations of Voegelin's, Hannah Arendt's, Leo Strauss's, and Michael Oakeshott's works in editions of up to 20,000 copies have been published. Leszek Kolakowski, who emigrated from Poland in 1968, has had 50,000 copies of his *Metaphysical Horror* published there. "His three-volume critique of Marxist thought, by exposing in detail its character as an anti-philosophy, is more responsible than any single agency save the economy for the demise of Marxism as a respectable theoretical discipline in Poland."[14] In Hungary there is the further dimension of a search for a new constitutional and legal foundation adapting the Anglo-American tradition of liberty and free government that is stunningly signaled by the establishment in 1989 of a Henry Bracton Society in the law school of the Eotvos Lorand University in

Budapest, by much work being done in English, and by conscious emulation of the U.S. Constitution in Hungary's own constitution-making process.

The classic and Christian analysis of reality that is patent in the writings of many of the members of the new eastern European leadership forms the foundation of the alternative to Marxism, even if their language still betrays residues of a cast of mind now essentially repudiated. The previously noticed opposition between pseudo reality and true reality, between Truth and Lie, is familiar to readers of Voegelin's political philosophy with debts to Plato's *Republic* (the "True Lie") and to Robert Musil's and Heimito von Doderer's novels ("Second Reality"). In Voegelin's powerful formulation, "True humanity requires true theology; the man with false theology is an untrue man. 'To be deceived or uninformed in the soul about true being *[peri ta onta]*' means that 'the lie itself *[hos alethos pseudos]*' has taken possession of the 'highest part of himself' and steeped it into 'ignorance of the soul.' "[15]

Solzhenitsyn's emphasis on the spiritual poverty of the West in his Harvard address, which so outraged his audience and much of American public opinion as he condemned atheistic humanism and pointed to the kindred forms of such reductionist views in American liberalism and in Marxism alike, included the reminder that

> in early democracies, as in American democracy at its birth, all individual human rights were granted on the ground that man is God's creature. That is, freedom was given to the individual conditionally, in the assumption of his constant religious responsibility. . . . Two hundred or even fifty years ago, it would have seemed quite impossible, in America, that an individual be granted boundless freedom with no purpose, simply for the satisfaction of his whims. . . . In the past decades, the legalistic selfishness of the Western approach to the world has reached its peak and the world has found itself in a harsh spiritual crisis and a political impasse. All the celebrated technological achievements of progress, including the conquest of outer space, do not redeem the twentieth century's moral poverty, which no one could have imagined even as late as the nineteenth century.[16]

These same themes are sounded by the leaders of the nations of central Europe. Thus, Václav Havel remarks:

We are going through a great departure from God which has no parallel in history. As far as I know, we are living in the middle of the first atheistic civilization. . . . I feel that this arrogant anthropocentrism of modern man, who is convinced he can know everything and bring everything under his control, is somewhere in the background of the present crisis. It seems to me that if the world is to change for the better it must start with a change in human consciousness, in the very humanness of modern man. . . . He must discover again, within himself, a deeper sense of responsibility toward the world, which means responsibility toward something higher than himself. . . . [O]nly through directing ourselves toward the moral and the spiritual, based on respect for some "extramundane" authority—for the order of nature or the universe, for a moral order and its suprapersonal origin, for the absolute—can we arrive at a state in which life on this earth is no longer threatened by some sort of "megasuicide" and becomes bearable, has, in other words, a genuinely human dimension. This direction, and this direction alone, can lead to the creation of social structures in which a person can once more be a person, a specific human personality.[17]

IV

As these statements show, a differentiated experience of reality has been recovered out of the suffering of the people of central and eastern Europe that restores to the contemporary world a sense of human dignity and personality largely eclipsed both in Marxism and in other prevailing currents of Western thought. "There are some things worth suffering for," the eminent Czech philosopher Jan Patočka affirmed in his valedictory *Political Testament*, and he paid with his life to prove it.[18] The recovery of the reality obscured by second realities undertaken by such leading modern thinkers as Voegelin and Solzhenitsyn is important in itself. That it can be discerned as structuring a renaissance of liberty and free government in sectors of the world where such things are culturally all but unknown may be epochal. To see Solzhenitsyn struggle in his latest reflections to find the "grass roots" of a feasible Russian "democracy" in the Russian tradition based expressly on theoretical foundations established by Plato and Aristotle is a little breathtaking:

Plato, and Aristotle after him, discerned and named three possible types of state systems. . . . It appears that nobody has actually created anything since then that has not fit this pattern;
it was merely augmented by constitutional forms. If we were to
disregard the form of complete lack of authority (anarchy, the
power of anyone who is strong over anyone who is weak) and
avoid being caught again in the trap of totalitarianism, which
was invented in the 20th century, we could not say that we have
much choice: Judging from the entire flow of modern times, we
will opt for democracy.[19]

If we hear the counsel of those most expert on the subject by virtue
of decades of subjection, the future of socialism in its authoritarian
guise is oblivion. Not Autonomous Man but, it is hoped, a creaturely
man who humbly bears the image and likeness of his Creator, one
who is a person potentially restored to the dignity of his being
under God, will form the paradigm for the new politics. Such a
man is no mere nodal point in the ensemble of social relations in
the Marxist reduction. Rather, he is the true man of philosophy and
revelation. Social structures must serve him, and not he them, in a
dominion of man over nature that harmonizes with Psalm 8 and is
not preoccupied with the material, consumer, and technological dimensions of existence—important though these unquestionably are
in the hierarchy of being. The political theory of the latest victims of
socialism aspires to communities formed by friendship and virtue so
as to ameliorate, if it cannot eliminate, the ruthless clash of interests,
factions, and parties characteristic of modern democratic politics and
its own fundamental crisis today. Both Havel and Solzhenitsyn, for
instance, tend to be small-republic men in somewhat the same sense
as were the anti-Federalists during the American founding and the
debate over ratification of the U.S. Constitution. Thus, Solzhenitsyn would dismember the USSR (a development he believes inevitable in any case) so as to leave a more cohesive Slavic core of
republics animated by a common ethnic foundation and faith. The
dehumanization of man has gone far enough, as has the idolatry
of materialism, communist or capitalist, from this perspective. So
the private property and free market economies that are urgently
sought as admittedly indispensable to genuine personal liberty and
independence must somehow be so moderated as to serve not only

individual well-being but the common good in fostering prosperity and happiness.

The great question, then, is not so much the future of socialism per se: *real socialism* (as the Czechs call it) of historical fact, the kind experienced in central and eastern Europe over recent anguished decades, may soon be as extinct as the dinosaur as a political system of choice—unless (as Solzhenitsyn says) men again fall into the totalitarian trap. The great question, one of utmost urgency we may say in a moment of great nobility of soul, is how to avoid utopianism and its traps while effectively seizing a unique opportunity to institutionalize liberty under law in moderate regimes in the only world we have. Perhaps it is not impossible for the politics of poetry once again to succeed—as it may truly be said to have done once upon a time when the Glorious Cause, against all odds, carried the day in the American Founding. And perhaps a right beginning can be found in the hard-won wisdom of Russia's leading political philosopher:

> Political life is by no means man's main style of life. . . . Politics should not swallow up the people's spiritual energies and creative leisure time. In addition to *rights*, man needs to protect his soul and liberate it for a life of wisdom and feeling. . . . The destruction of *souls* for three-quarters of a century is the most frightening thing.[20]

2

Liberty and Rule of Law in Czechoslovakia and East-Central Europe

THIS COMMENTARY MIGHT EASILY be titled "random thoughts stirred by a recent trip to Czechoslovakia," *or* "twenty-odd things that spring to mind about creating democratic free government in Czechoslovakia after forty-odd years of communist Russian tyranny."[1] Even the name of the country is contested, since it is now dubbed the Czech and Slovak Federative Republic (CSFR) in official parlance. And thereby hangs a tale, about which more anon. But I will begin in the middle, with thoughts arising after a year of planning for a conference on *The Federalist Papers* held in that country (May 26–June 2, 1991) and many conversations then and with experts at the University of Virginia subsequently on the prospects for constitutional government in the former Iron Curtain countries of central and eastern Europe. The uncontested premise of all these discussions, it may be stressed, is that some kind of modern democratic republic is the only acceptable option. Deliberation, therefore, revolves around *how to make the jump* from long-term authoritarian, totalitarian, and collectivist experience to solidly institutionalized free governments and market economies and how to do so expeditiously. It is a long way, indeed, from a splendid vision to a settled constitutional political order: examples of the former abound; the latter is seldom seen in the turbid flow of history.

1. Neutrality of lawyers. Perhaps because these reflections were first jotted down in the midst of a conference of lawyers, John

Marshall Scholars from the six countries of central and eastern Europe and from the Soviet Union, there arose the impression of technical rather than substantive interest in liberty and justice among these lawyers. This is, of course, not a observation about personal or moral shortcomings but about professional attitudes. Missing seemed to be a sense of the advocacy of liberty and justice of the kind palpable in the likes of Sir John Fortescue, Sir Edward Coke, James Otis, John Adams, Abraham Lincoln, or (in recent memory, for my money) Sen. Sam J. Ervin Jr., who reflected supreme devotion to the justice of the fundamental law or Constitution and to the liberty of the people as the substantive centers of their merely technical expertise. Admittedly, I have mentioned great names from half a millennium of common law and American constitutional history. Yet such a devotion to justice and truth is an essential and vocal part of the seismic events of central and eastern Europe since 1989, even if they have typically not been led by members of the legal profession there. The great moral stature of President Václav Havel of the CSFR (now of the Czech Republic), who was wonderfully characterized by Pavel Bratinka as "a cross between Saint Teresa and George Washington," might fittingly be appropriated as the stance of the entire leadership of the country—not least of all by the members of the legal profession who will draft, execute, and adjudicate the constitution and statutes of the new regime.

A distinguishing element here may well be the rather anomalous adversary system of courtroom trials held before an impartial judge and/or jury and the general public, pursued through every lawful means by rival prosecuting and defense attorneys who are, themselves, officers of the court both equally dedicated to seeing justice served, a proceeding premised on the innocence of the accused person, unless he can legally be proved beyond reasonable doubt to be guilty of specific violations of specified statutes. Such a pattern of administering justice is generally characteristic in Anglo-American litigation, and it also can be found, by way of analogy, in designed adversarial political institutional checking at all levels of American government. The assumptions and relationships premised here stand in significant contrast to those of the inquisitorial system followed in European civil law jurisdictions and in drastic contrast to those in communist states where arrest brings a presumption of guilt.

This large question cannot be explored here. But it can be noted that, while there is variation in different civil law jurisdictions, the role of the judge (typically one member of a multi-judge court, in contrast to the single-judge courts at common law, an institution whose concentration of power disturbs civil lawyers) in this system traditionally affords much leeway for him to become an active inquisitor in charge of the different phases of a trial, including the conduct of the inquiry into the guilt or innocence of the accused. Moreover, the degree to which an accused person benefits from the protection of any legal presumption of innocence varies considerably. Generally, there is today a tendency for the familiar impartiality of the judges and other protections of common law and American courts to be assimilated in the practice of civil law systems, a trend deserving encouragement.

Be that as it may, with constitutions now being drafted throughout the region, the Velvet Revolution, for better or for worse, is ineluctably being handed over to lawyers. They all would do well to follow the emblematic step of the Eotvos Lorand University's School of Law in Budapest and found a "Henry Bracton Society." Bracton's words against tyranny, nearly coeval with Magna Carta, and in favor of rule of law have rung true since the thirteenth century and sent King Charles I to the block for murder, arbitrary rule, and tyranny in the seventeenth century.

The much invoked "rule of law" to be emulated (if it is not to degenerate into a tired cliché and vacuous shibboleth) is not merely the observation of technical and procedural niceties by officials that— viewed as sovereign or incontestable command—has been used to send tyrannized subject peoples to the gulag or some other miserable fate with legal propriety for decades, even centuries. Rather, *rule of law* in Anglo-American tradition rightly signifies subservience of government to justice and personal liberty, which are to be protected against substantive as well as procedural infringement in the ordinary workings of public institutions and social practices.

The watchdog of this arena in British and especially in American practice (imperfectly, as with all human institutions) is the legal profession and especially an independent judiciary. It is simply unimaginable that free government can truly be secure and endure without some such analogous alliance between the legal profession and the executive and judicial officers of the new regimes now being shaped in Europe and Russia. And that, in turn, requires not a neutral but a committed legal profession. A legal profession accustomed to serving as institutionalized handmaidens of the KGB in effecting systematic oppression—observing the technical niceties on the way to the gulag—obviously is poor precedent for the new situation. A whole tradition of law and lawyering will have to be revamped, and the study of Bracton, Fortescue, and Coke and even the adoption of something along the lines of the American Bar Association's *Model Rules of Professional Conduct* suggest plausible starting points for reform. As with other fundamental reforms, this is easier said than done.

    2. Policy and constitutions. The Solonic axiom that the fundamental law of the constitution needs to be so terse and plain that a rider on horseback can read it as he passes is not being observed in the documents now under preparation. They are so long and so filled with policy matters as to resemble codes more than constitutions.[2] Policy might better be left as far as feasible to subsequent statutory enactment rather than be included in the constitution itself where the optional and essential become hopelessly entangled to the detriment of the latter. What Publius wrote regarding laws in general has application here (however egregiously abandoned since 1788 in America itself): "It will be of little avail to the people that the laws are made by men of their own choice, if the laws be so voluminous that they cannot be read, or so incoherent that they cannot be understood" *(Federalist No. 62).* The U.S. Constitution is about six thousand words long and can be read in twenty minutes; it has been amended twenty-seven times in two hundred years (including ten amendments ratified together in 1791 as the Bill of Rights); and it is the world's oldest existing constitution still in force. Its statement of essential principles can profitably be consulted by anybody wishing to find a way toward a durable and lasting rule of law securing liberty and dedicated to the happiness of the people. Of course, such knowledge is no panacea but merely a starting point for finding means to institutionalize free government; no wholesale transfers to vastly different societies and cultures ever are possible. Beautifully written constitutions did not foster liberty under Stalin or save Germany from Hitler; in and of themselves they are mere parchment barriers of little force and effectiveness in securing liberty and justice (see *Federalist No. 48* and *No. 73*).

3. Too little attention to fundamental principles. The converse of the above is a lack of clarity about what is fundamental and what peripheral in establishing free government. The study of *The Federalist Papers* is valuable as an antidote to this malady, as our conference in Chudobin Castle, near the famed city of Olomouc and its Palacky University in Moravia, emphasized.[3]

4. Constitution as fundamental law. A supremacy clause is a vital provision of any constitution if it is to be distinguished from ordinary legislation or from a code, and if effective government over an extended territory of semisovereign states is, in fact, to be established. In the American Constitution this clause reads: "This Constitution, and the Laws of the United States which shall be made in Pursuance thereof; and all Treaties made, or which shall be made, under the Authority of the United States, shall be the supreme Law of the Land; and the Judges in every State shall be bound thereby, any Thing in the Constitution or Laws of any State to the Contrary notwithstanding" (art. 6, sec. 2). It may be that the ethnic hostilities emerging between the Czechs and the Slovaks will make such a federal arrangement impossible and confederation the practicable arrangement. That these animosities cannot be underestimated is demonstrated by the dissolution of Yugoslavia through secession of Croatia and Slovenia and the onset of violence that could result in full-scale civil war as a fatal contagion of balkanization. Here the standard has to be that of the Federal Convention: to find the best constitution that the people will receive, not the best that can be devised. Free government rests upon the twin pillars of consent and justice with only the weak reed of persuasion to reconcile these hostile sisters. It is easy to forget that the ultimate foundation of all political entities sovereignly organized for action in history, whether they are free or not, is supplied by power. For instance, the American political order was consolidated through more than a decade of warfare—the Revolution and the Civil War—in addition to warfare with Spain and the conquest of the indigenous peoples across the continent in a sporadic centuries-long process.

5. Liberty and free government. A desire for liberty and rule of law seems to be the premise of all efforts in the region and ought to be seen as the foundation of constitution writing. The pattern of individual (and thereby enforceable) liberty, rather than social liberty, sets the tone for free government dependent upon the consent of the people for its laws, judgments, and rulers, thus necessitating systems of election and representation. These principles compose the other face of the coercive dimension of rule of law, which follows from the supremacy principle just mentioned. At the same time it must be stressed that free democratic government is essential to free market economies and that the latter will not automatically produce the former, as much Western opinion seems to assume. As one observer has remarked: "East Europe's 'Goulash communism'—ideology without rational economics—failed; but 'Goulash capitalism'—economic reform without democracy—is certain to fail too. . . . Democracy remains the most valuable of Western goods we have to offer."[4]

6. **Proemium(ia) or preamble(s).** In order formally to identify and elucidate the consensus of the community as to the goals and principles basic to the constitution, a persuasive introduction to the entire document or to the principal segments of it might be composed so that the foundation of government will be concisely and publicly formulated for the citizenry. This thereby might become an instructive standard and text for the inculcation of laws and liberties of the people that bind rulers and ruled alike in fundamental political matters. A preamble partly satisfying this suggestion is included in the draft CSFR Constitution, perhaps under inspiration from Plato's *Laws,* since classicists were involved in drafting the document.

7. **Limitations and empowerments.** A pattern of delegating powers and enumerating them by class so as to empower the government sufficiently to govern effectively should be balanced by limitations on the sphere of governmental authority vis-à-vis the people and the constituent states or political entities composing it. The essence of constitutionalism is (a) to limit the powers of government, and (b) to establish procedures sufficient to enforce those limits. The famous principle of separation of powers and the system of checks and balances woven into the U.S. Constitution and much admired in central and eastern Europe are designed to move from flimsy rhetorical and parchment barriers to a politically rooted self-equilibrating institutionalization of limited government as an "auxiliary" strategy—

where a virtuous citizenry that insists on accountability is present as a precondition—that has a chance of approximating just rule of law, the triumph in government of reason over ambitious desires for power, wealth, and vengeance (see *Federalist No. 51*). In other words, this "mechanism" is as effective as it is primarily because it is grounded in a thoroughly realistic theory of human nature shrewdly institutionalized with insightful attention to historical facts and social and cultural conditions.

But the quest for balance and reason is a matter of constant adjustment and compromise. Otherwise, public paralysis can become the price paid for undue solicitude of rival opinions impeding effective exercise of governmental power. Impotence and stalemate in the name of liberty replace the threat of despotism as the chief maladies to be avoided, as the history of the United States under the Articles of Confederation attests. And it must be said that much of the political literature of the region is reminiscent of American anti-Federalist rhetoric in evoking the republic of virtue and consensus. Unfortunately, this is a stance that cannot be maintained in the midst of highly factionalized heterogenous communities riven by profound religious and ethnic animosities. Moreover, if we are to believe *Federalist No. 10*, such unity of consensus is not even desirable if liberty is to be served and the inquisitorial spirit of repression and dogmatic enthusiasm avoided.[5] Interest-driven politics may not have to be the entire solution. But if there is to be something resembling free government it must be a significant part of any solution, and pitting interest and virtue against one another suggests a false dichotomy and distortion. Overreliance on rule by the pure of heart in a politics of angelic virtue evokes, as a matter of fact, an unattainable ideal, one suspiciously akin to the old ideals of Marxism-Leninism. The old perfectionism and absolutism of the theologians and ideologues will inevitably creep back in, ever ready to "solve" disorder through force and repression in the name of truth. A mix of virtue and interest is the only workable alternative in free government. Human beings must somehow have peace if they are to live, and, whether it is just or unjust, experience dictates that almost any peace is better than anarchy. The key drafters of the new constitution for the CSFR, such as Daniel Kroupa, M.P., who attended the *Federalist* conference in Chudobin, seem alert to these considerations.

8. Emergency powers. These should be eliminated wherever and whenever possible as too subject to abuse and too easy to invoke at the slightest provocation, especially in societies prone to embrace authoritarian rule from long, even immemorial practice.

9. Judicial power. It is doubtful whether any better balance against despotic rule can be devised than an independent judiciary exercising judicial review and generally practicing *stare decisis* on the basis of published decisions and opinions. This is the linchpin of rule of law in America—to the extent that it actually exists—where liberty and justice are the criteria of constitutional government. These institutions may well seem foreign to the region under consideration, but so too are liberty and rule of law, in the substantive (as opposed to procedural) meaning of the terms. If there is any comparably effective substitute for this institutional strategy for securing the supreme ends of personal liberty and good government, it is unknown to me.

10. Free press. With much of the communications media still in government hands, it becomes of pressing importance to accelerate the transition to free press and free communications. This is to allow the free flow of information as a vital end in itself and one essential means of educating populations inexperienced in self-government. Communication at all levels—mail, telephone, television, radio, newspapers—needs priority attention. Progress has been made in the Czech Republic, where nineteen independent radio stations had been licensed by the summer of 1991 and most of the large newspapers are privately owned and operated, although a state agency controls distribution. The Slovak Republic maintains tight controls on broadcasting, and the newspapers are officially owned. Telephone communication is not always reliable. Station licensing for radio and TV broadcasting is closely held by the government. But apart from the latent threat of censorship, this does not contrast greatly with the situation in other countries, including the United States, where regulation of the airwaves developed at the request of American broadcasters through enactment of the Radio Act of 1926 and the subsequent establishment of the Federal Communications Commission.

11. Politics of free government. After forty-two years of totalitarianism, and with only twenty years of republican experience (from 1918 until 1938, when Adolf Hitler and Western appeasement ended the experiment, with British Prime Minister Neville Chamberlain declaring that these are "people of whom we know nothing"), Czechoslovakia is today embarking for the first time in most people's memory on a course of political rule. This is unknown territory on both the micro and the macro levels. A subject population ruled by terror does not constitute a political people. Citizenship is an unknown role and a little-understood concept to the persons who compose these populations, and the Czechoslovakian population may be more advanced than others of the region in this respect. As is well known, the Soviet, Marxist-Leninist, communist totalitarian police state ruled through terror, repression, and unlimited brutality. This is an apolitical system of domination. Accordingly, politics itself has to be learned from the ground up. It must then become a habit of mind for the members of these now free societies—an enormous undertaking of highly uncertain outcome, even under the most favorable of circumstances.

Indeed, this may well be *the* greatest challenge facing the newly liberated countries of the region, since it involves nursing to life a democratic political culture and consciousness among the general run of the people themselves. In speaking of the Soviet mind-set, a prominent political writer for *Izvestia* bluntly stated: "The problem is that, after centuries of czarism and decades of communism, there is basically only slave's blood in our veins, so that we need to squeeze it all out. We need a complete transfusion."[6] In contrast, the ancient Hellenic standard of civic culture may be invoked through the words reported of Pericles:

> Our public men have, besides politics, their private affairs to attend to, and our ordinary citizens, though occupied with the pursuits of industry, are still fair judges of public matters; for, unlike any other nation, we regard him who takes no part in these duties not as unambitious but as useless. . . . Athenians are able to judge at all events [even] if we cannot originate, and instead of looking on discussion as a stumbling-block in the way of action, we think it an indispensable preliminary to any wise action at all.[7]

Citizens in free political regimes share in ruling and being ruled by turns, as Aristotle long ago taught in writing of the *politeia* or mixed regime (*Politics* III.2.7). In fact, an important component in learning politics and citizenship would be a systematic study of the fundamental classical texts on the subject, Aristotle's *Nicomachean Ethics* and *Politics*, the cornerstone of political culture in Western civilization.

Meanwhile, the old apolitical ideological rule of gnostic elites—who are charged with transforming man and the world into the Marxian Realm of Freedom through atrocity and brute force in which the populace is considered merely dehumanized material for the building of socialism—has to be attenuated in favor of something like the classical and Christian model of human beings, each of whom is equal before God and the law and possessed of ineradicable dignity and worth. The constitution—one cannot properly say reconstitution—of the theoretical foundations of rule of, by, and for the people looms as an enormous challenge, one not to be met in a day. The notion of a "free-man *[liber homo]*" of Magna Carta[8] and the Anglo-American common-law tradition more generally, as nurtured by religious and philosophical sources, which found expression eight centuries ago and lives into the present, may be ready to be stirred to life in central and eastern Europe. But this universal goal—if it truly is a universal goal—will require creation of a political culture and civic consciousness of responsible self-government in modes congenial with the historically nurtured unique customs and traditions of each of the countries and districts of these nations—a formidable task. Moderate politics with its compromises, imperfect justice, and partial truths can be defined on the basis of Winston Churchill's maxim: "Democracy is the worst form of government except for all the others."[9]

The starting point for such a process of developing a democratic political culture and consciousness will be the lowering of expectations. The way to salvation is a religious and not a political enterprise. This will be the hard lesson to learn after millennia of confusion of the two spheres from theological and ideological perspectives. The apocalyptical mentality of modernist gnostic apolitical rule has to be expunged and what J. L. Talmon termed "political messianism" abandoned.[10] Politics as a distinctively human affair aimed at happiness and justice in moderate regimes through self-government must replace it. Politics is everyman's affair in the In-Between realm of human striving. "Think small!" becomes an appropriate slogan. More elegantly, Thomas Jefferson's adage can be embraced: "That government is best which governs least."

Ultimate reality belongs to the realms of love, faith, hope, art, music, poetry, and speculative philosophy—activities of mind and spirit attainable in personal experience, communion, and expression and socially represented by extrapolitical institutional communities— but it inheres only peripherally in politics, messianic or otherwise. "My kingdom is not of this world" (John 18:36) is the Gospel's lodestar. It thereby becomes imperative—if there is to be any chance for peace, liberty, and rule of law—to wring fanaticism out of political process and supplant it with moderation, toleration, and civility. Socialistic total-rule suffers from, among other things, public overload and an attendant annihilation of private personal existence. At the same time, of course, justice, truth, and morality remain primary requisites for any political order, if it is to be fit for human habitation and conducive to happiness. We confront a central set of paradoxes structuring the human condition. No wholly satisfactory political resolution of them is possible. At the end of a century drenched in ideological fanaticism and now enjoying resurgent old-time religious fanaticism, the moderation of democratic liberalism takes on renewed appeal. The trouble with that, however, is a matter of fact: most of the people of the world are not secular-minded Anglo-American liberals. Rather, religion and ethnicity define their very being and way of life as enduring reality. Witness post-communist Yugoslavia!

The complexities cannot be exaggerated. To find adequate therapy for the indicated range of problems is a tall order, indeed, for a region overlaid with multiple kinds of patriarchal rule, low self-esteem on the part of individuals apart from the collective, and fiercely divided by tribal and ideological hatreds that are taken for—and cynically manipulated as—the substance of patriotism and life in this world. It is not inevitably necessary, however, to hate the man who disagrees with you and to kill or imprison the opposition because of their political incorrectness—to use the liberal totalitarian rhetoric of American academe's own latest fanatics. This is to inculcate the counsel of moderation and the essence of a sentiment wonderfully stated by the "judicious" Richard Hooker in facing fanatics of an earlier age: "Think ye are men, deem it not impossible for you to err!"[11] If democracy is to have any chance at all, infallible rule must give way to the politics of imperfection—of truth, justice, peace, and liberty to be sure, but only so far as these great goods can be attained in the In-Between existence of an imperfect world by fallible and sinful human beings none of whom possesses a monopoly on truth. This (or so, at least, it seems to me) is a flat requirement—if decent democratic regimes are to take root amid the desolation left by the Communists throughout this part of the world. Since, however, it is so much easier, satisfying, and historically ingrained to loathe rather than civilly to tolerate those who embrace evident error in a universe of Manichaean black-and-white convictions, the prospects for the success of political moderation are gloomy at best.

12. American advice. Because of the pervasiveness of gnostic-ideological thought and the attendant deformation of reality in the contemporary world, it has been often and rightly observed that American academics tend to be left-leaning. Thus, the American (and the British) universities remain, along with Red China, among the chief remaining redoubts of true believers in the Marxist-Leninist apocalypse of collectivist man, economics, and society abandoned elsewhere by civilized humankind as flawed and failed. Advice coming from these sources must, therefore, be received with this skewed perspective in mind and *cum grano salis*. It is with regret that I mention this caveat about what may be boringly obvious. In the words of one writer, the American college "campus culture is so far behind in the battle for hearts and minds that one wonders why the dominant culture [in the country] worries. The left may have the power on campuses, but so what? The campus has merely isolated the left and allowed it to wallow in irrelevance." Or as the Czechoslovak Finance (and later Prime) Minister Václav Klaus bluntly put it: "We are not interested in the market socialism dreams of the leftist liberal economists on the East Coast of the United States. Right now, the main obstacle to our development is ideological infiltration from the West!"[12]

13. Decommunization. While it is well recognized among the new leaders in Czechoslovakia and elsewhere that the rot in society associated with four decades of communist oppression is far from remedied, and that enclaves of the old order still persist, no systematic decommunization ("lustration") effort has been undertaken comparable to the de-Nazification of Germany after 1945. The Trojan Horse threat remains, and the resolve to deal with this problem seems not yet to have been found. The matter is perplexing and complex, with the CSFR ministries of Interior and Defense still largely in the old hands, and the universities' sociology, political science, and law faculties now staffed by tenured professors who formerly worked for the KGB—a grotesque situation. Tenure is a great democratic institution, as all academics know.

Consider also the celebrated "pink tank" episode in Prague of April and May 1991. A remaining Soviet memorial to the liberation of the city during World War II in the form of a tank was painted pink and "crowned by a giant papier-maché middle finger" by a Charles University art student named David Černy—to symbolize the fading of red rule in his country and his low opinion of that era. He was arrested under the infamous article 202 of the criminal code for "hooliganism" and "disturbing the peace" (*Vytrznictvi* in Czech)—the very law used to put Václav Havel in prison just a few short months before the Velvet Revolution in 1989. Some thirty deputies from the Federal Assembly, after the tank had been painted military green again by the police, subsequently demonstrated solidarity with Černy's gesture. To the cheers of a large crowd they themselves repainted the tank with fresh coats of pink paint, although without replacing the original's most startling artistic adornment. The Czech ambassador to the USSR was given a stiff reprimand in Moscow; a mortified deputy foreign minister of the CSFR (Zdenik Matejka) apologized to the Soviet ambassador in Prague; and Federal Assembly Chairman Alexander Dubček publicly slammed the deputies' actions and scurried off to Moscow, where he televised his nation's abject apology to the Soviet people. When I viewed the still very pink tank on June 1, a large banner carrying the words *Trojan Horse* was draped from the turret. Thus, the Velvet Revolution gained a new comic symbol, a force called the "Pink Coalition" emerged in Czech politics, and the student was extricated from his trouble. The old cadres still wield substantial influence, obviously. President Havel himself nervously fretted over the incidents, fearing a breach with the USSR, and publicly scolding the parliamentarians for breaking the law and invoking parliamentary immunity while doing so. A student newspaper reporter, on the other hand, was sure that this "was the best action since the revolution."[13]

With all Soviet forces now out of the country, more energetic steps to decommunize would seem to be in order. But the pink tank and the reactions to it suggest the touchiness of the situation. Decommunization would logically extend to preventing the old *Nomenklatura* from enjoying windfall benefits from the transition to private ownership of property (as is now occurring) and from, thereby, also establishing a secure and central new power base in the emerging social and economic order. Such revolutionary leaders as Pavel Bratinka, M.P., are taking a strong stance on this matter. As long as more than one hundred thousand Soviet troops remain in the former East Germany, the problem is particularly delicate. Such cancerous pollution underlying the democratic surface of these societies jeopardizes reform.

14. Secret police and internal spying. The residual ubiquity of informants (an estimated 140,000 in preliberation Czechoslovakia) and of the supposedly disbanded secret police is a problem that remains to some degree long months after the Velvet Revolution of November 17–December 29, 1989. A free society with personal liberty and responsible government cannot be thus maintained. This is to play the preliberation game of *als ob* all over again under potentially lethal conditions.

15. Politics of civility. The generic problem of supplanting total-itarian tyranny with a political regime might benefit from a good dose of Lockean liberalism, as previously hinted, especially with respect to the noisiest and most notorious problems of the region, that is, the ethnic hostilities and rivalries. The purposeful cultivation of toleration as policy has helped to dampen (but not eliminate) bigotry and bloodletting in western Europe and America. It is in-dubitably a very great good that black and white people, Catholics and Protestants, Christians and Jews, are not obliged to hate one another as part of state policy or social duty. It was a sound and serviceable insertion into the American Constitution of 1787 that "no religious Test shall ever be required as a Qualification to any Office or public Trust under the United States" (art. 6, sec. 3). If these solutions are far from perfect—and the English-Irish terror of Northern Ireland and ethnic politics in America plainly testify that they are imperfect—they nonetheless help to establish benchmarks that men and women of reason and goodwill can refer to in the face of irrational alternatives. Some such means may warrant consideration before the next surge of separatism and balkanization sweeps the quest for free government back into the dark ages from whence millions of worthy human beings are just now emerging. To think that Russia with Boris Yeltsin in June 1991 conducted its first election in one thousand years is, at once, breathtaking and depressing. Every means must be sought to blunt ancient animosities, so as to avoid a collapse into despotism by the fragile free governments struggling into existence.

Even when every allowance is made for the enormous property confiscations, savage persecutions, and terrible suffering of churches and clerics under the Communists, Pope John Paul II's passionate homilies in Poland in June against separation of church and state—even urging a merger of the institutions—can only be deplored. This stance may be understandable counsel intended to keep peace and fortify the vigor of faith by extending the "solidarity perspective" against the twin evils of "the Communism of the Soviet Union and the secularism of Western Europe."[14] Justice and truth must be served here as elsewhere, to be sure. But this is counsel certain to inflame dogmatic passion and zealotry—the infamous *dogmatomachy,* by far modernity's deadliest of all curses—to the plain detriment of toleration, civility, peace, and life itself. It is poorly calculated to foster anything resembling liberty through law or a genuinely political order. At best, this is to pursue prescribed benign orthodoxy in the entire society by every available means. The spirit of the pope's message is curiously reflected in a nearly nostalgic lamentation by Roman Catholic Bishop Vladimir Filo of Bratislava, Slovakia, on the high price being paid for the newly gained freedom: "There are so many problems that did not exist before. In those days [under communism], there was one sole enemy. Now we have several enemies, for example the sects. They are active in schools, television and the press."[15] At worst, something more forbidding comes to mind: a sort of clerical theocracy (not historically unknown in seventeenth- and eighteenth-century Bohemia and elsewhere, to be sure) seems to be advocated, a perversity unforgettably caricatured by Dostoevsky's nightmarish "Legend of the Grand Inquisitor" in *The Brothers Karamazov.*[16]

16. Private property. The sine qua non of free governments no less than of free enterprise economies is widespread private property with secure commercial transactions based on inviolable contracts. Private property and all that goes with it do not deserve to be derided by moralizing pundits of whatever stripe by equating them with corrupting consumerism and Western secularist banality—especially not under existing conditions of collapsing economic and social order in countries emerging from the never-never land of "real socialism," the Realm of Freedom Soviet style. Such counsel and criticism, however unwittingly, lend aid and comfort to the gravediggers of liberty under law in a region groping toward decent and workable social orders. They bear some affinity to the ironical advice to those starving for bread that they could eat cake instead.

A different line of discussion would be more to the point. Thus, when Edmund Burke in the eighteenth century insisted that liberty was indissolubly tied to property in English historical experience, he was not merely giving voice to an Anglo-Saxon idiosyncracy. In a world of corporeal reality where individuality, personal identity, and well-being implicate the material dimensions of being—the reality of the human condition as inextricably participant in *all* levels of being—private property remains basic to an independent citizenry, personal virtue and morality, vital social and economic relationships, and justice in society. Sir Dudley Digges, speaking in the House of Commons in 1628, did not exaggerate when he asserted this humble but abiding truth:

> Be pleased then to know, that it is an undoubted and funda-mental point of this so ancient common law of England, that the subject hath a true property in his goods and possessions, which doth preserve as sacred that *meum et tuum* that is the nurse of industry, and mother of courage, and without which there can be no justice, of which *meum et tuum* is the proper object.[17]

These relationships were protected for good reason under the Constitution of 1787. James Madison's Princeton mentor, President John Witherspoon, concisely drew the lesson of seamless human reality for free government and personal liberty in these two sentences: "There is not a single instance in history in which civil liberty was lost, and religious liberty preserved entire. If therefore we yield up our temporal property, we at the same time deliver the conscience into bondage." It is easy to overlook the substance of these golden words since today Marxist ideological thought pervasively deforms understanding of the relationship between material reality and other dimensions of existence. It may be recalled, however, that the defense of private property, contract, and commerce is not merely an economic matter but is properly ontological, as Aristotle suggested long ago when he rejected Socrates' proposed communism of women, children, and property.[18]

17. Federalism. This celebrated principle is less than a panacea in the highly charged post–Cold War world of central and eastern Europe with nationalism rampant and Yugoslavia verging on civil war because of ethnic friction and separatism. One must bear in mind that American federalism was not firmly settled until after the Civil War, in human terms the most costly war in American history. Moreover, it originated out of a desire on all hands to come together into a single union, while most of the hankering for "federalism" in central and eastern Europe arises from the desire to separate from central authority so as to gain or preserve autonomy—an opposite impulse. The contemporary Czechoslovak situation has been summarized in this way:

> The achievement of substantial autonomy within a federal system of government has been the Slovak goal since the republic was founded over seventy years ago. That goal was also an unfulfilled promise of the Prague Spring. Devising and adopting a system that creates a central government with enough authority to deal with the many daunting economic, ecological, social, political, and international problems that Czechoslovakia faces, while allowing the Slovaks the degree of autonomy they demand, will be very difficult. . . . Along with . . . ethnic disputes, communism, with its tyranny, corruption, and inefficiency, has increased public skepticism of all forms of central government, even democratic ones. The result is a trend toward centrifugalism that has manifested itself in a widespread demand throughout Eastern Europe for devolution of central authority into a loose form of federalism, with power shifting from the center to the regions.[19]

It is possible, of course, that the vexed nationalities problem in the CSFR might be alleviated through one of several means that would make federalism a workable principle. Obdurate extremists could moderate their positions in the face of a Yugoslav disaster and its sobering lessons, for instance, so that cooler heads and sounder counsels might prevail. The embrace of toleration (a policy not unknown in Czechoslovak history) might allow a workable federation to be established. The possibility is being considered of working with a triad rather than the unmanageably seesawing dyad of states or provinces by adding Moravia-Silesia to Slovakia and Bohemia as constituent and representable units. This could finesse the threatened stalemated government made possible by a de facto absolute veto of legislation in the upper house of Parliament (the Chamber of Nations) where Slovak and Czech representation is equal (seventy-five members each) and super-majorities are requisite for key legislation. Slovaks, jealous for their autonomy, vigorously oppose such a step, however. Another theoretical possibility might be to devise a scheme of representation on the basis of units other than constituent states, such as election districts composed of metropolitan areas or other population units not keyed to geographic location, a pattern employed in earlier times; or bicameralism in Parliament might be sacrificed in favor of a unicameral national legislature, a step that could be accompanied by strengthening the legal and constitutional responsibilities of the republics to make them more truly "constituent" with concurrent taxing and police powers. It has been observed that the kind of federalism now seen in the CSFR is imposed from the top down, rather than emerging from the bottom up to the central government.

A further suggested palliative of ethnic preoccupations would be to bring constitutional provisions into line with those demanded for membership in the European (Economic and Political) Community (EC). Admittedly, the precise character of the EC is still in flux, so exactly what its ultimate nature and authority might become are murky questions. Still, Czechoslovakia's leaders are eager for admission on economic grounds, since the country's primary trading partner of recent decades, the Soviet Union, has been lost. Meeting the conditions for EC participation is viewed in Prague as utterly vital—if up to a decade away—to the future well-being of the country. Czechs and Slovaks may be able to parlay their agreement on this cardinal matter into effective internal political agreements making the CSFR a viable national entity. Something of the kind will have to be done before the French, at least, are prepared to admit the CSFR even to associate membership, to judge from recent statements by French President François Mitterrand. With the decisive turn of Czechoslovakia toward Europe, however, the avenues for ameliorating internal divisions seem most likely to lie with the developing EC and with the Conference on Security and Cooperation in Europe or so-called Helsinki process. These extraordinarily significant supranational economic, political, and prospectively military unions pointing toward some kind of United States of Europe or European Union have gained great momentum since they first began to germinate in 1950. They promise to be the "federalism" of the future and decisive in shaping the resolution of internal political problems in Czechoslovakia and elsewhere. Paradoxically, some kind of supranational therapy for the nationalities' problems seems in prospect. The result could be a country that becomes newly independent at the expense of a significant part of its very sovereignty, as the age of nation-states enters the twilight.

18. Personal liberties. Declarations of rights need to be accompanied by provisions stating qualifications of standing to sue and by definitions of jurisdictions, to the end of both (a) restricting access to courts and (b) placing protection of personal liberties at the center of the jurisdiction of constitutional protection. The latter objective also might be achieved by putting other judicial institutions into an appellate hierarchy under a single supreme judicial body like the U.S. Supreme Court. Otherwise, the anomaly appears that personal liberties can be affirmed to no real effect in actually remedying abuses by executive and legislative agencies and magistracies. Again, the play government of the people may be subverted in practice by the real government of the bureaucracy à la Bolshevism.

19. Universities. The independence and integrity of the universities as preserves for the cultivation of science and the pursuit of truth will have to be established and protected, perhaps by constitutional provision. These institutions of higher learning need to be protected against politicization or co-optation from any direction. This protection will have to extend to the protection of property rights during the ongoing transition from state ownership of everything to a predominantly private property system. The Communists' destruction of education throughout the region was one of the great atrocities of the Russian yoke of the past forty-odd years, especially perhaps in Czechoslovakia, where standards were wonderfully high. A new threat in the name of restoring property to "original" owners can result in a kind of power grab—for instance, by the Roman Catholic Church, which lays claim to the entire University of Palacky in Olomouc as church property. Once again, this is not a problem without precedent in Bohemian and Moravian history. But if democratic government and pursuit of public well-being through consent of the people are the settled objectives of the country, then some way of finding compromise in such situations and of insulating the universities and other educational institutions from control through ownership of property titles would appear to be imperative. Several roads lead to serfdom, F. A. Hayek would doubtless concede.

20. Local government. Throughout the region a cultivation of local autonomy and government would seem to be imperative, if a democratic culture is to be nursed to life. The celebrated New England town meeting may be overrated but remains a useful model to be considered. The school of self-government cannot convene solely at the national level. Many activities best done on the basis of local responsibility should be done there in democratic fashion— not simply administered as arms of the central government. This is termed "division of powers" in the jargon of American government where overlapping, concurrent, and exclusive jurisdictions form the texture of federalism both joining together and freeing up central, state, and local governments (see *Federalist No. 39*). The desideratum is a grassroots political process and a structure charged with local authority. Alexis de Tocqueville in his great classic study of American democracy extolled the jury as the preeminent school of citizenship in America, and such schooling at the local level is an urgent need in central and eastern Europe.[20] Solzhenitsyn suggests revitalization of the *zemstvos* in Russia as a native-growth institution of local government that could be nurtured as the school for democratizing a highly authoritarian society. Other such historically stunted institutions might be revived in other countries. Of course, Czechoslovakia is a relatively small country of 17 million inhabitants in a territory the size of New York State, Poland is more than twice as large with 38 million people, and the Russian Republic (RSFSR) is vast with a population of 150 million, so circumstances vary widely.

Still, local self-government affording the utterly novel opportunity of practicing home rule—finding local solutions to local political and economic problems, as far as possible—is basic for formation of democratic character and resilient self-governing polities.

21. Elections. A universal franchise and participatory, referenda-like elections appear to be the almost inevitable format of democratic process in the CSFR. Failing other means, adoption of genuinely proportional representation in both houses of Parliament would obviate the Slovaks' ability, with only one-third of the population, to block legislation not to their liking through their equal representation in the Chamber of Nations. As mentioned earlier, a unicameral parliament might achieve the same objective, as would also the creation of Moravia-Silesia as a represented state. The electorate is splintered at last count among twenty-three parties in the CSFR, which seems baffling to American eyes, but is far less fragmented than the situation in Poland, where some seventy parties are represented with another sixty-plus vying for recognition. Such fracturing gives every faction its say, to be sure, but threatens calamity on every significant vote and undermines prospects for coherent policy formulation backed by stable aggregates of population and party. Single-member representational districting coupled with winner-take-all elections—characteristic in the United States and essential for two-party government—effectively address the range of problems associated with political instability and government by volatile coalition. These strategies allow consensus building and provide means for citizens to express consent: (a) to officials' selection and tenure at all levels of government; and (b) to legislative enactments and tax measures. But under present conditions in the CSFR (it is argued) such arrangements would unduly magnify communist and procommunist representation and might negate the achievements of the Velvet Revolution in the CSFR. Struggling in Poland with related problems made more acute by Communist Party control of two-thirds of the Sejm's (lower house's) seats, President Lech Walesa in late June 1991 threatened to dissolve Parliament and vetoed a bill that would have allowed the electorate to vote for individuals rather than for an entire party slate of candidates, which he desires. He cited as justification of the veto the destabilizing tendency of such a rule for elections and its aggravation of the faction problem, thereby impairing consensus building and concerted political action. A constitutional crisis looms.

22. Conclusion. Many other matters deserve comment, but the gist of some of the problems and their complexity will have become apparent. On one hand, this unquestionably is a magic moment such as is seldom experienced. The nations of an entire region of the globe have the opportunity to reinvent government for themselves. On the other hand, the overt and hidden constraints that condition and impede this process may be so massive and intractable as to derail it altogether. It would seem that Czechoslovakia, Hungary, and Poland have the best chances to make a satisfactory transition from servitude to free governments and market economies. Zealotry in multiple guises threatens on every hand in the jockeying for power. The old Communist Party members and their clients who have come to rely upon the certainties of socialist bread are lying low, waiting for a debacle that will play into their hands. The centrality of private property and individual liberty to functioning free government is inveighed against as secularist Europeanization and consumerism by church leaders who champion human rights philosophically while remaining serenely oblivious to the economic and political foundations vital to realizing in this world the very purposes they rhetorically espouse.

The question remains, how will things turn out? It may be a bumpy ride, but the genie is out of the bottle. Liberty will triumph, truth prevail. Three cheers for the noblest endeavor of our time—and Godspeed.

3

The Politics of Truth

Ideological pseudo-reality . . . is built on a very unstable foundation. It is built on lies. It works as long as people are willing to live within the lie.

All of us, East and West, face one fundamental task from which all else should follow. That task is one of resisting vigilantly, thoughtfully, and attentively, but at the same time with total dedication at every step and everywhere, the irrational momentum of anonymous, impersonal, and inhuman power—the power of ideologies, systems, apparat, bureaucracy, artificial languages, and political slogans. We must resist its complex and wholly alienating pressure, whether it takes the form of consumption, advertising, repression, technology, or cliché—all of which are the blood brothers of fanaticism and the well-spring of totalitarian thought. We must draw our standards from our natural world, heedless of ridicule, and reaffirm its denied validity. We must honor with the humility of the wise the limits of that natural world and the mystery which lies beyond them, admitting that there is something in the order of being which evidently exceeds all our competence. We must relate to the absolute horizon of our existence which, if we but will, we shall constantly rediscover and experience. . . . We must trust the voice of our conscience more than that of all abstract speculations. . . .

> We must not be ashamed that we are capable of love,
> friendship, solidarity, sympathy, and tolerance, but . . .
> we must set these fundamental dimensions of our hu-
> manity free from their private exile and accept them as
> the only genuine starting point of meaningful human
> community. We must be guided by our own reason
> and serve the truth under all circumstances as our own
> essential experience.
>
> —*Václav Havel*

D URING THE FIVE YEARS in which it has been my pleasure
to collaborate in conducting here our series of colloquia on
liberty and rule of law, we have sought to reflect especially
on the abiding things, those that potentially elevate human existence
above the brute to make man a little lower than the angels. Your
illustrious Rector Josef Jařab, scholar and patriot that he is, has
proved to be a kindred spirit and an able ally in this quest.[1]

The setting for our deliberations, of course, has been a background
of recovery from a half-century of grinding tyranny and the effort
to reestablish free government out of the rubble. The premise of
our modest efforts is that government exists for men, not men for
government. Our focus has been to seek in history, philosophy, and
reflection resources for fostering human nurture and flourishing in
freedom. The concrete individual person as man and citizen is the
prime human reality always in the foreground of such seemingly
abstract statements. The point may be stressed at the end of a century
of horrendous collectivism and statism: the integrity of the person
is the cardinal consideration in a valid theory of politics. While we
have discussed and debated matters of weight and consequence,
and may not have agreed on everything, a thread of consensus has
so far emerged that is as instructive for America as it is for the Czech
Republic and other nations emergent from totalitarianism.

The imperative arises that justice and liberty be served and tyranny resisted. It may be objected that these are old-fashioned ideas.
They now are spurned and denigrated by trendy academics and intellectuals who also have abandoned reality, truth, and philosophy in
favor of criticism, correctness, and deconstruction. Forgive me if I decline to be fashionable. To the contrary: I regard these quasi-Marxist

postures as calculated theoretical obfuscation and camouflage. We detect therein the latest disguises of that old wolf *nihilism* decked out in new sheep's clothing. It is, indeed, little more than old-fashioned *libido dominandi* once again parading as liberation but, in fact, engaged in the further destruction of human reality.

The people of our century, especially those of central and eastern Europe, have experienced in unprecedented degree the mystery of evil in the world. After decades of falsehood and manipulation, there now is some hope that the politics of truth may for a time supplant the antipolitics of the lie. From Jan Hus to Václav Havel, this is a familiar Czech theme. The second realities of the ideologues cannot withstand scrutiny and questions but must give way before honesty and vision. Such convictions seem to be as widely held in this country as in my own. Such convictions may even serve to define the better selves of America and the Czech Republic. We also verge on the territory that philosophers symbolize as universals.

America early became famous for asserting a set of universals as self-evident truth: that all men are created equal, endowed by their Creator with certain unalienable rights, among which are life, liberty, and the pursuit of happiness; and that to secure these rights governments are instituted among men, drawing all of their just powers from the consent of the governed. Five centuries before these self-evident universals were articulated, the greatest Christian philosopher found it self-evident that the Good is that which all things seek after. From this self-evident truth about the creature man, the philosopher derived the whole natural law. For it thereby follows as the basic precept of the law of nature that Good is to be done and striven for and evil avoided, and this law is evident through reason in our observed inclinations to the range of goods. These include our inclinations to self-preservation, to reproduce ourselves and educate and nurture our young, to know through reason and experience the truth about God and reality, and to live in society as the natural means of fulfilling the quest for the highest good attainable by action, each person's search for happiness and blessedness.

Perhaps it is only my weakness for self-evident truth. But it has seemed, and still does seem to me, in experiential terms, that Thomas Jefferson's and Thomas Aquinas's self-evident universals are cogent and strikingly complementary. Both have a classical and Christian ring, and both powerfully illuminate human reality in structure and process. That unalienable rights arise on the basis of the laws of nature and of nature's God is a not unreasonable implication. Moreover, both sets of truths clearly bear on the understanding of constitutionalism and personal liberty that at once appeals to a customary (or historical) as well as to a natural (or hierarchical) jurisprudence—the actual jurisprudence of England and America and, until absolutism and revolution negated it, of our civilization back to Cicero and the Greeks. Thus long centuries before Thomas (and reiterated by him) it was pertinently affirmed by *Antigone* that an unjust law is no law at all—a universal devastating for the lie (whatever positivists say about it), one that echoes through history from Hippo to Birmingham Jail to the gulag.

Devotion to the politics of truth—with each and every person laying claim to it as the natural birthright of free men, the groundwork of personal as well as social order—is heady business, however. The core of the politics of truth is not a system of doctrines, dogmas, or ethical teachings, it may be stressed, but the living experience of each person's participation in the transcendent divine ground of being as the foundation of ineradicable dignity and worth. Spiritual experience—noetic and pneumatic apperception, as philosophers say—lies at the heart of human existence. From it flows order and its articulate symbolization in all spheres of reality. This understanding is, of course, deeply feared by all tyrants, their lackeys, and other purveyors of the lie of all times and places. The politics of truth strives to embody the idea in history, to the limits of possibility. But it must do so mindful of the demands of individual freedom. The community's right to resist tyranny is an obligation of free men: the principle is that eternal vigilance is the price of liberty, and it is as old as Demosthenes.

Certain cautions deserve mention. To begin with, truth's blazing luminosity cannot sustain itself perfectly given the facts of refractory historical existence, not least of all the vividly attested mystery of evil. The politics of truth thereby implies some degree of prudential tempering, if it is not to succumb to perversion. It is here that the idealist becomes impatient, indignant, or even disgusted with the statesman. Compromise appears to be necessary, and this always seems an unwholesome business. How can the vulgar necessity of compromise be made more palatable? Perhaps by reexamining truth itself. A political order depends only partly upon mind and spirit. Pure vision—whether philosophical or religious—has never been the regimen of any polity in history: Plato and Aristotle, for instance, discriminated between the *bios theoretikos* and the civic life, Augustine between the *civitas Dei* and the *civitas terrena*. A political order is not entirely rational. This is principally because human beings themselves are not purely rational, disembodied shades, nor are they capable of being rigorously governed in all things by reason, justice, and truth whether individually or socially. In fact, my axiom of politics (a minor contribution to science) is this: *human beings are virtually ungovernable.* After all, human beings in addition to possessing reason and gifts of conscience are material, corporeal, passionate, self-serving, devious, obstreperous, ornery, unreliable, imperfect, fallible, and prone to sin if not outright depraved. And we have some bad qualities besides.

It is part of the very truth of politics that private property and security in our persons and possessions are essential to human well-being and happiness, according to all credible accounts from Aristotle to John Locke. The trick of politics and the demand of statesmanship are to embody the idea—truth and justice—in recalcitrant human reality within tolerable limits. And what may be possible or desirable can be determined only by the *phronimos* (as Aristotle called his prudential virtuoso) or statesman concretely on a case-by-case basis. Experience—the culture of habit and the institutions available to the society and its political leadership—is generally a limiting factor, but the particulars always are decisive. In fact, the plausibility of the argument in favor of the rule of law rather than of men always has been that law is the distillation of reason and justice. But men possess an element of the beast, so that anger and passion pervert the minds of rulers, even when they are the best of men. Aristotle first said this, and James Madison and the American founders believed him and partly based their constitutional design of separated powers with checks and balances on the validity of this anthropology.

To single-mindedly pursue the politics of truth heedless of other considerations is to risk plunging into the reductionist trap and, however inadvertently, to become hostage of the gnostic fallacy of immanentizing the Christian eschaton. No truth is immune if dogmatically insisted upon. By seeking perfection in the here and now—heaven on earth—we paradoxically open the gates to the lie. Ideological politics perfectly exemplifies this paradox, whether in the seductive versions of progressivism and utopianism or in the brutal guise of Marxist-Leninist revolutionary activism.

If we can acknowledge that politics is art as well as science, and that even as science it can never be more precise than its subject matter permits, we set foot on the road to sound government. Truth as grasped in human cognition is, thus, neither monolithic and doctrinaire nor comprehensive. The truths of the human realms of time and space, historical truth, must be distinguished from eternal or everlasting verity. Even under the best of circumstances, human knowledge achieves no more than representative truth grounded in the perspective of participation, and it is never the comprehensive Truth of omniscience that is pretended to by system mongers. Philosophy ineluctably remains love of wisdom, never its absolute possession. The noetic differentiation of reality in terms of immanent and transcendent being with human existence participant in both as the In-Between realm *(metaxy)*, therefore, implies limits on human capacity and grandeur. Politics is and must remain the art of the possible. One's fondest dreams and most cherished hopes are channeled in the material reality of culture, nationality, place, time, and mortality. Politics is thereby seen to be a limited and mediocre affair, not the way to salvation; and the pretension to eschatological pseudopolitics, however well-intentioned, prefigures the loss of reality and a slide into the total state and its waking nightmare.

This leaves, then, the aspirations to the noble and the true, the experiences of which shape human consciousness as being more than merely mortal. Through poetry, art, music, science, philosophy, and above all faith, we are drawn to become participant in the realm of the divine and transcendent. While structured by such experience, these realms of mind and spirit are understood to lie beyond the merely political as superior to it in rank and beauty. Moreover, since private property is essential to free government and to the formation of responsible civic consciousness in a citizenry that understands itself as composed of persons who rule and are ruled by turn, each one having personal standing and material stake in society, a further limitation on political power is suggested. Additional limitation is imposed by respect for individual volition and intelligence, by respect for the ontological integrity of personality that thus argues for minimal government and public restraint, in the interest of private satisfactions and liberty. For example, it is out of this consideration that the American bills of rights (federal and state) are intended to put certain natural and civil liberties beyond the ordinary reach of majorities; and occasionally the First Amendment rights of conscience are claimed to be absolute by jurists. The nineteenth-century American humorist Josh Billings quaintly averred that most of the happiness in this world consists in possessing what other people can't get! This parody of liberal politics has its attractions. At the present juncture in history, we may find it infinitely more appealing than the heady salvific projects of overreaching Autonomous Man. At least it is honest.

The modesty of the political realm, its limitations, provides a precondition for openness toward the horizon of reality. This fosters nurture of the core tension toward the divine ground constitutive of man's attunement to the transcendent in various modes of ascent historically fashioned by persons, traditions, and communities. Happiness as a state of feeling and consciousness is not primarily a political project. The desideratum, then, is a politics of moderation. Surely we have by now had enough of the total state and the deification of the dialectic of history at the expense of persons.

Throughout history the Czech and American peoples, in widely differing ways to be sure, have wrestled with and served the politics of truth. We thus draw common lessons. Truth is by all means to be embraced in politics, but embraced with a circumspection attentive to its perspectival character and to the sense of limits intrinsic to the human condition. An aspect of our devotion to truth and its universality is our attentiveness, also, to the plurality of truth as seen in the uniqueness of traditions, habits, institutions, and political capacities. These change over time. Free government is a historical rarity and the greatest political challenge; ochlocracy is its viral disease, inviting the socialist demagogue and constantly threatening every liberal democracy with extinction.

The celebrated Tomas Garrigue Masaryk once remarked that "our vulgar liberalism fears the ultimate questions of life as the devil fears holy water." But he found such a view to be contrary to the "entire meaning of Czech history and Czech spirit."[2] In a time when liberal democracy appears to be the only practicable alternative to authoritarianism or worse, it is precisely requisite that the ultimate questions of human existence be explored and, so far as possible, that the truth of reality be recovered as a living possession. Only thus can it be woven into the fabric of representative free government as the texture of political order, civic consciousness, and institutionalized statecraft in service of the good life. This, it appears to me at least, is the world-historic task of an authentic politics of truth—if a plunge into the abyss is to be averted.

Masaryk admired a prayer of the great Jan Hus, and he urged his auditors of 1910 to "heed it well." This good advice and Hus's memorable words can suitably conclude my own remarks today:

> Seek truth, listen to the truth, learn the truth, love the truth, speak the truth, keep the truth, defend the truth with your very life![3]

4

Philosophical and Religious Dimensions of the American Founding

T HE FOUNDATION OF THE American regime was deeply influenced by the rationalist mood of Enlightenment thought, primarily in its English and Scottish aspects. But it began and remained more fundamentally an antimodernist recovery and rearticulation of Western and English constitutionalism on the classical and medieval patterns identified with the seventeenth century of Sir Edward Coke, a principal figure of the Elizabethan Renaissance, and John Locke, himself a principal enlightener. Moreover, all aspects of the political, constitutional, and philosophical debate were strongly conditioned by an ethics and ontology grounded in the ample range of religious convictions of an American Protestant Christianity dominated by Dissenter or Nonconformist perspectives.

While (given the empirical evidence) all of these elements certainly cannot be homogenized or blended into a perfect harmony and generalized as such, there still remained sufficient consensus or near agreement on fundamental principles to sustain independence, fight the revolution, and conclude with the Constitution. This process soon was capped by adoption of the Bill of Rights (a condition of ratification in some states), which affirms natural and traditional liberties of persons and states by placing them beyond the ordinary reach of majorities. There is no attempt here to deny differences of many kinds, even multitudinous and profound differences—most obviously among the Loyalists, of course. But one must concede that without some sort of effective consensus to structure the new community and to allow its organization for political action in history, there could have been no founding and there would be no United States of America. This essay will consider several aspects of this consensus and glance at its religious and philosophical underpinnings.

I

Since novelty and revolution mesmerize contemporary consciousness, the relative lack of novelty in the American founding seems counterintuitive and requires emphasis at the outset. The institutional forms were new in degree, but the underlying theory was often very old and highly traditional. There is thus a strong contrast with much of our contemporary world and its recent past.

To begin with, the conceptions of human existence and of comprehensive reality prevailing during the American founding were not ideological in the strict sense of the term. By this at least the following is meant. The American founders (as a rule) did not hold out the promise of a humanistic transformation of time and the world as a goal within the reach of action and revolution—apart from the traditional Christian faith in the transfiguration of the world at the end of time as consistent with eschatological expectation of the Parousia, the Second Coming of Christ in power, glory, and judgment.

The founding was not significantly infected by the radical humanistic egophanic rebellion that supplants God through the apotheosis of Autonomous Man as the center and ground of reality. To the contrary, a transcendental-immanent worldview is reflected in the core of the American founders' thought, as is plainly expressed in the Declaration of Independence's proclamation that "all men are Created equal and are endowed by their Creator with certain unalienable rights" and elsewhere. Perhaps the most persuasive expression of this orientation in reality is voiced in Alexander Pope's *Essay on Man* (1734). Evoked there is the millennial image of the great chain of being with man the middle link, an image whose genesis lies in the distant antiquity of Anaximander's *apeiron* as developed by Plato and Aristotle into the ontological hierarchy epitomizing the whole philosophy of human affairs. Pope wrote so compellingly as to make the poem favorite reading for eighteenth-century Americans:

> Vast Chain of being! which from God began,
> Natures aethereal, human, angel, man,
> Beast, bird, fish, insect, what no eye can see,
> No glass can reach; from Infinite to thee,
> From thee to nothing.[1]

The founding was not "utopian" in expectation nor in its assessment of the world. Thus the reality of the American founders while distinctly hopeful was nonetheless considered a stable site of human striving in nature and in a process of history governed by beneficent and responsive providence, a time when fallible human beings might seek the joys of life and anticipate the bliss of salvation and eternal beatitude. Reality itself was conceived as the fourfold God, man, world, and society of classical philosophy and traditional understanding. To again illustrate from Pope's picture of human reality:

> Plac'd in this isthmus of a middle state,
> A being darkly wise and rudely great,
> With too much knowledge for the sceptic side,
> With too much weakness for the stoic pride,
> He hangs between; in doubt to act or rest;
> In doubt his Mind or Body to prefer;
> Born but to die, and reas'ning but to err; . . .
> Chaos of Thought and Passion all confus'd.
> Still by himself abus'd, or disabus'd;
> Created half to rise, and half to fall,
> Great lord of all things, yet a prey to all;
> Sole judge of Truth, in endless error hurl'd;
> The glory, jest and riddle of the world.[2]

Government under such conditions was pronounced (by James Madison in *Federalist No. 51*) as the "greatest of all reflections on human nature." Because human beings are neither angelic nor brute but in between, capable of virtue and inclined to vice, the first task of government is to control the governed; the second task is to oblige the rulers to control themselves. "Ambition must be made to counteract ambition."

We are thus reminded of the cautious view of man as flawed and sinful, graced with reason but inclined to follow passion and selfish interest. Madison's language in *Federalist No. 51* may be more fully quoted. For there the core constitutional innovation of separation of powers and a system of checks and balances is explained as the means of attaining a government of laws and not of men—even though, paradoxically, there are only human beings available to rule. The underlying analysis for the constitutional mechanisms is sketched as follows:

> The interest of the man must be connected with the constitu-
> tional rights of the place. It may be a reflection on human nature
> that such devices should be necessary to control the abuses of
> government. But what is government itself but the greatest of
> all reflections on human nature? If men were angels, no gov-
> ernment would be necessary. If angels were to govern men,
> neither external nor internal controls on government would be
> necessary. In framing a government which is to be administered
> by men over men, the great difficulty lies in this: you must
> first enable the government to control the governed; and in
> the next place oblige it to control itself. A dependence on the
> people is, no doubt, the primary control on the government;
> but *experience* has taught mankind the necessity of auxiliary
> precautions.[3]

Finally—and deserving of utmost consideration—there is the ubiquitous criterion of experience just encountered in the passage from *Federalist No. 51*. Experience, illumining the present and future by the light and lessons of the past, is the cardinal touchstone of validity. It also is the one that indelibly distinguishes the American founders from those they ironically helped greatly to inspire, the soon-to-appear Jacobin revolutionaries of France inebriated with utopian rationalism. By comparison the American founders were a sober lot. Thus, John Dickinson in August 1787 famously observed during the convention that "experience must be our only guide. Reason may mislead us."[4] Perhaps nothing better marks the mind of the American founders than this conviction. It runs like a thread through all of their deliberations. It is the enduring prophylaxis against the siren songs of apocalyptic revolution and utopian antipolitics that so savagely beset modern existence into the present. Rule of law grounded in both natural and historical jurisprudence distinguishes American constitutionalism, as does also a political order devoted to *salus populi* and to the protection of every individual person's life, liberty, and property within the limits of possibility.[5]

What, indeed, may be possible can be decided only by prudential judgment anchored in experience. Briefly to dwell on this bedrock principle, we find Publius in *The Federalist Papers* using such phrases as these: "Let *experience,* the least fallible guide of human opinions, be appealed to" (No. 6); "the best oracle of wisdom, *experience*" (No. 15); "*Experience* is the oracle of truth; and where its responses are unequivocal they ought to be conclusive and sacred" (No. 20); "Let us consult *experience,* the guide that ought always to be followed whenever it can be found" (No. 52); "*experience* is the parent of wisdom" (No. 72).[6]

Alexander Hamilton concludes *Federalist No. 85* with a quotation from David Hume's *Essays* (1742) that underlines this good sense from our birthright. For Hume demonstrates the abject inability of reason alone to guide philosophy toward truth. He thereby finds himself compelled to take account of the whole experiential horizon as context, if reason is reliably to serve inquiry and direct men toward truth and happiness. To do otherwise would be to fall into the hubris of autonomous reason that ends either in despair or in the ataraxy of radical skepticism—or (more frequently) in the disaster of evoking Autonomous Man after the fashion of generations of immanentizing ideologues from 1789 into the present.[7] From this prudential perspective, then, Hamilton quotes Hume as follows:

> To balance a large state or society whether monarchial or republican, on general laws, is a work of so great difficulty, that no human genius, however comprehensive, is able by the mere dint of reason and reflection, to effect it. The judgments of man must unite in the work: *Experience* must guide their labour: *Time* must bring it to perfection: And the *feeling* of inconveniences must correct the mistakes which they *inevitably* fall into, in their first trials and experiments.[8]

These representative sentiments signal the sober, realistic, undogmatic yet hopeful outlook of American politics at its inception. Whatever the historical lapses, they supply the standards nurtured to this day.[9]

II

Liberty and the truth that makes men free go hand in hand in political and religious discourse of the American founding era. There was general agreement that political and religious truth are vitally intertwined: "Year after year the preacher reaffirmed from his high pulpit that both revelation and reason pointed to a single set of principles which outlined the best form of government."[10] Nor was this merely a Puritan or New England affair, as recent scholarship attests. Robert M. Calhoon stated in 1994 that "Evangelical political thought, discipline, and use of the Bible—among other expressions of its activity and vision—formed a coherent whole and functioned as a persuasion in the early South. It was an eclectic, improvised mixture of intellectual assumptions, behavioral norms, and Scottish common-sense teachings about the interconnectedness of all knowledge and revelation."[11]

The old interpretation is, with refinements, now becoming the new interpretation of scholars, it would seem. Religion gave birth to America, Tocqueville long ago observed. On the eve of revolution, in his last-ditch attempt to stave off impending catastrophe, Edmund Burke reminded the House of Commons of the inseparable alliance between liberty and religion among Englishmen in America. A recent student has called America the nation with the soul of a church. Another has elevated the political sermon considered as jeremiad to the rank of the primary symbolic form of the American mind. Yet another has exclaimed of the Americans on the eve of the Revolution, "who can deny that for them the very core of existence was their relation to God?"[12]

Given modern predispositions, and despite new developments, our point of departure may still have to be negative. It requires that we abandon what Perry Miller over three decades ago called "obtuse secularism" as a reflexive habit of mind so as to enter into a quite different attitude.[13] Miller's bristling phrase as emblematic of the prevailing climate of opinion probably still is justified. God-centered existence is not the twentieth-century commonplace among literate Britains and Americans that it was among our eighteenth-century brethren. For all the differences among them, American preachers of the eighteenth century premised an unsurprisingly biblical vision that includes a stratified, differentiated reality, an ontological Whole experienced as the community of being articulated into the familiar fourfold structure of God, man, world, and society.[14] The human and the divine are tensional polarities of this reality, the one unintelligible without the other. The modern reductionist deformations of being into a contracted reality of Autonomous Man lodged in an equally autonomous nature do not reflect the intellectual horizon of any significant segment of the thinking public of the time, although radically secularizing influences of the French Enlightenment were pushing them that way. Thomas Paine and Ethan Allen, and the more ambiguous instance of Thomas Jefferson, rightly are adduced as evidence of the presence of such influences. But they plainly are exceptions. And even the so-called rationalistic elite probably can best be understood in religious terms, as historians recently have begun to argue—even from the vantage point of the ratification process near the end of the founding era. Thus, Stephen A. Marini wrote in 1994:

> it was primarily among Anglicans and Congregationalists and the political, economic, military, and literary elites they dominated that a movement of Enlightenment religious liberalism burst into full flower. Thomas Jefferson, the Virginian who shared Voltaire's theological skepticism yet penned passionate defenses of an innate moral sense and committed the sayings of Jesus to memory, Benjamin Rush, the Philadelphia physician who embraced Unitarianism and Universalism while campaigning passionately for temperance reform and the abolition of slavery, and Benjamin Franklin, the transplanted Bostonian who provided the new nation with a wealth of moral aphorisms and a model of toleration by contributing to all churches of Philadelphia, epitomized the sort of *religious liberalism* that swept through America's cultural elite during the late eighteenth century. . . . In its advocacy of a benign Creator, a benevolent cosmos, human reason and free will, and a thoroughgoing moral optimism, Enlightenment religious liberalism supplied a powerful theological and philosophical foundation for the cosmopolitan republican culture of the 1780s . . . the Deism of Paine and Ethan Allen failed dramatically to become the new American faith, especially after the French Revolution. In 1787, however, Enlightenment religious liberalism still flourished widely in America's urban churches, universities, and plantation parishes.[15]

Prevalent American ontology reflects the familiar biblical image of Creator and creation, of fallen and sinful men, striving willy-nilly in a mysteriously ordered historical existence toward a personal salvation and an eschatological fulfillment. These goals are themselves paradoxically attainable only through the divine grace of election, a condition experienced as the unmerited gift of God discernible (if at all) in the mode of hopeful human responsiveness called faith in Christ that alone yields assurance of eternal beatitude. The relationships are variously symbolized by personal and corporate reciprocal covenants ordering individual lives, church communities, and society as a whole in multiple layers productive of good works, inculcating divine truth and attentiveness to providential direction according to the "law of liberty" of the sovereign God revealed in the lowly Nazarene.[16]

The bare externals of these relationships so regulate the visible community as to beckon everyone to open their souls to truth and thereby enjoy in appropriate measure more perfect participation as members of the mystical body of which Christ is head. The communion of the faithful, those actuated by the love of God even to the contempt of self, comprises the invisible church of the regenerate (in America often the gathered, visible church itself) made one through love of God as like-minded persons chosen to reign with the Lord as his saints forever.[17] The picture that emerges is not parochially Puritan or Calvinist but palpably Augustinian, thoroughly biblical, and often Arminian. Even so, it will be salutary to avoid misgivings by recalling Ralph Barton Perry's indispensable admonition against the *Fallacy of Difference* as we reflect on American religious experience with one eye on its Puritan background. He writes, "Puritanism was an offshoot from the main stem of Christian belief, and Puritans, equally with Catholics, claimed descent from St. Paul and Augustine. [Thus, it can be defined as] theocratic, congregational-presbyterian, Calvinistic, protestant, medieval Christianity."[18] Even institutionally this was so. For, although Baptists and Quakers felt obliged to secede, orthodox New England Puritans gave allegiance to the Thirty-Nine Articles and remained within the national communion of the Church of England well into the eighteenth century. Although they might call themselves congregationalists, this was primarily descriptive of a form of church polity that they insisted was true to the New

Testament and apostolic so that "in their heart of hearts [they] remained convinced that [theirs] was no more than the most reformed portion of the universal church."[19]

The intricacies of the varieties of belief cannot be much explored here, but at least a few hints must be given. For though our primary focus is on political dimensions—and thus exceptional expressions of the faith of a people who looked not primarily to history but to the eternal beyond for perfect fulfillment of their pilgrimage through time in partnership with God—the spiritual root of that collaborative enterprise as directed by divine Providence requires clarification.

It has been persuasively argued that a revolution in the spiritual and social life of America began with what is called the (First) Great Awakening. There is considerable reason to suppose that religious and political lines of development are intimately, perhaps decisively, linked. Narrowly construed as occurring in the years 1739 to 1742, the Great Awakening designates the outburst of religious revival that swept the colonies in those years.[20] It reached from Georgia to New England and affected every stratum of society. There had been a quickening of religious impulses even earlier, but the First Great Awakening was a spiritual earthquake, one that, as Alan Heimert and Perry Miller argue, "clearly began a new era, not merely of American Protestantism, but in the evolution of the American mind."[21] A turning point and crisis in American society, it rumbled and echoed through the next decades. Colonial life was never the same again. American events could be seen as part of the general rise of religious sentiment traceable in Europe between 1730 and 1760, particularly in Great Britain, where major catalysts were the itinerant Anglican priests John and Charles Wesley, the founders of Methodism, and their compatriot George Whitefield. These men played a large part in rescuing England from the social debauchery and political corruption associated with the Gin Age, aspects of the period portrayed in William Hogarth's paintings and prints and in his friend Henry Fielding's novels.[22] The so-called Second Great Awakening began after 1790 in revival camp meetings on the frontier and in the backcountry. The great political events of the American founding, thus, have a backdrop of resurgent religiousness whose calls for repentance and faith plainly complement the calls to resist constitutional corruption and tyranny so as to live virtuously as

God-fearing Christians and, eventually, as responsible republican citizens.[23]

It should be emphasized in this context, perhaps, that Stephen Marini argues for a surge in religiousness *during* the time of the American Revolution: religion prospered during the revolution. Indeed, there was a "Revolutionary revival." This 1994 judgment merely confirms one that Perry Miller made in 1961: "The basic fact is that the Revolution had been preached to the masses as a religious revival, and had the astounding fortune to succeed." And Patricia Bonomi in 1994 in no way recants her 1982 and 1986 views on the thriving and increasing of religious consciousness in all parts of the American community during these same years, including the colonies and subsequent states of the Middle Atlantic and Southern regions of the country. These judgments challenge the old orthodoxy; to quote Marini: "Far from suffering decline, religion experienced vigorous growth and luxuriant development during the Revolutionary period. It occupied a prominent place in public culture and a disproportionately large number of religiously active men served in the new nation's constituent assemblies. In a host of ways, both practical and intellectual, the church served as a school for politics."[24]

With this perspective on the Awakening and religious development during the remainder of the century in mind, understanding the earlier surge of religiousness becomes all the more urgent. In fact, the preeminent awakener in America throughout much of this whole period was the English evangelist George Whitefield, who first visited the colonies in 1738 and made six more preaching tours of the country, and who died one September morning in 1770 just before he was to preach in Newburyport, Massachusetts. Whitefield was regarded as not only the most controversial preacher of his time but also as "perhaps the greatest extemporaneous orator in the history of the English church," and it is his view of the human plight and its therapy that will best give a clue to the thrust of the awakening as formative of the American mind.

> The theme of his preaching is that of evangelicals in every age: in his natural state man is estranged from God; Jesus Christ, by his death and Atonement, has paid the price of that estrangement

and made reconciliation with God possible; to achieve salvation man, with the guidance and the grace of the Holy Ghost, must repudiate sin and openly identify himself with Christ. To Whitefield religion, when properly understood, meant "a thorough, real, inward change of nature, wrought in us by the powerful operations of the Holy Ghost, conveyed to and nourished in our hearts, by a constant use of all the means of grace, evidenced by a good life, and bringing forth the fruits of the spirit." There was, of course, nothing new in this belief. Its special appeal for eighteenth-century audiences lay partly in the fact that it answered an emotional need the established Church had for too long tried to ignore, and partly in the charismatic personality of the man who revived it.[25]

It is worth stressing in a secularized age that the mystic's ascent and the evangelist's call, although conducted in different forums, have a common root and purpose. For each seeks to find the responsive place in a person's consciousness where vivid communion with God occurs. The consequence is that such communion becomes the transformative core of personal existence for the individual person who therewith feels himself made anew. Initially this is manifested in the conversion experience (understood as a spiritual rebirth) and subsequently in the continuing meditative nurture of the soul pursued by every means but chiefly, in the American Protestant horizon, through prayer, sermons, and study of the Bible. Whitefield's words—those of an Oxford graduate and ordained Anglican priest, we may remember—can thus in some respects be compared with a remarkable passage in Augustine's *Confessions* where a great mystic tells of, with Christ's help, finding his way to God:

> And being thence admonished to return to myself, I entered even into my inward self, Thou being my Guide: and able I was, for Thou wert become my Helper. And I entered and I beheld with the eye of my soul, (such as it was,) above the same eye of my soul, above my mind, the Light Unchangeable. Not this ordinary light, which all flesh may look upon, nor as it were a greater of the same kind, as though the brightness of this should be manifold brighter, and with its greatness take up all space. Not such was this light, but other, yea, far other from all these. Nor was it above my soul, as oil is above water, nor yet as heaven above earth: but above to my soul, because It made me; and I

below It, because I was made by It. He that knows the Truth, knows what that Light is; and he that knows It, knows eternity. Love knoweth it. O Truth Who art Eternity! and Love Who art Truth! and Eternity Who art Love! Thou art my God, to Thee do I sigh night and day. Thee when I first knew, Thou liftedst me up, that I might see there was what I might see, and that I was not yet such as to see. And Thou didst beat back the weakness of my sight, streaming forth Thy beams of light upon me most strongly, and I trembled with love and awe: and I perceived myself to be far off from Thee, in the region of unlikeness, as if I heard this Thy voice from on high: "I am the food of grown men; grow, and thou shalt feed upon Me; nor shalt thou convert Me, like the food of thy flesh, into thee, but thou shalt be converted into Me." And I learned, that *Thou for iniquity chastenest man, and Thou madest my soul to consume away like a spider* (Ps. 38:14). And I said, "Is Truth therefore nothing because it is not diffused through space finite or infinite?" And Thou criedst to me from afar; "Yea verily, *I AM that [who] I AM*" (Exod. 3:14). And I heard, as the heart heareth, nor had I room to doubt, and I should sooner doubt that I live, than that Truth is not, *which is clearly seen being understood by those things which are made* (Rom. 1:20).[26]

The appeal of the evangelist is analogous to the quest of the mystic. It is to stir response to the actualizing attraction of the divine pull as far as he can, both in himself and in those with whom he communicates. The intent is steadily to find in the soul the place of communion with the divine and, thereby, eagerly to vivify the life of the spirit through ever better—more perfect—participation in the transformative experience of transcendent divine Being. Such living communion with God—experienced as a passion in Whitefield and in the awakened Americans no less than it is in Augustine, himself a matchless preacher—lies at the heart of the Awakening and revivalism more generally as mass phenomena in eighteenth-century Britain, America, and elsewhere. Hence its power and effectiveness both personally and socially as well as historically.[27]

The cry was for a converted ministry able to revive religious communities lacking vitality and zeal, to make the presence of God with his people a palpable reality. Such hortatory preaching and intent were the hallmarks of the so-called New Light Presbyterian and New Side Congregationalist clergy, along with the Baptists, Quakers, Anglican-Methodists, and other evangelicals, as contrasted with their opposites who eschewed emotion and experimental religion. Many of the former, like Whitefield himself, had no church of their own but traveled the country preaching in homes and pastures or wherever they could. *Conversion* as the criterion of election involves a personal experience of regeneration at least somewhat along lines classically drawn by Augustine. The individual is flooded with a sense of divine presence and intense participation or union with God such as that intimated by Augustine's words: "I am the food of grown men; grow, and . . . be converted into Me!" A further mark is complete assurance of blessing and of feeling the embrace of Truth itself, so that the moment becomes supremely authoritative for whomever it befalls. Thus, Augustine's words convey all the energy language can bear and fall like hammer blows: "I heard, as the heart heareth, nor had I room to doubt, and I should sooner doubt that I live, than that Truth is not."

Such robust experiences made the Awakening what it was. And it cannot be too surprising that its sociological dimensions manifested emotionalism, sometimes rising to the level of frenzy, we are told. Comparable intensity lies close to the surface of the account of such experience by the likes of Augustine, a spiritual virtuoso of world historic stature. Such experience, one Virginian explained, came with surrender or an abandonment of his own efforts at reform, and with the consequent realization that "my guilt was gone, my conscience at rest, and my soul at liberty." As a church covenant stated in matter-of-fact language, the power of this freeing came through "faith" understood not as "an act of man's free will and power but of the mighty, efficacious grace of God."[28] The criterion, thus, was "an experience of grace" that both made faith possible and succored the soul through liberation and forgiveness. As Robert Calhoon wrote, quoting George Whitefield: "The immediacy of Christ's sacrifice brought ecstasy and the 'indwelling of the spirit' into the consciousness of the convert; evangelical Christianity combined Calvinist assumptions about human depravity and divine majesty with the Arminian appreciation of God's desire to flood all humanity with grace; evangelical converts felt and communicated a contagious desire to be bonded spiritually to others." At the core of the evangelical political theology, Stephen Marini argues, "was 'the necessity of the New Birth,' the requirement that all true Christians experience an episode of conscious spiritual regeneration modeled on the accounts of the New Testament."[29]

One concern of the preachers, however, was to maintain a balance between reason and emotion so as to avoid the opprobrium of being seen as enthusiasts. What concretely resulted from the kind of evocative discourse that Whitefield and his fellow evangelists practiced in proclaiming the Word, then, was a strengthening of conviction regarding fundamental truth, righteous resolve, and palpable moral reform. First encountering Whitefield in Philadelphia in 1739, Benjamin Franklin not only found his preaching personally moving beyond all expectation but also became his printer and testified to the good he did:

> [Whitefield] was at first permitted to preach in some of our Churches; but the Clergy taking a Dislike to him, soon refus'd him their Pulpits and he was oblig'd to preach in the Fields. The Multitudes of all Sects and Denominations that attended his Sermons were enormous, and it was matter of Speculation to me who was one of the Number, to observe the extraordinary Influence of his Oratory on his Hearers, and how much they admir'd and respected him, notwithstanding his common Abuse of them, by assuring them they were naturally *half Beasts and half Devils.* It was wonderful to see the Change soon made in the Manners of our Inhabitants; from being thoughtless or indifferent about Religion, it seem'd as if all the World were growing Religious; so that one could not walk thro' the Town in an Evening without Hearing Psalms sung in different Families of every Street.[30]

It is against the experiential background of such preaching that the political teaching of the preachers of the eighteenth century is to be seen as it came into powerful display in the crisis of conflict and revolution. A sketch of their views might begin with the representative statement of the famous lexicographer and biblical scholar Noah Webster, who was himself caught up in the fervor of the Second Awakening.

> It is extremely important to our nation, in a political as well as religious view, that all possible authority and influence should be given to the scriptures; for these furnish the best principles of civil liberty, and the most effectual support of republican

government. They teach the true principles of that equality of rights which belongs to every one of the human family, but only in consistency with a strict subordination to the magistrate and the law. The scriptures were intended by God to be the *guide of human reason*. The Creator of man established the moral order of the Universe; knowing that *human nature*, left without a divine guide or rule of action, would fill the world with *disorder, crime and misery*. . . . The principles of all genuine liberty, and of wise laws and administrations are to be drawn from the Bible and sustained by its authority. . . . [T]here are two powers only which are sufficient to control men, and secure the rights of individuals and a peaceable administration; these are the *combined force of religion and law,* and the *force or fear of the bayonet.*

    The Bible is the chief moral cause of all that is *good,* and the best corrector of all that is *evil,* in human society; the *best* book for regulating the temporal concerns of men, and the *only book* that can serve as an infallible guide to future felicity.[31]

This biblical perspective can be illustrated, then, by a representative exposition of the human condition and its political implications such as that sketched in Rev. Gad Hitchcock's anniversary sermon given at Plymouth on December 22, 1774. He began from the premise that man is a moral agent living freely in a reality that is good as coming from the hand of God: "And God saw every thing that he had made, and behold, it was very good."[32] His responsibility is to live well, in accordance with God's commandments and through exercise of his mind and free will. Thus, he longs for knowledge of God's word and truth and seeks God's help to keep an open heart so as to receive them. Among the chief hindrances to this life of true liberty is the oppression of men, who in service to evil deceive with untruth and impose falsehood in its place proclaiming it to be true. Man, blessed with liberty, reason, and a moral sense, created in the image and likeness of God a little lower than the angels and given dominion over the earth (Gen. 1:26; Ps. 8; Heb. 2:6–12), is the chief and most perfect of God's works. Among his perfections is his capacity freely to hold communion with God and, through this intercourse, to improve in natural and moral science and perfection, controlling appetites by his superior principles and growing into full personality through acts of love, gratitude, and obedience toward

God and fellow human beings. Pursuit of these authentic goods, then, defines responsibility.

Liberty is an essential principle of man's constitution, a natural trait that yet reflects the supernatural One whose image man is, and who freely created him and the world. The growth of virtue and the perfection of being depend upon free choice, in response to divine invitation and help, in a cooperative relationship. Liberty is most truly exercised by living in accord with truth and is, therefore, the correlate of responsibility. Man's dominion over the earth and other creatures therein, his mastery of nature through reason, is subject to no restraint but the law of his nature, which is the perfection of liberty; his obligation to obey the laws of the Creator is only a check to licentiousness and abuse. Liberty is thus God given. However, this gift of freedom to do right and live truly carries the opposite possibility as well, that is, rebellion and rejection. This, in turn, leads to the necessity of government to coerce a degree of right living and justice from a mankind fallen from the high road of willing obedience to the loving Father. Moreover, coercive law can be inflicted in ways not merely just and conducive not to truth, righteousness, and union with God but frequently to their very opposites. This biblical understanding of the human condition is reflected, as we have seen, in the most famous passage of *The Federalist Papers* (No. 51), which turns on the sentiment that, if men were angels, there would be no need for government, for what is government but the greatest of all reflections on human nature? It remains true, however, James Madison went on, that "Justice is the end of government. It is the end of civil society. It ever has been, and ever will be pursued, until it be obtained, or until liberty be lost in the pursuit."

Hence, the Royal Psalmist prays: "Deliver me from the oppression of man: So will I keep thy precepts" (Ps. 119:134). The prayer is that he be delivered from human oppression so that he can keep the truth of God. This is thus a prayer for just and free government wherein responsibility to the civil laws conduces to the perfection of virtue and truth in concrete lives of concrete societies of men. The psalmist does not endorse but, rather, condemns enforcing evil in the name of justice and propagating lies as truth, thereby perverting reality and the lives of a people who would, then, imbibe and embody corruption. Such perversion would create an abomination standing in the holy place. It would deform everything it touched. Indeed, by such misrule not liberty but slavery is enforced, inasmuch as living in accordance with an evil will necessarily result in being enslaved to the passions of *libido dominandi,* the lust for power that is the nadir of pride (*superbia vitae,* 1 John 2:16) productive of tyranny or dictatorship. So to live is to abandon both God and our true selves, to forfeit liberty while proclaiming it, and to mutilate the divine image that animates the noble conception of man and reality reflected in Psalm 8, which is rightly called the Magna Carta of humanity. Hence, Thomas Jefferson's personal seal carried the famous motto: Rebellion to Tyrants Is Obedience to God!

While it seems to be true that the Federal Convention did not embrace the aged Benjamin Franklin's suggestion for prayer, there is little doubt that Franklin evoked the sentiment of the country no less than of the clergy when he remarked to that great assembly, presided over by George Washington himself,

> I have lived, Sir, a long time, and the longer I live, the more convincing proofs I see of this truth—*that GOD governs in the affairs of men.* And if a sparrow cannot fall to the ground without his notice, is it probable that an empire can rise without his aid? We have been assured, Sir, in the sacred writings, that "except the Lord build the House they labour in vain that build it." I firmly believe this; and I also believe that without his concurring aid we shall succeed in this political building no better than the Builders of Babel.[33]

Nathan O. Hatch has remarked that "the right to think for oneself became . . . the hallmark of popular Christianity" in America. Such pre-Revolutionary figures as the Presbyterian Reverend David Caldwell in North Carolina and the Baptist Reverend Richard Furman in backcountry South Carolina sought political truth in history and in the Bible all the while emphasizing "the autonomy of the individual conscience."[34] At the heart of this autonomy lay the conviction of the individual's capacity to read and understand the Bible. The consequences are incalculable. As Hatch has emphasized, for example:

> Deep and powerful undercurrents of democratic Christianity distinguish the United States from other modern industrial democracies. These currents insure that churches in this land

do not withhold faith from the rank and file. Instead, religious leaders have pursued people wherever they could be found; embraced them without regard to social standing; and challenged them to think, to interpret Scripture, and to organize the church for themselves. Religious populism, reflecting the passions of ordinary people and the charisma of democratic movement-builders, remains among the oldest and deepest impulses in American life.[35]

A prime example is the message of the popular Baptist Elder John Leland, a friend of Thomas Jefferson and James Madison who joined them—or they him—in arguing that the conscience ought to be "free from human control," who insisted that "religion is a matter between God and individuals," and who roundly dismissed as snobbery and worse the contention that "the ignorant part of the community are not capacitated to judge for themselves." On the contrary, Leland asked:

> Did many of the rulers believe in Christ when he was upon earth? Were not the learned clergy (the scribes) his most inveterate enemies? Do not great men differ as much as little men in judgment? Have not almost all lawless errors crept into the world through the means of wise men (so called)? Is not a simple man, who makes nature and reason his study, a competent judge of things? Is the Bible written (like Caligula's laws) so intricate and high, that none but the letter learned (according to the common phrase) can read it? Is not the vision written so plain that he that runs may read it?[36]

Confidence in the "natural" clarity and unity of the Bible to the ordinary intelligence is a theme not merely of the eighteenth and nineteenth centuries. It is as old as the English Bible itself, as John Wycliffe already stressed in the prologue to his translation:

> he that kepith mekenes and charite hath the trewe vndirston-dyng and perfectioun of al holi writ, as Austyn preuith in his sermoun of the preysing of charite. Therefore no simple man of wit be aferd vnmesurabli to studie in the text of holy writ, for whi tho ben word is of euerlastyng lif, as Petir seid to Crist in the vj. chapitre of Jon; and the Holy Gost stired hooly men to speke and write the wordis of hooly writ for the coumfort and saluacioun of meke cristen men, as Petir in the ij. epistle

in the ende, and Poul in xv. chapitre to Romayns witnessen. . . .
Symple men of wit moun be edified mych to heuenly lyuyng bi
redyng and knowyng of the olde testament, for in the bigynnyng
of Genesis they moun knowe, hou God made heuen and erthe
and alle creaturis of nout, and made man to his owne ymage
and licnesse, and to haue blisse in body and soule with outen
ende.[37]

The unity and intelligibility of the Bible to the average person was
increasingly a motif of major importance in subsequent centuries. It
also was reflected in the preachers' approach to textual exegesis from
the pulpits. The basic principle, following Augustine and Calvin,
was that the Bible is reflexive in the sense of providing its own
explanation of its meaning in an overall consistent whole. The key
to finding that unity according to William Perkins's manual entitled
The Arte of Prophysying (1592, translated in 1607) was to begin the
mastery of the Bible by first mastering Paul's Letter to the Romans;
then, and only then, ought the student move to the remainder of the
New Testament and subsequently to the Old Testament. The result of
this, because of the emphases in Romans, is a stress on justification,
sanctification, and true faith. Meaning is to be found through the
three methods (which cannot be entered into in detail here) called
circumstance, collation, and application. Thus, it is the task of the
preacher as interpreter to place any text into its circumstances and
context, collating it with similar texts elsewhere in the Scriptures,
and to find consistent meaning—then to finish the text of the sermon
by making it and his preaching conform to the "analogies of faith."
This means that any statement made had to be in harmony with or
contained in the *Apostle's Creed*.[38]

For the ordinary believer and individual person the consequences
of habitual Bible reading were enormous. The reliance upon individual judgment of the terms of eternal salvation largely based on
private Bible study may be said to lie at the heart of the formation
of the civic consciousness of responsible individuals. It greatly contributes to the rise of the American republican ethos and citizenry
during the period leading up to independence and in the decades
subsequent to it. As George Trevelyan more generally remarks, "the
effect of the continual domestic study of [the Bible] upon the national
character, imagination, and intelligence for three centuries—was

greater than that of any literary movement in the annals, or any religious movement since St. Augustine."[39]

III

The political implications canvassed by Alice Baldwin remain serviceable today:

> southern Presbyterian ministers based their political concepts upon the Bible. The idea of a fundamental constitution based on law, of inalienable rights which were God-given and therefore natural, of government as a binding compact made between rulers and peoples, of the right of the people to hold their rulers to account and to defend their rights against all oppression, these seem to have been doctrines taught by them all. . . . in the South as in New England, the clergy helped in making familiar to the common people the basic principles on which the Revolution was fought, our constitutional conventions held, our Bills or Rights written and our state and national constitutions founded.[40]

These views were reenforced and amplified by Patricia Bonomi in 1994:

> To be sure, religious differences alone did not bring on the American Revolution. . . . But the striking thing about the dissenting mentality is how easily it flowed in with the emergent republican understanding of the political radicals. Habits inculcated over more than 150 years by such Nonconformist practices as the gathering of congregations, electing of leaders, and then sharing power with them under the principle of majority rule proved far more congenial to republican forms than to the imperial alternative. . . . We may stop well short of proposing religious differences as the primary "cause" of the American Revolution. It may nonetheless be asserted that the state of mind in which American colonials moved toward separation is nowhere better seen than in the realm of religion.[41]

The complexities are not to be minimized for the good reason, as Jonathan Clark has stated, that "early-modern societies [are] far more theoretically articulate than the societies which succeeded them, and their social relations were expressed to a much larger degree in terms of grand theory." "In America a new and programmatic civil religion provided an evangelical impetus for society unlike any the world had seen before: at once more ethical and more materialistic, more libertarian and more deferential to the sovereignty of collective opinion."[42]

Finally, as I earlier tried to summarize a part of this subject elsewhere:

> The great frame of biblical symbolism is comprehended in Exodus, Covenant, and Canaan. That the American Israel understood itself as continuing this history through its pilgrimage to the American wilderness in analogy with the Mosaic adventures is well known but bears repeating. The fact that Americans organized themselves by covenants for civil as well as religious purposes and even in federations of covenants is clear; and that the Constitution itself is framed in the spirit of the covenant, compact, contract symbolism is evident. That this symbolism is indebted to Christian theory is also acknowledged, "Without the strong link that Augustine forged between consent and will, social contract theory would be unthinkable, since it defines consent in terms of will" [writes Patrick Riley]. But then, the whole sequence of biblical covenants linking consent and will lay behind Augustine. That the symbolism of Exodus can be applied to the departure of America from the British Empire through independence also is clear and in keeping with the tenor of the religious literature of the period. That the Revolution was theorized as a just war is explicit in the resolutions of the Congress and even in Tom Paine's writings. That the fulfillment of time in the dawn of the millennium in America by establishment of *novus ordo seclorum* of Constitution and republic is a palpable hope of a faithful people and a theme that has played a role in American consciousness into the present century. Who could doubt that America is a special and favored nation? Could this not be the beginning of time transfigured into the eternal Sabbath of the Eighth Day? Such apocalyptical enthusiasm, however, was generally kept in check by the robust good sense of the founders, and the watchful, hopeful waiting typified by President Ezra Stiles [of Yale] seems to be consonant with general sentiment.[43]

It is from some such a general perspective, one emphatically open to the horizon of being, that not only the ringing lines of the

Declaration of Independence are to be read and understood but also the Constitution and Bill of Rights and the order they represent— if we mean to understand them as Americans of the time did. Or at least so it seems to me. This, in turn, might serve to direct our inquiry toward the philosophical and natural law foundations of the American political and constitutional order so as to trace its sources into Renaissance, medieval, and perhaps still earlier times. As Harold Berman has written, from the religious perspective on law and Constitution, "history is a revelation of divine providence, a spiritual story of the unfolding of God's own purposes, and more particularly [it teaches] that God works in history, in part, through his elect nation . . . which is historically destined to reveal and incarnate God's mission for mankind."[44] Then, when we are satisfied that we have the story straight as to origins and meaning, we still have to face the question of the importance of even an essentially true account for present and future concerns—the famous *So what?*—that is, the theoretical, political, and existential consequences for the conduct of life in truth. But these are tasks for another day.

5

Religious Liberty and Religion in the American Founding

R ECENT WRITERS ON THE subject of religious liberty in America today paint a picture that would have both aston-ished and appalled even the most enlightened members of the founding generation of this country. For this was quite plainly a Christian country from the perspective of the founding generation generally, and even those of its luminaries who for whatever reasons disdained denominational affiliation or public worship held biblical religion in high esteem as fundamental to the civilization and the public virtue of the rising new republic. The point is tellingly made by an anecdote recounted by Reverend Ethan Allen. Thomas Jefferson was hurrying to church one Sunday morning "with his large red prayer book under his arm when a friend querying him after their mutual good morning said which way are you walking Mr. Jefferson. To which he replied to Church Sir. You going to church Mr. J. You do not believe a word in it. Sir said Mr. J. No nation has ever yet existed or been governed without religion. Nor can be. The Christian religion is the best religion that has been given to man and I as chief Magistrate of this nation am bound to give it the sanction of my example. Good morning Sir."[1] The fact verges on self-evidence, to quote one authority: "Who can deny that for them the very core of existence was their relation to God?"[2]

1. Tendencies toward radical privatization of religion and their effects. In considering the perspectives of those who laid the foun-dations of liberty in America, including freedom of conscience, it seems useful to pause at the outset to notice the quagmire into which American society has plunged on the subject of religious freedom— if legal literature is any indication, at least. Jurisprudence in this area has been called "a maze," "in significant disarray," "a conceptual disaster area," "inconsistent and unprincipled," and not unlike the adventures of "Alice in Wonderland."[3] The flavor is given in 1993 by another legal writer who begins his analysis from that oracle of postmodern nihilistic deconstructionism, the nineteenth-century German thinker Friedrich Nietzsche, whose Zarathustra exclaimed: "God is dead! God remains dead! And we have killed him!" The writer concludes his essay as follows:

> The effect of selective post-modernism is to allow secular ide-
> ologies to use political muscle to advance their causes, including
> using the public schools to inculcate their ideals, without even
> the psychological constraint of liberal neutrality, but at the same
> time to preserve liberal formalism in court to ensure that religion
> is not included in the public dialogue. Thus, in New York City
> the children are read *Heather Has Two Mommies* in the first grade
> and given information on anal intercourse in the sixth; but, as the
> Tenth Circuit recently held, *The Bible in Pictures* must be removed
> from the shelf of the fifth grade classroom library.

If you dispute the fact that God is dead, the author continues, "you have the inalienable right to sing, weep, laugh, and mumble, so long as you do it in private. That is the freedom of religion in the postmodern age."[4]

Perhaps this is merely hyperbole—or a sign of salutary social progress, depending on how one looks at it. But the alarm has been sounded by distinguished scholars. Thus, from their perspective, radical privatization of religion is a tendency to be reckoned with in contemporary America. It has as one of its most objectionable effects, as Michael McConnell indicates, leaving by default the avowedly religiously neutral atheism of the politically correct secular state as the officially sanctioned ideology inculcated in public schools. Harold J. Berman concurs. As he wrote as long ago as 1979, the result closely approximates in George Washington's America the pattern of institutions and state-imposed ideology fostered through the unquestionable orthodoxy of Marxism-Leninism in the former

Soviet Union. "The Soviet Constitution provides for the separation of church and state and for freedom of religion. . . . Thus atheism, by claiming to be not a religion, but a science or a philosophy, is in fact 'established,' and traditional religions such as Christianity, Judaism, and Islam are withdrawn from public discourse. It seems to me that this example shows quite well that it is not, in and of itself, the constitutional guarantee of freedom of religion from governmental control or support that is our final protection against religious oppression."[5]

It should also be noticed that the quest for a sufficiently innocuous and comprehensive definition of the *religion* that Americans may, after all, be free to exercise under terms of the First Amendment leads one commentator to the reductionist extreme of identifying it in terms of primitive totemistic belief systems that our founders are likely to have considered a caricature.[6] Religious substance is and has been a principal care of Americans because it lies at the core of our culture. Whatever the broad applications, the precious heritage of America is biblical faith and religious liberty on the biblical pattern. Totemism, proceduralism, and broad classification working hand-in-hand with deconstructionism are unsatisfactory in this sphere. Such exceptionalism may pose significant problems in an age of generics, but it lies inconveniently close to the heart of the matter.[7]

Similarly, the United States has prized personal liberty generally on the pattern of, and in continuity with, the English Whig and common law traditions distantly represented by Sir Edward Coke, Magna Carta, and the ancient constitution of England as that tradition was reaffirmed in the seventeenth century and revivified during the founding as a central element. Thus, American liberty is not Jacobin liberty, it is argued.[8] Religion and liberty were understood by the founders to be linked in important ways. In reflecting on the spirit of '76 late in life, John Adams pointedly summarized matters in a letter to Thomas Jefferson:

> The *general principles,* on which the Fathers Atchieved Independence, were the only Principles in which that beautiful Assembly of young Gentlemen [representing the numerous religious denominations of the country at the time of the Revolution] could Unite. . . . And what were these *general Principles?* I answer, the general Principles of Christianity, in which all those

> Sects were United: And the *general Principles* of English and
> American Liberty, in which all those young Men United, and
> which had United all Parties in America, in Majorities suf-
> ficient to assert and maintain her Independence. Now I will
> avow, that I then believed, and now believe, that those general
> Principles of Christianity, are as eternal and immutable, as the
> Existence and Attributes of God; and those Principles of Liberty,
> are as unalterable as human Nature and our terrestrial, mundane
> System.[9]

The treasury of Anglo-American civilization's religious and constitutional attainment as manifested in the founding is a triumph
of faith and reason of millennial significance, as the founders themselves tended to believe. If one looks to the founding for any guidance, it ill accords with this fact for its substance to be equated
in contemporary jurisprudence of the Constitution with irrational
primitivism in religion and fundamentalistic positivism, a philosophy averse to all "transcendental moonshine."[10] Their common root
Perry Miller three decades ago identified as "obtuse secularism,"[11]
a persuasion now often heard in the trendy babel of neo-Marxian
dialects. Such a decoding of their intent or meaning, it seems safe to
say, definitely was not what any of the founders had in mind. And it
seems not to be what the general run of the American public today
has in mind, either.[12] If such critics as McConnell and Berman are
right, those in public policy positions and charged with husbanding
the American system of ordered liberty may have occasion to reflect
on the ancient adage of good government: *salus populi suprema lex
esto*—the well-being and security of the people is the supreme law.[13]

In this vein, there is the elementary premise that, under free
government, in the liberal tradition that has shaped our politics
since the seventeenth century, there exists the indispensable requirement of nurturing a community's cohesion and well-being—a point
suggested by the drift of the Preamble's "promote the general Welfare, . . . secure the Blessings of Liberty to ourselves and our Posterity." Otherwise there can be no possibility of free government at all,
but only the alternatives of anarchy or coercive apolitical oppression.
As James Madison and Publius remarked on more than one occasion,
representative majority rule (government of, by, and for the people)
is the republican principle that must inevitably be served, even as

we seek the means to avoid majoritarian evils leading to tyranny and, thereby, to preserve individual liberties. We are unaccustomed to thinking of Madison as a champion of the community's well-being and popular government as first priorities. As Marvin Myers remarks, "Madison's lifelong concern with the dangers of majority rule has sometimes obscured the source of that concern: his prior commitment to popular government."[14]

That a community unified by fundamental convictions beyond the calculation of merely material interests actually existed, and that it was considered vital for the success of America's republican experiment, was attested by John Jay writing as Publius near the beginning of *The Federalist Papers:* "It has until lately been a received and uncontradicted opinion, that the prosperity of the people of America depended on their continuing firmly united, and the wishes, prayers, and efforts of our best and wisest Citizens have been constantly directed to that object. . . . I have . . . often taken notice, that Providence has been pleased to give this one connected country, to one united people, a people descended from the same ancestors, speaking the same language, professing the same religion, attached to the same principles of government, very similar in their manners and customs, and who, by their joint counsels, arms and efforts, fighting side by side through a long and bloody war, have nobly established their general Liberty and Independence. . . . A strong sense of the value and blessings of Union induced the people, at a very early period, to institute a Federal Government to preserve and perpetuate it."[15]

A century before Publius wrote, John Locke justified majoritarian rule on the principle that the community is vital to free government, and a community must move in one direction: this can only be that of the greater number and force, as the sine qua non of free government—that is, government based on the consent of the people.[16] This theory of politics as grounded in consent and consecrated to liberty and justice is given authoritative statement in the opening lines of the Declaration of Independence. From it arises the indispensable fiction that every man's consent to law is given in an act of Parliament or of the legislative body more generally. As Sir Thomas Smith, who was secretary of state to Queen Elizabeth, stated the principle in 1589:

all that ever the people of Rome might do either in *centuriatis comitiis* or *tributis,* the same may be done by the parliament of England which representeth and hath the power of the whole realm, both the head and the body. For every Englishman is intended to be there present, either in person or by procuration and attorneys, of what preeminence, state, dignity or quality soever he be, from the prince, be he king or queen, to the lowest person of England. And the consent of the parliament is taken to be every man's consent.[17]

Those of our citizens today who evidently find the American political tradition so odious as to seem intent on dismantling or transforming it have grasped the essentially political nature of our constitutional system, even as they reach for levers of power. Perhaps citizens who prudently regard democracy as the worst form of government except for all the others, who wish to preserve and continue to adapt rule of law and ordered liberty as these have historically evolved since 1776, need to nurture consensus in the politically effective community before it is fractured beyond all repair. Ingenuity moderated by the kind of common sense reflected in Justice Robert H. Jackson's "celebrated warning" in the 1949 *Terminiello* case may be to the point: "There is a danger that, if the Court does not temper its doctrinaire logic with a little practical wisdom, it will convert the constitutional Bill of Rights into a suicide pact."[18] And that, too, was not the founders' intention.

2. Theoretical and historical basis of religious liberty. My principal concern here is to clarify something of the historical and theoretical ground of American religious liberty as it emerged in the founding generation with particular attention to the role of James Madison. In addition, I hope to suggest the cogency of this perspective as an enduring legacy of American freedom considered, not merely as a time-bound and parochial achievement, but as a philosophically acute and politically astute insight into the institutionalization of just order in society. To these ends I shall briefly reflect on the concern with religion and religious liberty as matters of compelling importance to human beings, discuss several justifications for toleration leading to the principle of liberty of conscience, and pay attention to the role especially of James Madison in the institutionalization of religious liberty in Virginia. That activity, it turned out, became the immediate background for the drafting and ratification of the federal Constitution and Bill of Rights.

To begin with, there are certain philosophical considerations. Thus, the key problem underlying the matter of religious liberty is the theoretical question of the right relationship between the temporal and spiritual realms of reality, and secondary to that, the practical question of how the relationship can optimally be institutionalized in ordering society. To use the New Testament terms favored by James Madison, for instance, this requires that the community "Render . . . unto Caesar the things which are Caesar's; and unto God the things that are God's." It also means taking to heart the Gospel's principle: "My kingdom is not of this world."[19]

Human experience intimates that reality is not exhausted by the temporal and spatial sphere but that the civilized existence is surmounted or comprehended by the divine, eternal, and transcendental reality apperceived as the spiritual realm called God. Such a layered or stratified structure of reality, articulated in levels from the material to the divine and participated in by men through a human nature that is the epitome of being, was—despite the inroads of radical French Enlightenment—still the common coin of Western civilization for Americans into the period of the eighteenth-century founding. It supplies the background for any discussion of our subject that wishes to avoid hopeless anachronism or the obtuse secularism that often vitiates inquiry. We can rightly be reminded of the injunction to understand the founders as they understood themselves as a worthwhile standard, provided only that we be allowed to draw the implications of their thinking from a theoretical perspective. From the specific perspective of our subject, the following observation has recently been made:

> It is important to remember that the framers and ratifiers of the first amendment found it conceivable that a God—that is, a universal and transcendental authority beyond human judgment—might exist. If God might exist, then it is not arbitrary to hold that His will is superior to the judgment of individuals or of civil society. Much of the criticism of a special deference to sincere religious convictions arises from the assumption that such convictions are *necessarily* mere subcategories of personal moral judgments. This amounts to a denial of the possibility

of a God (or at least of a God whose will is made manifest to humans).[20]

As has been suggested, Americans at the time of the founding were virtually unanimous in embracing such views—not merely as hypotheses in Enlightenment fashion, but as articles of their living faith.

In the eighteenth-century horizon of our inquiry, *liberty* (including religious liberty) is distinguished from *license*. The understanding endures that the genuinely free man is one who lives in accordance with truth and justice, so that liberty, law, reason, and revelation are interrelated symbols of order that cannot be separated from one another. Sir Edward Coke's *Institutes*—along with his *Reports* the hornbook of John Adams and Thomas Jefferson, and also the basis of legal education in America into the late 1770s—expounds this understanding of the relationship between liberty and law. Coke writes that the primary meaning of *libertates* in Magna Carta is "the Laws of the Realm, in which respect this Charter is called, *Charta libertatum*. . . . It Signifieth the freedomes, that the Subjects of England have."[21] This is in harmony with the philosophers' insight that a free man is precisely one who lives in accordance with reason and highest truth. Reason *(nous)* is related to the individual in the same manner that law *(nomos)* is related to society, so that rule of law is the governance of God and reason. Conversely, the slave is any human being (regardless of social status) who so deforms or perverts his nature that life is dominated by ungoverned passions. These reign in a brutish dominion wherein instrumental reason secures the ways to gratification, whether of private desire or of political *libido dominandi,* as in the tyrannical man of Plato—or, perhaps, the putative normal man of Hobbes.[22] From the horizon of evangelical Protestant Christianity (the controlling horizon of our founders and of the communities they represented), the free man is the man of faith who stands in divine grace, in the law of liberty of Christ's embrace symbolized as "the way, the truth and the life," out of a free response of the contrite heart to the divine appeal expressive in *amor Dei* and, within mortal limitations, a blameless life: "whoso looketh into the perfect law of liberty, and continueth *therein,* he being not a forgetful hearer, but a doer of the work, this man shall be blessed in his deed."[23]

These convergent lines of insight into order pose the problem of the founders as much as they convey something of the background of their convictions. For it is manifestly possible, and appears from all I know to be likely, that the representatives of the American communities of the time that we collectively designate as our founders were both men of conviction and men of sufficient divergence in their specific convictions as to embrace liberty of conscience not merely as the prudential device of statesmen but, as reflective men of faith and varying degrees of zeal, out of humble recognition of the limits of human knowledge. In other words, there is an unavoidable need to separate the question of exactly what the founders believed from the question of what they saw as requisite to the establishment of a compound republic that would not founder on the rock of religious division, the bane of modern Western history. "Torrents of blood have been spilt in the old world, by vain attempts of the secular arm, to extinguish Religious discord, by proscribing all difference in Religious opinion," Madison wrote in 1785. Moreover, the zeal with which they and their several communities sought to serve and propagate the truth of ultimate reality was effectively curbed by taking to heart the judicious Richard Hooker's timeless maxim of moderation: "Think ye are men, deem it not impossible for you to err."[24] This admonition plants the seed of toleration and propagates the saving doubt essential to any free government that is ineluctably grounded in the consent of heterogeneous communities. It fosters civility and squarely places reliance upon persuasion as the basis of liberty of conscience for individual persons and of peace for society.

3. American tradition and liberty of conscience for religious reasons. Some such set of considerations would seem to underlie the American political decisions of prohibiting a religious establishment and of ensuring freedom of conscience. These are compromises, but they are ones without which the country probably could not have been constituted and almost certainly could not have endured. Behind these compromises looms, however, the whole array of problems arising from concerns about the moral and philosophical rectitude of a political establishment not formally anchored in the community's nurture and acceptance of a coherent account of the good that attends to all levels of reality, including divine Being. How is the bridge between the philosophical and theological anthropology of classical philosophy and general Christianity—the core structuring elements of the American community at the time of the founding—to be erected and sustained so as to ground the political life of the country morally and ontologically without formal institutional support? What seems to be lacking in the American experiment with free government is coercive means to make men free, to maintain the consensus along lines of the philosophical and biblical teachings universally embraced at the time. Put otherwise, where and how would the sustaining fundamental core agreement about matters of first importance upon which free republican institutions finally depend (because resting upon consent of the people) be renewed and vivified without some authoritative orthodoxy of belief? Are the solutions of Lockean toleration or of Madisonian and Jeffersonian liberty of conscience merely seductive subterfuges, a dark calculus whereby a radical secular Enlightenment propagating outright atheism is in time expected to claim the personal and social life of the country for itself, as long ago feared and lately reasserted?[25] Let us reflect upon these questions.

In discussing religious liberty it is important not to leave out the religious dimension of the subject, whatever one may conclude (or not conclude) about the spiritual interests and convictions of such luminaries as Washington, Adams, Jefferson, Madison, and Franklin. Such an impartial student as Alexis de Tocqueville makes the fundamental point that in America, perhaps uniquely in the world, "two perfectly distinct elements which elsewhere have often been at war with one another . . . somehow . . . incorporate into each other, forming a marvelous combination. I mean the *spirit of religion* and the *spirit of freedom.*" This amazing feat is possible, Tocqueville believes, because the English colonists

> brought to the New World a Christianity which I can only de-
> scribe as democratic and republican. . . . There is not a single
> religious doctrine hostile to democratic and republican institu-
> tions. . . . America is the place where the Christian religion has
> kept the greatest real power over men's souls; and nothing better
> demonstrates how useful and natural it is to man, since the coun-
> try where it now has widest sway is both the most enlightened
> and the freest. . . . It was religion that gave birth to the English
> colonies in America. One must never forget that. In the United

States religion is mingled with all the national customs and all those feelings which the word fatherland evokes. For that reason it has peculiar power. . . . Christianity itself is an established and irresistible fact which no one seeks to attack or to defend.[26]

If Tocqueville's status as founder or contemporary of the founders be questioned, a word from a famous Pennsylvanian can supplement these statements. Dr. Benjamin Rush, a confidant of Jefferson, Franklin, and Adams, along with other leaders of his time, subscribing as did most of his contemporaries to the proposition that liberty cannot be established without morality nor morality and a virtuous citizenry without religion, wrote: "The only foundation for a useful education in a republic is to be laid in RELIGION. Without this, there can be no virtue, and without virtue there can be no liberty, and liberty is the object and life of all republican governments. . . . The religion I mean to recommend in this place is the religion of JESUS CHRIST. . . . A Christian cannot fail of being a republican . . . for every precept of the Gospel inculcates those degrees of humility, self-denial, and brotherly kindness which are directly opposed to the pride of monarchy and the pageantry of court . . . his religion teacheth him that no man 'liveth unto himself.' . . . [H]is religion teacheth him in all things to do to others what he would wish, in like circumstances, they should do to him."[27] An evangelical Christian consensus that, whatever the diversity of creeds, generally marked America at the time of the Revolution was a fundamental of the society and recognized as such by leading figures.

The conventional understanding of religious toleration, religious liberty, or liberty of conscience reconciles it to one or the other of two models, one resting on political or rationalist principle and the other on religious principle. The view was given succinct statement by James Lord Bryce a century ago in his famous book, *The American Commonwealth.* The political principle, he wrote,

> sets out from the principles of liberty and equality. It holds any attempt at compulsion by the civil power to be an infringement on liberty of thought, as well as on liberty of action, which could be justified only when a practice claiming to be religious is so obviously anti-social or immoral as to threaten the well-being of the community. . . . The second principle . . . starts from the

conception of the church as a spiritual body existing for spiritual purposes, and moving along spiritual paths. It is an assemblage of men who are united by their devotion to an unseen Being, their memory of a divine life, their belief in the possibility of imitating that life, so far as human frailty allows, their hopes for an illimitable future. Compulsion of any kind is contrary to the nature of such a body, which lives by love and reverence, not by law. It desires no state help, feeling that its strength comes from above, and that its kingdom is not of this world. . . . Least of all can it submit to be controlled by the state, for the state, in such a world as the present, means persons many or most of whom are alien to its beliefs and cold to its emotions. The conclusion follows that the church as a spiritual entity will be happiest and strongest when it is left absolutely to itself, not patronized by the civil power, not restrained by law except when and in so far as it may attempt to quit its proper sphere and intermeddle in secular affairs.

Lord Bryce concludes, "The former much more than the latter . . . has moved the American mind." As a consequence of this happy arrangement, "There are no quarrels of churches and sects. Judah does not vex Ephraim, nor Ephraim envy Judah."[28]

This is important testimony to the prudential success of the founders' approach to reconciling religion and politics in America, given a century after their work was done. These observations, however, do not quite do justice to the view of religious liberty held by many eighteenth-century Americans. Perry Miller has written, perhaps thinking mainly of the established churches, that the "Protestant churches did not so much achieve religious liberty as have liberty thrust upon them." Generally speaking, they did not so much contribute "to religious liberty, they stumbled into it, they were compelled into it, they accepted it at last because they had to, or because they saw its strategic value."[29] The situation was more complex and contradictory than either Bryce or Miller suggests, and the direct role of the dissenting churches, perhaps the Baptists chief among them, in establishing religious liberty as it took shape in the generation of the founding is unquestionably great.

A leading historian of the subject, William G. McLoughlin, contradicts Lord Bryce's judgment that primarily the political or rationalistic justification of religious liberty has moved the American mind:

neither of the two approaches delineated above has prevailed. The establishment of the principle of disestablishment in 1791 [through adoption of the federal Bill of Rights] was a temporary, fortuitous and unresolved alliance between the two. And what applied to the federal government did not apply to any of its constituent states. For the major part of our history the pietistic approach has been dominant, though since 1925 the rationalist approach (which underlies most of the decisions of the United States Supreme Court) has become so. Still, the tension exists today as powerfully as it did in 1791.[30]

Related to and defining religious liberty are several distinct elements that impact both politics and religion. Much of the struggle for "soul liberty" in America, once toleration had been achieved (in 1691 in New England), was for disestablishment of the Standing Order Congregational Church in New England and of the Anglican Church in much of the remainder of America and the rise of separatism or voluntarism in its stead. But exactly what was meant by establishment varied. One thing it tended to mean was the payment of taxes to support a church and its ministers whether or not one was a member of that church, a "dissenter" being subject to sometimes severe penalties including imprisonment and public whipping. A second element related to the quest for acceptance and equality by dissenting communions that suffered physically and psychologically from discrimination and disabilities, both social and legal, that branded them as inferior. Thus, the quest for liberty was one for equality as well, for respectability and leadership in society on a common footing with the members of other sects. A third element that complemented voluntarism and pluralism was pietistic-perfectionism, a major symbolism of America itself as a city on a hill with a world-historic providential destiny to fulfill in an eschatological triumph of spirit. Since both the established and the dissenting communities were pietistic in America, the spectrum of attitudes ranged along related forms of pietism. These included the search for moral order, the thirst for religious freedom, and the interaction with Enlightenment philosophies that played an important role from the 1750s onward. In comparing attitudes of the Baptist leader Isaac Backus with those of Thomas Jefferson, McLoughlin remarks: "Both Jefferson and Backus wanted separation of church and state so that the truth would prevail, but for Backus truth came through the heart by grace, whereas for Jefferson it came through the head by reason."[31] A fourth element was the relation of the progress of religious liberty to the process of democratization itself as, in the wake of the founding, that matured to shape the rise of Jeffersonian and Jacksonian democracy with its individualism and laissez-faire attitudes.[32] These attitudes were undergirded by the revivals or Great Awakenings that had first stirred, and then tended to universalize, American religious experience so as to insist upon personal conversion, to maintain the priesthood of all believers, to oppose public support of religion, and to organize individual churches on the principle of congregational autonomy—subject to no authority for their communicants' faith but God, Scripture, and conscience. These originally religious attitudes conditioned and indelibly schooled American citizenship itself in the rising democratic nation.

All in all, as a result the "old religious myth of the errand into the wilderness, the city upon a hill, the Bible Commonwealth that was an outpost looking backward toward Europe, was rejected for the new nationalist myth of divinely directed manifest destiny." McLoughlin is the historian of the New England Baptists, primarily, but the story can rightly be generalized. Nor is it all rhapsodic. "The trend toward individualism ends in the tyranny of the majority; the ardor of pietism is cooled by the necessity of institutionalization; the courageous dissenters are often intolerant conformists; the advocates of religious liberty practice religious discrimination; the non-conformist becomes the status-seeker; the fight for disestablishment ends in the creation of a new kind of establishment—the White, Anglo-Saxon, Evangelical Protestant 'establishment.' " Still, the American quest for liberty through the belief that all men are created equal rose and fell but never completely subsided after 1776. Nor did conviction falter among evangelical Christians in the nation's oft-proclaimed providential destiny "to play the crucial role in advancing the Kingdom of God on Earth."[33]

As nurtured especially (not exclusively, of course) from the religious impetus, then, liberty of conscience may be said to have moved through three phases of development: from *toleration* viewed as a reluctant but necessary concession to dissenters wrung from the established order for the sake of peace, to an assertion of *liberty of conscience* based on the conviction of human equality before God, to the claim of *perfect freedom of belief and practice* conceived as essential to truth itself and to a life lived in accordance with truth. These stages generally can be identified with the writings and work of John Locke, Roger Williams, and Isaac Backus, respectively.[34] And it will have been seen that, whatever the ambiguities and inconsistencies involved, American claims to religious liberty did not annul the proclamation of Christian truth, retard its propagation, or dim hope for the universal triumph of that truth. The drive toward religious freedom in the 1780s was part and parcel of the American evangelical movement itself. It was a fervent religious conviction of such Baptist leaders as Isaac Backus in Massachusetts and, between 1776 and 1791, of Elder John Leland in Virginia, where the latter became Madison's obstreperous constituent and political ally in Orange County. Simply said, establishment equated with political control of religion and stifled spiritual growth and initiative. Moreover, the dissenting sects had much to gain by breaking the monopoly of the old established churches. "The greatest support for disestablishment and free exercise therefore came from evangelical Protestant denominations, especially Baptists, Quakers, but also Presbyterians, Lutherans, and others."[35]

4. Prudential justifications for religious liberty: Madison and Jefferson in Virginia. If we turn our attention from the primarily religious to the primarily political concern for religious liberty (to the extent that the dichotomy is serviceable), we come face-to-face with the handiwork of Virginians, especially Thomas Jefferson and James Madison. Both of these men championed religious liberty throughout their careers, and especially Madison reacted in anguish and anger as a young man to Virginia's harsh persecution of dissenters that intensified in 1768 against the Baptists. When twenty-two years old he wrote his college chum William Bradford expressing attitudes he would hold for the remainder of his long life:

> [I] have nothing to brag of as to the State and Liberty of my Country. Poverty and Luxury prevail among all sorts [here in Virginia]: Pride, ignorance, and Knavery among the Priesthood, and Vice and Wickedness among the Laity. This is bad enough. But it is not the worst I have to tell you. That diabolical Hell-conceived principle of persecution rages among some and to

their eternal Infamy the Clergy can furnish their Quota of Imps for such business. This vexes me the most of any thing whatever. There are at this [time?] in the adjacent County [Culpeper?] not less than 5 or 6 well meaning men in close Gaol for publishing their religious Sentiments which in the main are very orthodox. I have neither patience to hear talk or think of any thing relative to this matter, for I have squabbled and scolded abused and ridiculed so long about it, [to so lit]tle purpose, that I am without common patience. So I [leave you] to pity me and pray for Liberty of Conscience [to revive among us.].

An editorial note to this letter adds: "Apparently it was religious issues, more than tax and trade regulation disputes with England, which were rapidly luring JM away from his beloved studies and arousing his interest in contemporary politics."[36]

Madison's activities in personally defending jailed Baptist ministers marked the beginning of a public career that next saw him helping to frame the Virginia Declaration of Rights, defending his state against the advocates of religious establishment through authorship of the "Memorial and Remonstrance against Religious Assessments," securing passage of Jefferson's long dormant Bill for Religious Freedom (January 1786), playing a pivotal role in the Philadelphia Convention in framing the Constitution of 1787, leading the drafting and passage of the federal Bill of Rights in the First Congress under the Constitution in 1789, enforcing it as president, and never deviating throughout his long lifetime in his devotion to liberty of conscience. Madison regarded securing the enactment of the Virginia Act for Establishing Religious Freedom (the official title) as his most gratifying legislative achievement. "We now give full credit to the contribution of James Madison, mediating with consummate skill among Baptists, Presbyterians, and liberal Anglicans, putting through the Statute while Jefferson was in Paris," Henry F. May writes. "The troops were Baptists and Presbyterians and the tactics were Madison's, but the words—with a few minor corrections made by the Assembly—were Jefferson's. These were and are wholly representative of the Revolutionary Enlightenment."[37]

"Religious liberty," Madison's biographer Ralph Ketcham observes, "stands out as the one subject upon which Madison took an extreme, absolute, undeviating position throughout his life." He continues:

There is no evidence that Madison's defence of religious liberty reflected any hostility to religion itself or to its social effects. On the contrary, he argued repeatedly that freedom of religion enhanced *both* its intrinsic vitality and its contribution to the common weal. He believed that attitudes and habits nourished by the churches could and did help importantly to improve republican government. He believed just as strongly that complete separation of church and state saved the church from the inevitably corrupting influence of civil authority. . . . Throughout his long public career he received cordial support from Protestants, Catholics, and Jews who admired his forthright stand on religious liberty. . . . Madison bespoke fully and cogently what came to be the characteristically American attitude toward the relation between religion and politics.[38]

The Virginia Declaration/Bill of Rights of 1776 was drafted by George Mason, and it was especially Article 16 that was revised in one key phrase at young James Madison's suggestion, in his first legislative triumph. It reads in final form as follows:

16. That Religion, or the duty which we owe to our Creator, and the manner of discharging it, can be directed only by reason and conviction, not by force or violence; and, therefore, all men are equally entitled to the free exercise of religion, according to the dictates of conscience; and that it is the mutual duty of all to practice Christian forbearance, love, and charity, towards each other.[39]

A half century later, Madison believed that the effect of his emendation was to substitute for the word *toleration* "inadvertently adopted" by Mason "phraseology which—declared the freedom of conscience to be a natural and absolute right."[40] This was certainly the drift of his convictions and intentions more generally. The distance of the pietism of Isaac Backus from the Virginians' version of religious liberty can be gauged from the following article that the former proposed for inclusion in the Massachusetts Constitution of 1780:

As God is the only worthy object of all religious worship, and nothing can be true religion but a voluntary obedience unto his revealed will, of which each rational soul has an equal right to judge for itself; every person has an inalienable right to act in all religious affairs according to the full persuasion of his own mind, where others are not injured thereby. And Civil rulers are so far from having any right to empower any person or persons to judge for others in such affairs, and to enforce their judgments with the sword, that their power ought to be exerted to protect all persons and societies within their jurisdiction from being injured or interrupted in the free enjoyment of this right under any presumption whatsoever.[41]

The more specifically Christian appeal in Backus's language is to be observed. The pattern of calculated vagueness displayed by Madison, to avoid any sectarian identification, persisted throughout his career.[42] It is "God" who alone deserves "worship," and "true religion" is nothing but a voluntary obedience to his "revealed will," in Backus's language. Of course, the final clause in the Virginia document counseling "Christian forbearance" remained unchanged from Mason's original draft—as did also the first clause with its appeal to "reason and conviction"—and cannot be attributed to Madison. The latter notion is reflected in Backus's text, which claims for every rational soul the liberty to judge religious truth for itself and makes explicit the inalienability of every person's "right to act in all religious affairs according to the full persuasion of his own mind."

5. The "Memorial and Remonstrance against Religious Assessments" and its aftermath. The great document outlining Madison's case for religious liberty came with the "Memorial and Remonstrance against Religious Assessments" in 1785. Here an elaborate argument is advanced that clearly does do what Madison believed years later he had done by modifying the language of the Virginia Declaration of Rights in 1776. It takes the form of a listing of fifteen arguments against enactment of a bill to support teachers of the Christian religion, this being seen as a device for reestablishing religion in Virginia. The issue was so treacherous politically that Madison kept his authorship secret for forty years, only acknowledging it in 1826. After all, in a religious time, with Christianity understood as the very foundation of life and morals, why should not its teachers be at least partly compensated from public funds? Were opponents really opposed to Christianity itself? The way out, politically, was through alliance with the Baptists and Presbyterians, who stoutly opposed all forms of civil support of religion.

The deluge of arguments given in the "Memorial and Remonstrance" touches every level of appeal. It begins and ends with quotation of the Virginia Declaration of Rights, which embraces all of the liberties most sacred to society. It is, thus, both fundamental law and undeniable truth that religion cannot be coerced but is strictly a matter of reason, conviction, and the conscience that is unalienable and subject only to each person's inner judgment. Religious duty is precedent to all claims of civil society, and thus derives from a natural right resting on higher law. "Before any man can be considered as a member of Civil Society, he must be considered as a subject of the Governour of the Universe"—Creator, Universal Sovereign, and Supreme Lawgiver, as God is variously named. The absolute superiority and priority of the freedom of conscience is such "that in matters of Religion, no man's right is abridged by the institution of Civil Society and . . . Religion is wholly exempt from its cognizance." Compulsion by any majority in civil society in matters of religion is ultra vires—a trespass against the minority's rights, since these are strictly beyond the reach of any civil process whatever. To overstep this limit is to plunge the society into slavery and tyranny. In a passage reminiscent of *Federalist No. 51*, Madison argues that the "preservation of a free Government requires not merely, that the metes and bounds which separate each department of power be invariably maintained; but more especially that neither of them be suffered to overleap the great Barrier [of unalienable natural rights and higher law] which defends the rights of the people." To do so exceeds the outer limits of legitimate authority.

Paragraph 3 subtly plays on the language of the hated Declaratory Act of 1766, which so galvanized the American colonies against Britain when it claimed the right to bind them in all cases whatsoever, including in matters religious by threatening to send a bishop to America to secure uniformity. Madison recalls the three-pence tax on tea as well, conjuring the worst fears of an audience ready to believe that great monstrosities can grow from tiny afflictions. "Who does not see that the same authority which can establish Christianity, in exclusion of all other Religions, may establish with the same ease any particular sect of Christians, in exclusion of all other Sects?" This was a devastating line of argument from the perspective of the Elder Leland and his Baptist communicants. In Paragraph 8 the contrast with tyranny is drawn and just government identified as one that protects every citizen's enjoyment of religion in exactly the same way that it protects his property and person. The horror of persecution resulting in the Inquisition is evoked, as is also the futility of attempting to torment believers into unanimity of belief by coercing orthodoxy, the "[t]orrents of blood" of the old world offered as conclusive evidence. Thus, as a pragmatic matter, the cure has been discovered: equal and complete liberty, which has dawned at last in America.

A further practical matter attaching to the unenforceability of such coerced support of religion is the enervation of all law. The consequent demonstration of impotent rule inevitably follows, undermining all public authority and pushing society toward the brink of anarchy and civil strife. If, despite all reason, such a policy will be pursued, then it ought at least to have the support of a clear majority of the people, which it currently did not have. Madison concludes by pointing out that infringing the religious liberty guaranteed in the Declaration of Rights will at the same time weaken the protection of and potentially violate all of the most precious rights of free men under the Constitution. Freedom of the press and trial by jury will fall; next the separation of powers itself will be obliterated by concentrating all power in the hands of the legislature, who can then end the suffrage itself and therewith establish a hereditary power so as to tyrannize without stint.[43]

Madison's comprehensive line of argument, ranging from divine and natural law to social and existential catastrophe, made all the more persuasive through living memories of tyranny and vivid present evidence of persecution, supplies the frame of reference for understanding less articulate justifications of religious liberty. The defeat of the assessments bill followed. This paved the way for enactment six months later of Jefferson's Statute for Religious Freedom, which premises that "Almighty God hath created the mind free." Jefferson regarded the passage of this statute as one of the three great achievements of his life, ranking with writing the Declaration of Independence and founding the University of Virginia. Its enactment, Madison claimed, had "in this country extinguished for ever the ambitious hope of making laws for the human mind."[44] The framing of the First Amendment to the Constitution came less than four years later, but the battles over the meaning and extent of free exercise of religion had largely been fought out in Virginia by the very personalities who would take the lead in devising the Constitution's Bill of Rights.[45]

What, then, is the solution proffered by freedom of conscience? Madison's tenacity in holding to the position of the 1780s is exemplified in many places, not least of all during old age when he and Jefferson collaborated in founding the University of Virginia, whose rectorship Madison then assumed after Jefferson's death in 1826. It was to Madison that Jefferson turned when it came to selecting theological books for the new library. But there would be no professor of theology, and no instruction in the subject would be provided. Madison crisply explained the reasons to Edward Everett in 1823.

> A University with sectarian professorships becomes, of course, a Sectarian Monopoly: with professorships of rival sects, it would be an Arena of Theological Gladiators. Without any such professorships, it may incur for a time at least, the imputation of irreligious tendencies, if not designs. The last difficulty was thought more manageable than either of the others. On this view of the subject, there seems to be no alternative but between a public University without a theological professorship, and sectarian Seminaries without a University. . . . The difficulty of reconciling the Xn mind to the absence of a religious tuition from a university established by law and at the common expense, is probably less with us than with you. The settled opinion here is that religion is essentially distinct from Civil Govt. and exempt from its cognizance; that a connection between them is injurious to both; that there are causes in the human breast, which insure the perpetuity of religion without the aid of the law; that rival sects, with equal rights, exercise mutual censorship in favor of good morals; and if new sects arise with absurd opinions or overheated imaginations, the proper remedies lie in time, forbearance, and example; that a legal establishment of religion without a toleration could not be thought of, and with a toleration, is no security for public quiet & harmony, but rather a source itself of discord & animosity; and finally, that these opinions are supported by experience, which has shewn that every relaxation of the alliance between Law & religion, from the partial example of Holland, to its consummation in Pennsylvania Delaware N.J., &c, has been found as safe in practice as it is sound in theory. Prior to the Revolution, the Episcopal Church was established

by law in this State. On the Declaration of independence it was left with all other sects, to a self-support. And no doubt exists that there is much more of religion among us now than there ever was before the change; and particularly in the Sect which enjoyed the legal patronage. This proves rather more than, that the law is not necessary to the support of religion.[46]

6. Religious liberty, constitutionalism, and higher law. From what we have considered, it can be concluded that the religious and the philosophic appeal go hand in hand in fashioning the basis for religious liberty in America. The axiom emerged (shall we say) that liberty of conscience stands above and apart from the power of the state to legislate as a God-given, inalienable natural right of every individual person. It is antecedent to citizenship and independent of it, woven into human nature as inseparable from man's very being or specific essence. This is the high ground theoretically claimed and politically won in the struggle for religious liberty, as the victory was conceived by Madison, his supporters, and his associates. Jurisprudentially, such a view underlines the meaning of *limited* free government in America: certain individual rights are beyond the reach of majorities in just governance, and to violate them is tyrannical.

From this perspective, the free-exercise clause of the First Amendment has been called the "most philosophically interesting and distinctive feature of the American Constitution . . . [because it] represents a new and unprecedented conception of government and its relation to claims of higher truth and authority."[47] How such an argument will fare in the courts remains to be seen. But it asserts a claim readily and rightly linked with the historic lineage of higher law convictions fundamental to the consensus of the American communities that declared independence, fought the American Revolution, and framed the basic instruments of government in the states and nation at the time of the founding.[48]

Truth to say, this perspective is far from new or esoteric in American jurisprudence. As one scholar recently stated:

> the framers *were* seeking to promulgate fundamental, higher law, which legislators and judges in later ages would apply to their own, altered circumstances. . . . Unless one accepts the idea that "those who have framed written constitutions contemplate them as forming the fundamental and paramount law

of the nation" . . . and also accepts the abiding vitality of the
great principles of republicanism, liberty, the public good, and
federalism, then the United States can scarcely regard itself as a
constitutional polity. . . . What Justice Jackson called "legal principles and . . . fundamental rights," dependent on no majority
votes or transient conditions, must be understood as higher
law, to be used as enduring standards, if the United States is
to be a constitutional polity. The Constitution makes little sense
either as mere rules of thumb used to make decisions in an ever-
changing world, or as a two-hundred-year-old repository of specific injunctions to resolve current problems. The proper middle
ground is to see its persisting principles—republicanism, liberty, the public good, and federalism—as general guides for the
present and the future. That is what the judges, if they are truly
faithful to "original intent," should say the Constitution is.[49]

Another scholar supplements this argument by identifying rule of
law itself, as developed in America, with an indispensable appeal to
a transsocietal source of justice or higher law:

> The underlying philosophy of American constitutionalism rests
> not only on a historical jurisprudence, as in England, but also on
> an implicit theory of natural law. It is presupposed that certain
> kinds of moral principles, rooted in reason and conscience, have
> binding legal force. Their basic terms are expressed, to be sure, in
> written form in a legal document, the Constitution, and thus they
> are embodied in positive law, but they are ultimately derived
> (in the words of the Declaration of Independence) from "Nature
> and Nature's God," and their meaning transcends their written
> form. This means that they can be consciously and deliberately
> adapted by the courts to new situations from generation to
> generation.[50]

There also is to be noticed the massive shift in constitutional law
after the mid-1950s known as the "civil rights revolution," whose
theoretical foundation and moral fervor lay—beyond mere positive
law legalities or, even, express Constitutional provisions—in ancient
higher law principles such as those invoked, for example, by Martin
Luther King Jr. in his *Letter from Birmingham Jail:*

> One has not only a legal but a moral responsibility to obey
> just laws. Conversely, one has a moral responsibility to disobey

unjust laws. I would agree with St. Augustine that "an unjust law is no law at all." Now, what is the difference between the two? How does one determine whether a law is just or unjust? A just law is a man-made code that squares with the moral law or the law of God. An unjust law is a code that is out of harmony with the moral law. To put it in terms of St. Thomas Aquinas: An unjust law is a human law that is not rooted in eternal law and natural law. Any law that uplifts human personality is just. Any law that degrades human personality is unjust. All segregation statutes are unjust because segregation distorts the soul and damages the personality.[51]

As policy, the freedom of conscience constitutionally protected under the religion clauses of the First Amendment aims at securing individual liberty, thereby fostering diversity and pluralism in pursuit of truth in the life of the mind and the spirit of the people. However, this can be done only within limits imposed by the nature of the system itself and by the consensus of the general public whose security and well-being are the primary concerns of government, unless the Bill of Rights is to incline toward becoming the "suicide pact" Justice Jackson warned of in his *Terminiello* dissent. Such a sense of political moderation runs through American history as a standard that already was stated in the Federal Convention of 1787: "We must follow the example of Solon who gave the Athenians not the best Government he could devise; but the best they would receive."[52] Concretely, this means achieving most of what the Baptists, Presbyterians, Quakers, and other dissenting sects intended to achieve when they supplied the political muscle to secure religious liberty in Virginia and elsewhere in the country during the founding. "To them, the freedom to follow religious dogma was one of this nation's foremost blessings, and the willingness of the nation to respect the claims of a higher authority than 'those whose business it is to make laws' was one of the surest signs of its liberality."[53]

The overwhelming majority of Americans in the period under discussion, throughout the nineteenth century, and during most of the twentieth century have assumed this is a Christian country and expected government to uphold the generally agreed upon

Protestant ethos and morality.[54] And this fact lies at the root of some of our current difficulties.

> In many instances, [Americans] had not come to grips with the implications their belief in the powerlessness of government in religious matters held for a society in which the values, customs, and forms of Protestant Christianity thoroughly permeated civil and political life. The contradiction between their theory and their practice became evident . . . with the advent of a more religiously pluralistic society, when it became the subject of disputation that continues into the present.[55]

7. Conclusion: problems and prospects. What James Madison might think today seems, at first glance, evident enough: truth is great and will triumph—with the help of sound institutions and laws. The historian of the American Enlightenment, however, has doubts. He reflects on the splendid Jeffersonian Moment that found an unlikely coalition of philosophes, statesmen, and enthusiasts achieving a work of millennial significance, and then parting company. They became separated by a great cultural chasm after 1800 through the acceleration of the Second Great Awakening in the backcountry and on the frontier and with the rise of the common man. "For the rest of the century," May writes, "I think it is fair to say, most Americans believed at the same time that man was a sinner dependent on unmerited grace and that he was endowed with the right and ability to govern himself. Anybody who can understand this paradox . . . can claim to understand . . . America. . . . [It] could never have been predicted, approved, or under[stood] by any prophet of the eighteenth-century Enlightenment."[56]

There is room to worry on other grounds as well. On the one hand, the substance of the American solution to religious liberty with the prohibition of establishment is one of the triumphs of the constitutional founding. Not least of all this is because it has served to thwart the worst tendencies of religious zealots to persecute minorities with whom they disagree about ultimate truths. No one who considers the carnage presently being inflicted over Ulster or over Palestine or over the territory of former Yugoslavia, among other hot spots in the world, can doubt the service to peace in

America of our constitutional solution to the religion problem. No religion is acceptable in America unless it premises and practices toleration, even against its better judgment.

In addition to this wonderful success, and despite the possibilities for aggressiveness, the American civil theology—especially as it came into play in Manifest Destiny, the abolitionist movement, and the Civil War—has never metastasized as ethnic imperialism such as has engendered soteriological nationalism and ideological totalitarianism in much of the modern world since the French Revolution. Those developments depended upon atomizing the societies down to isolated individuals and, at the same time, eternalizing the nation with the aid of ideology. The fatherland thereby became the Absolute Good into which all other goods were collapsed and submerged. Only in such terms were personal and social identity meaningful.[57] There is, by contrast, something of an Augustinian quality about the American solution that somewhat paradoxically, to be sure, has kept (and still keeps) apart the spiritual and the secular. This is a true legacy of the distinction drawn between the city of the world and the city of God as transmitted by the dissenting Protestant tradition central to American consciousness.[58] The relationship between society and religion has been symbiotic, ambiguously reciprocal, throughout American history and never, in fact, so absolute as the "wall of separation" metaphor implies.[59]

The moral fervor nourished by Christian faith has marked every crisis faced by the country from the onset of the movement for independence in the 1760s down to World War II, which took on the character of a crusade against iniquity incarnate; not to forget the Cold War of the past half-century, which regularly conjured visions of Armageddon and found the president of the United States as late as 1983 describing the Soviet bloc as "an Evil Empire."[60] Thus, when Rev. Thomas Coombe in 1775 quaintly exclaimed that "patriotism without piety is mere grimace," he unwittingly spoke for all generations to come, with God and country typically invoked in the same breath.[61] Yet a distance was and has been maintained between the two spheres.

In stark contrast, modern soteriological nationalism and ideological totalitarianism arise out of the vacuum of identity created by the "death of God"[62] and the collapse of Christianity in Europe so that a substitute is found for social and personal identity solely in the nation, or in the transnational apocalypse of mankind through ideological totalitarianism, or in a conflation of the two: the mystical body of Christ is transmogrified into the mystical body of the nation with its head in some party elite and leader. The careers of such deformations of human reality are at least superficially clear to us from the political adventures of Robespierre, Napoleon, Lenin, Stalin, and Hitler, even when the underlying etiology remains obscure or is carelessly forgotten. Solzhenitsyn's lamentation drives home a central lesson: "The destruction of souls for three-quarters of a century is the most frightening thing."[63]

So, on the other hand, our worry is with the "vacuum of identity," with the "hollow men"[64] and their proliferation through multiple sources of social disintegration, of which questions of free exercise of religion and no establishment are but elements of focus, but important elements. As we have seen, a major difficulty lies in the ostensible "neutrality" in the public schools, which in fact often serves to shelter expanding beachheads or safe havens for antireligious ideology and attacks on American society's moral convictions, radical doctrines ranging from political correctness to advocacy of homosexuality, and neo-Marxism parading as dispassionate science. Such a situation runs counter to any test that might be devised on the basis of community standards of acceptability. In effect, it verges on making the "state" precisely the "adversary" of religious believers in ways not envisaged by Madison and at least implicitly rejected as incompatible with the Constitution by Justice Black and the majority of the Supreme Court he spoke for in the *Everson* case.[65] Indeed, one can surmise that Madison would have detected oppression of free conscience in the de facto inculcation of principles of various radically secular ideologies (understood to be species of ersatz religion themselves)[66] in public schools under the rubric of religious neutrality. The crisis in public education in the United States is profound enough without this sort of abuse. The matter is likely to attract the public's attention, as is suggested by Congress's enactment in 1993 of the Religious Freedom Restoration Act, a straw in the wind.

Especially because of the rise of statism and of the expansive American positive administrative state, with more and more government at all levels—municipal, state, and national—there looms a related set of potential issues whose mention verges on thinking about the unthinkable.[67] To the degree that pseudoscience and radical privatization of traditional religion tend to disparage faith as merely subjective, irrational surmising, a matter of no more than personal "value choices" (as positivists insist) without any objective validity—thus as scientifically unworthy and publicly irrelevant to education and to concerns that count in social existence—the crisis of identity is exacerbated. That the vacuum will be filled we have no doubt from familiar recent history. The experiential appeal to transcendent divine reality that underlies the Anglo-American higher law tradition and is the substance of Judeo-Christian faith becomes increasingly vulnerable. Indeed, such an appeal seems already to be a dead letter in much of the West, so this is hardly a far-fetched notion. The fundamental tension toward transcendent divinity can be rooted out of public discourse, of language, and of consciousness itself, denigrated and effectively excluded so as to widen the gulf of estrangement between the exercise of religion and socially approved activities of public life.

To the degree that this occurs, major disruption of the fragile processes forming individual character tends to dissolve personalities through conditioning into the emptiness of hollow men in a mass society increasingly bereft of effective competing authority centers that might be capable of countering the slide into ideological unreality. Just around the corner in this process of deculturation lie the deformations of human existence associated with the Autonomous Man of atheistic humanism, a familiar figure whose twentieth-century reign in Germany and Russia created a historically unprecedented chamber of horrors.[68] With this massive range of empirical evidence before us, shall we through inattention perhaps partly induced by our euphoria that the Cold War now is "over" invite some sort of repetition? Those who understand best, among them Václav Havel and his fellow countrymen, can tell us something about "Real Socialism," for instance.[69] Michael McConnell's nightmarish apparition of Nietzschean America begins to take on unanticipated plausibility.[70]

The founders, for their part, were clear on the point: no good institutions without good human beings first. One famous political scientist summarized the message of his edition of *The Federalist Papers* in these words: "no happiness without liberty, no liberty without self-government, no self-government without constitution-alism, no constitutionalism without morality—and none of these great goods without stability and order." The founders had added (Clinton Rossiter neglects to tell us), "that there can be no morality without religion."[71] George Washington's valedictory to the country in 1796, his "Farewell Address," resonates into the present on the very point:

> Of all the dispositions and habits which lead to political pros-perity, Religion and morality are indispensable supports. In vain would that man claim the tribute of Patriotism, who should labour to subvert these great Pillars of human happiness, these firmest props of the duties of Men and citizens. . . . [W]here is the security for property, for reputation, for life, if the sense of religious obligation *desert* the oaths, which are the instruments of investigation in Courts of Justice? And let us with caution in-dulge the supposition, that morality can be maintained without religion. Whatever may be conceded to the influence of refined education on minds of peculiar structure, reason and experi-ence both forbid us to expect that National morality can prevail in exclusion of religious principle. 'Tis substantially true, that virtue or morality is a necessary spring of popular government. The rule indeed extends with more or less force to every species of free Government. Who that is a sincere friend to it, can look with indifference upon attempts to shake the foundation of the fabric?[72]

It may be important to add that these convictions of George Washington and other of the founders are solidly affirmed by a leading legal scholar who lately wrote as follows:

> I start from the fact that every legal order requires for its vitality the support of a belief-system which links law not only with morality but also with fundamental convictions about human nature and human destiny. . . . In all societies religion and law, in the broad sense of those words, are interdependent and interact with each other. In all societies there are shared beliefs in tran-scendent values, shared commitments to an ultimate purpose, a shared sense of the holy: certain things are sacred. And in all societies, there are structures and processes of social ordering, established methods of allocating rights and duties, a shared sense of the just: certain things are lawful. The prophetic and

mystical sides of religion challenge, and are challenged by, the structural and rational sides of law. Yet the two are interdependent: each is also a dimension of the other.[73]

The virtue of the people, *The Federalist* teaches, is the primary reliance in republican government, and such virtue is rooted in individual personalities of character and intelligence. Even so, while necessary, human virtue is never sufficient of itself. The auxiliary precautions of sound institutions and adversarial checking are dictated by prudence and experience, the genius of the American system. As Publius remarks, "Had every Athenian citizen been a Socrates; every Athenian assembly would still have been a mob."[74] If, then, we acknowledge the institutions to be generally sound and sufficiently adaptable—a millennial achievement, one admirable in the history of civilization—the compelling questions remaining pertain to the substance of the human beings who will conduct the affairs of society: *Whence the requisite virtue?* And what of the American community itself as a force in history? If America historically has been above all an idea, a state of mind—one constituted by and consciously consecrating liberty on the pattern found self-evidently and abidingly true in the Declaration of Independence taken as a symbol, standard, and rallying point—how will American truth fare during the next two hundred years?

6

Sir John Fortescue as Political Philosopher

THE GREATEST ENGLISH POLITICAL thinker of the fifteenth century, Sir John Fortescue (ca. 1394–ca. 1477), served as an M.P. in eight parliaments, as chief justice of King's Bench for nearly two decades, and as lord chancellor of England to Henry VI, the last of the Lancastrian kings. He is chiefly known for the instructional dialogue he composed for the young heir apparent to the throne, Prince Edward, titled *In Praise of the Laws of England.*[1] The fame attaching to that work arises mainly from its prominence in the dispute two centuries later over the nature of the English monarchy and constitution conducted between the first Stuart kings (James I and Charles I) and Sir Edward Coke, John Selden, and Parliament leading up to the Petition of Right (1628) and the subsequent civil war. While quoted on both sides of the debate, Fortescue ultimately became a byword for the Old Whig cause of limited monarchy and parliamentary authority against the claims of royal prerogative and absolutism. He thus became a figure of pivotal importance for seventeenth-century English and eighteenth-century American conceptions of rule of law, liberty, and constitutionalism. Hence our own interest in this neglected figure.

In all of his major writings, Fortescue insists that England's government is and always has been not merely royal *(dominium regale)* but political and royal *(dominium politicum et regale)*. By this he particularly means that laws may not to be enacted nor taxes levied by the king without the assent of Parliament and that the monarch should be obedient to his own laws. These are principles reiterated by such later authorities as Richard Hooker (d. 1600) as forming the groundwork of personal liberty and free government in England and intended in the maxim "Laws they are not therefore which public approbation hath not made so."[2] Fortescue is the first writer who specifically asserts the power of Parliament to be a limit upon the authority of the king.[3] That supreme seventeenth-century oracle of the common law, Sir Edward Coke, so admired *Praise* that he thought it "worthy to be written in Letters of Gold for the Weight and Worthiness thereof."[4] In the history of liberty through rule of law, then, Fortescue stands in the line of celebrated English political, legal, and constitutional writers running from Henry de Bracton (d. ca. 1268) to Christopher St. Germain (d. 1540) to Richard Hooker through Sir Edward Coke (d. 1634) to Edmund Burke (d. 1797)—and so also to John Adams and the generation of American founders of the late eighteenth century who imbibed the writings of these authorities.

The most interesting and important theoretical work by Fortescue, however, is neither *Praise* nor its well-known sequel, *The Governance of England*, the first treatise on its subject written in the English language. Rather it is the largely neglected earlier and most extensive of his works, *The Nature of the Law of Nature*. This book provides the philosophical and religious foundations of the later political and constitutional writings without which they are not fully intelligible. It is of great value in its own right for first setting forth Fortescue's theories of law, justice, government, and human nature upon which all else depends.

The center of attention rightly remains on the political and constitutional aspects of the works under consideration, of course, for the obvious reasons that Fortescue is a great judge and common lawyer and that this is his own emphasis. His most important works were all written after his sixtieth year and all written on the fly, as it were: in Scotland as an attainted refugee after the Battle of Towton (March 1461), or during the seven years of exile in France, or under duress. He writes as a distinguished jurist with forty years of experience, twenty of these as chief justice, as chancellor (the persona adopted in *Praise*), as a statesman with extensive parliamentary experience, and as a man of affairs who for many years participated in the highest political deliberations and diplomatic dealings of the realm under Henry VI and afterward, for an undetermined period of time, as a member of the council of Edward IV, first of the York monarchs, a transition to the Tudor period that dates from 1485. Stanley Chrimes, the leading authority on Fortescue, in commenting on the character of the author of *Praise,* sums up as follows:

> We cannot but stand amazed at the robust vitality of this old man, more than seventy years of age, who composed this work after a life of such enormous exertion and such tribulation. The toughness of the common law itself is in him; there is no sign of failing faculties in this nor in any of his works. This work above all the rest has in it a freshness, an alertness of mind, a sprightliness, a dry humor, a humanity, an enthusiasm, and an almost boyish zest that are astounding in the circumstances. . . . We cannot avoid the feeling that we are reading the work of a great man in his own day and generation, of a great English-man. For Fortescue is very English. . . . He believes at once in hereditary monarchy, aristocratic society, and in the will of the people; he can reconcile in his mind something like autocracy with something like democracy. He is entirely convinced that English laws and institutions are the best in the world, and always have been. His pride of profession is immense, but he never entirely loses sight of the truth that his profession is only a means to a great and elusive end—Justice.[5]

All of Fortescue's writings are reflective of his career as a public man and, thus, cast in the mode of prudential concern and discourse. Moreover, he remained a partisan ("a partial man") of the Lancas-trian cause in mind, body, and sword until its definitive end at the Battle of Tewkesbury (May 1471) and Henry's probable murder in the Tower of London. Fortescue directly engaged in battle on more than one occasion as the so-called War of the Roses unfolded to the final defeat at Tewkesbury. There young Edward Prince of Wales (the "Prince" of *Praise*) was killed, and his mother, Queen Margaret, and Fortescue were captured by the victorious Yorkists. Fortescue's life was spared, and he submitted to Edward; in October 1471, he wrote the required repudiation of earlier views, entitled *Declaration Upon Certain Writings Sent out of Scotland.* He presented his new lord and master with a copy of *The Governance* when he assumed duties on Edward IV's council, and the substantive policy and institutional reforms proposed therein appear to have influenced in some degree the conduct of affairs under Edward and later on under the first

Tudor monarch, King Henry VII. The attainder finally was lifted in February 1475, and therewith Fortescue's property and standing were recovered. He is believed to have died about two years later, although a family tradition has him living past age ninety. He is buried in Ebrington Church, Gloucestershire.

Rather than attempt a summary of the arguments of his several works, it will be more to the point to reflect very briefly on the philosophical substance, range, and tenor of Fortescue's writings, considered as an important link from medieval to modern English political and constitutional thought.[6] For if we wish to understand the grounds of his devotion to liberty within the frame of a monarchy resting upon the consent of the realm as regularly registered through its representative institutions, and most particularly Parliament, the underpinnings of this devotion need to be at least roughly ascertained and placed in the author's context.

The heart of the matter becomes apparent in *Nature* and its searching account of human nature and man's participation in the comprehensive reality of time and eternity disclosed through philosophy and revelation. The participatory texture of human experience is the source of Fortescue's reflections. He is utterly clear on the point that man seeks the good and that the good he seeks is not exhausted by nature and the things of the world, with happiness being the highest end attainable by action (Aristotle). Rather, man seeks as his ultimate end the inexhaustible Good of the transcendent *summum Bonum*, supernatural Beatitude.[7] While the political vocation thereby finds a place of great importance in the hierarchy of being, it must ever remain distinctly secondary to man's spiritual quest. Fortescue's horizon of thought, in other words, is thoroughly Christian, classical, biblical, scholastic, and medieval Catholic, with elements of Renaissance humanism tending to modernize the whole. The theoretical explorations are often (but not always) for their own sakes as a search for truth and justice. But sometimes they are in the mode of the eristic—a mere lawyer's argument, as in the forensic exercise that is ostensibly the main concern of the second part of *Nature*, whose actual title is *Concerning the Right of Succession in Supreme Kingdoms*. This is even truer of the *Declaration*, which refutes *Nature* II's central contention with an almost comic sleight-of-hand lawyer's trick. It must have amused Fortescue himself, and presumably King Edward did not notice.

The theoretical efforts at their most brilliant are done with the humility of a man who knows his mortality and frailty and who, therefore, bows before God and king to defer his to their judgments and rightful authority. There is a constant mindfulness of human limits, a sort of Burkean sense that the individual is ignorant, the species wise. And this regard for views other than his own, conditioned by a recognition of the need to preserve the community of which he was part and of which he was also a steward, structures the political theory of Fortescue. He constantly preaches, as we might say, that two heads are better than one: government is political and royal when it is best *because* many men reflecting on problems of rule are more likely to judge truly and justly than is any one man alone. Even the king who rules in a royal dominion should seek aid and advice from wise counselors. There is an Aristotelian concern to maintain stable as well as just and secure rule as clearly better than the alternative of chaos and civil strife with which Fortescue was painfully familiar. There are reminders that men are naturally political and social beings living together in communities united by agreement on fundamental matters of truth and justice.[8] Agreement must constantly be renewed and nurtured through wide consultation. This core of concord is the "truth of justice" that is *phronesis* (moral wisdom), and is itself Reason, the very *Law of Nature* that Fortescue persuasively unveils and ultimately characterizes as "the truth of Justice which is capable of being by right reason revealed."[9] Such a mixed constitution as the one Fortescue describes as the *dominium politicum et regale* and sees as actually existing historically in England *is*, he insists, the very political order ultimately favored by Aristotle; it is also the mixed constitution that is Aquinas's choice as the best practicable regime, if not the absolutely best.[10]

Fortescue's restraint and counsel rest on more than a concern with legalities and protocol. They arise from a desire to live and rule in accordance with truth and in avoidance of error and sin. Consultation with the community through its leading members has a spiritual as well as an analytical purpose. Not only is one more likely to hit on the right and best policy but one is also prevented from self-serving decisions that lead down the primrose path of error and vice, to sin, tyranny, and finally servitude in self-indulgence and enslavement to base passion. True *liberty*, Fortescue constantly avers, is not the obvious thing found by willfully doing whatever you think you most want to do; rather liberty is only found in doing what you ought to do to live and, if king, to rule justly. This is a further reason "political and royal rule" is superior to merely "royal rule" and, at the same time (as the chancellor tutors the prince in *Praise*), despite first impressions to the contrary, the king's power actually is *greater* in the former kind of government than it is in the latter. This follows, the argument goes, because error and sin are acts not of power but of impotence; they are defections from truth, justice, and being in favor of nonbeing and the perfect nothingness of evil—as Augustine taught.[11]

A devotee of "consultation," Fortescue writes in consultation not merely with his own thoughts and direct experience (substantial as it is) but with those of all of the wise men of the ages so far as he can muster an acquaintance with them. Fortescue's pages seethe with references and allusions drawn far and wide from his reading and meditations. Scholars assure us that he was using crib books of popular maxims and pithy thoughts gleaned from a huge literature and really could not have read all the writers he cites. Perhaps not. But what is impressive about Fortescue and his sources is that he weaves his argument together with his citations to marshal a convincing if not quite seamless fabric of analysis. He cites not simply for the sake of authority but for the sake of illuminating his understanding by appeal to the deepest sources of wisdom. Especially is this true in the first part of *Nature*, which exemplifies the questing spirit of another great Englishman from centuries before, Anselm of Canterbury (d. 1109), who symbolized the path he followed as "faith in search of understanding *(fides quaerens intellectum)*."[12] Since, to a mind such as Fortescue's, Spirit and Justice must have human incarnation and institutional representation in order to achieve effectual ordering authority in history under conditions imposed by life in the world, he typically bows in overt deference to church and the law of the land, to pope and king. Life and well-being also must be protected against the harsh practices and penalties of the age, as the *Declaration* attests, so humility and prudence both are reflected in Fortescue's attitude. But there is no doubting the independent judgment of Fortescue as a great spiritualist and intellect and as a noble character of profound integrity.

Fortescue has broadly absorbed Christian religious, philosophical, and political culture in its English version, and Thomas Aquinas and his school are central to late medieval thought and plainly prominent in Fortescue. But there is more to it than that. Fortescue's independent judgment revalidates the insights of the thinkers he leans upon and makes them his own through a process of experiential confirmation and intellectual rearticulation. The analyses of man, society, politics, and the whole of reality given in the grandiose styles of Aristotle or of Augustine or of Thomas Aquinas, for instance, are not true because they said so; rather they said so because it is true— at least as far as faith and critical reason can see from their various perspectives. Fortescue draws upon all of these, and he reflects a concern to find the truth about the human condition within the limits of his inquiry and to do so with the help of the great truth finders of history.

Building on that foundation, then, the theory of human nature is basic to the theory of the community, and the historicity of the community moves progressively from merely royal or even despotic dominion toward the perfection of itself expressed in the intention of the people to assume the form of political and royal rule. The community is characterized as a *corpus mysticum* united by a common intention and governed by the king as head. The organic analogy is reminiscent of John of Salisbury, but it is drawn more directly from the Pauline conception of the church as the body of Christ through faith with the Savior as head.[13] Each of the individual persons as members constituting the mundane mystical body delineated by Fortescue contributes to and shares equally in the dignity and well-being of the common good of the political community.[14] Moreover, man as the creature of God bears his image and through grace enjoys fellowship with him. By faith he participates even in time in the eternal communion to be consummated personally and eschatologically in the world to come. Fortescue elaborately adopts the Trinitarian anthropology of Augustine that explains *imago Dei* in man in terms of memory, intellect, and will as these correlate with Father, Son, and Holy Spirit. The image of God's eternal unity is thereby exhibited in his creature man. Memory (*memoria*) is the font and matrix of the soul out of which all primary intuitions and all of our latent acquired ideas arise to generate the active intellect.[15]

The law of nature is thus impressed in the minds of all men as individuals and inclines them, even if imperfectly in their fallen state, to the good and most of all to the highest Good or *summum Bonum*. Human life so conceived is lived in tension toward the divine Ground of being at every step in the pilgrimage of man through time in partnership with God.[16] The general principles of the law of nature are not those of man in his bestial aspect (Aquinas's *fomes peccati, concupiscentia*); rather they are those that incline human beings to higher good in its several aspects: to preserving life itself; to propagating themselves in companionship with their spouses and protecting and educating their families and communities; and to knowing the truth about God and his eternal salvation, the Good beyond all earthly desire.[17] Such natural law, intrinsic to mankind and to every individual person among them as *imago Dei*, is itself a *participation* in eternal and divine law made possible through the crowning capacities of mind. Moved by his vision, Fortescue exclaims: "Oh, how great a thing is this participation!" Calling it the "higher part of reason," Fortescue powerfully writes of it experientially as "cleaving to God, and stretching itself out toward that which is eternal."[18] Variously identified as *ratio, intellectus, synderesis,* and conscience, this above all else is the specific essence of man and that in him whereby communion with the divine occurs.[19] All positive or human laws have validity insofar as they are in accordance with natural law and are null and void otherwise, even if in accord with custom.[20] Evil does not become good through long practice and reiteration. The law insists that life, the community, and the political order are justified only to the degree they serve the good.[21] Thus, the foundation of all law is the Golden Rule to do unto others as you would have them do unto you, for this sums up "the Law and the prophets."[22] The purpose of all governance is the well-being through peace and justice of the community, and its members must be inculcated by habit, instruction, and true laws with the virtues of human and divine excellence as the attributes of living well.

"The kingdom is not made for the king but the king for the kingdom."[23] A king, just as a pope, is most truly the servant of the servants of God.[24] Whenever any king departs from his high calling of service and justice, to that degree government loses the quality of kingship and derails into the kind of perverse misrule of coercion identified with the tyranny of Nimrod.[25] Such a tendency is naturally present in some degree everywhere since men, driven by

libido dominandi and *superbia vitae* (lust for power and pride of life),
are goaded by selfish ambition and brute passion "to be first" and,
consequently, must be bridled by instruction, habit, law, counsel,
and such institutional restraint as may be available in the kingdom.[26]
The restraint of parliament *(Praise)* and of an independent council
to the king *(Governance)* is included in Fortescue's own prescriptions
as emerging from English politics, law, and tradition as these look
toward a powerful, wealthy, and centralized monarchy that he hopes
may remedy ills of the realm. Contentiousness, he writes, quoting
Augustine, "is a great disease of the soul."[27]

Last, it may be noticed that *liberty* stands at the heart of Fortescue's
account of man and government. Thus, "freedom was instilled into
human nature by God."[28] The list of liberties enjoyed by Englishmen
sounds familiar in including jury trial, a required plurality of wit-
nesses, security against billeting troops in private houses, payment
for lodging them in public establishments, security of private property against arbitrary invasion or taking, no legal use of torture to
extract confessions, no taxation or changing of the law except with
parliamentary consent. The list smacks of Magna Carta, but that document is not mentioned. The stress on Parliament's role is the most
important distinction. For the fundamental liberty is to be subject
not to arbitrary government (such as the despotism exemplified by
France, as Fortescue often says) but solely to rule of law grounded
in the consent of the whole community as given by representatives
through established procedures.[29] This vital distinction has remained
the mark of free government from Fortescue's day until our own.

7

American Religion and Higher Law

1 EXTENT OF SUBJECT MATTER. The most familiar account of America's debt to something called *higher law* is the little book by Edward S. Corwin that carries the term in its title.[1] The most familiar reference to higher law is the Declaration of Independence's appeal to "the laws of nature and Nature's God." Natural, divine, and eternal law are understood to be "higher law." If we still inquire "higher than what?" the answer will be higher than merely human, or man-made, positive law such as that enacted by Congress, Parliament, or other legislative bodies. On the borderline as clearly man-made will be the Constitution of the United States whose article 6 proclaims it (and the laws made in pursuance thereof and all treaties made under the authority of the United States) to be the "Supreme law of the land" and, thus, itself intended to be higher law. Lastly, it has been observed that "the average American believes strongly that there is such a thing as Natural Law and that he has natural rights"[2]—a sociological fact of importance in a country whose laws and governments supposedly rest on the principle of consent.

2. Illustrations of the sentiment of transcendence. The attitude that invokes higher law is notoriously religious and philosophical in our secular age. For most of the past 2,500 years "theories of natural law have dominated" Western jurisprudence as fundamental to all law and societal order.[3] But today they are in almost total eclipse. Reigning supreme is positivism as descended from Hobbes and the Austinian jurisprudence of utility and power that dominates the thinking of lawyers and what courts do in the name of law and constitutional interpretation. Ever since the early Supreme Court decision in *Calder v. Bull,* which generated a lively but inconclusive debate between Justices Samuel Chase and James Iredell regarding the place of "fundamental principles of government" and "natural justice" in constitutional litigation, camouflaged vestiges of natural law jurisprudence have steadily remained in our law, although not expressly so. Natural law has been propounded under such rubrics as the several versions of substantive due process and substantive equal protection, extraconstitutional rights to privacy discovered as emanations of penumbras of explicit provisions, use of reasonableness and fairness as tests, and in other ways especially as devised during the past half century by an activist judiciary.[4] All of this will have to be left to another day.

More to the present point is to notice that American independence from James Otis's speech against the Writs of Assistance in 1761 to the Declaration of Independence in 1776 and beyond was argued largely on the basis of the old legal and constitutional traditions, as I shall briefly illustrate. But it is the religious and philosophical aspects that are the main focus of my remarks here as being fundamental, in my view, to our understanding both of the founding and perhaps of human reality simply.

The sentiment of openness to transcendent reality central to our subject is commonplace. It is movingly expressed, for example, in the third stanza of *America—My Country 'Tis of Thee,* which reads:

> Our fathers' God, to thee,
> Author of liberty,
> To the we sing.
> Long may our land be bright
> With freedom's holy light;
> Protect us by thy might, Great God our King.[5]

The outlook is evident also in Thomas Jefferson's motto—engraved on his personal seal and suggested by him as the motto for the United States itself: Rebellion to Tyrants Is Obedience to God.[6] Divine and natural orders are, thus, understood to shape the course of human affairs and communicate higher law dimensions of our national and civilizational destiny. In other words, this participatory tension toward the transcendent—in which higher law is embedded as one aspect—is experienced as constitutive of the human condition per se. As the illustrations suggest, the perspective is reflexively acknowledged on all hands in ordinary discourse. Thus, the Virginia Statute for Religious Freedom—whose adoption was engineered by James Madison and which Thomas Jefferson claimed in his epitaph as one of the three signal achievements of his lifetime—opens with the words "Almighty God hath created the mind free." The attitude is reflected by the prior of a Trappist monastery, Dom Christian de Cherge, who before being slaughtered by Algerian Islamic terrorists in 1996, movingly wrote of this anticipated end in a testimonial that evoked "the true strand of the Gospel learnt at my mother's knee, my very first Church"—where most of us first learn of higher things.[7] We remember also the cry of Shakespeare's *King Henry V* after the astonishing victory at Agincourt with hardly an English casualty:

> O God, thy arm was here;
> And not to us, but to thy arm alone,
> Ascribe we all!
> . . . Take it, God,
> For it is none but thine! . . .
> Let there be sung "Non nobis" and "Te Deum" (4.8)

3. Liberty and historical and natural jurisprudence. To attend briefly to the jurisprudential dimensions within our period of concern, it should be said that the Bill of Rights to the Constitution as conceived and adopted illustrates some higher law perspectives. It is substantively part and parcel of a tradition of common law liberty and natural law productive of what we refer to as constitutionalism or rule of law. Liberty and rule of law developed in medieval England from King Edward the Confessor (d. 1066) to Sir John Fortescue and were recovered, vivified, and perfected in seventeenth-century England during the lengthy contest between Parliament and the Stuart kings memorialized by revival of Magna Carta and culminating in the Glorious Revolution of 1688 and Settlement of 1689. Anything dated before the coronation of Richard I in 1189 and in continual usage since that time was regarded as prescriptive custom, as being before memory, in Littleton's phrase: "where a custom, or usage, or other thing, hath been used for time whereof the mind of man runneth not to the contrary" such rights and liberties were allowed by the common law.[8] Such remote antiquity took on the aura accorded the law of nature as resting on continual and universal assent.

This tradition as it survived into the period of the founding is especially evident in the great work of Sir Edward Coke, John Selden, and their associates in the House of Commons, as fashioned in the struggle over extension of royal prerogative and the attendant parliamentary resistance leading up to adoption of the Petition of Right (1628).[9] The fixing of this vision came through the debate surrounding political events from the English Civil War to the American Revolution and through the education of generations of lawyers by Coke's *Institutes* for the next 150 to 200 years—down to the late 1770s when Blackstone's *Commentaries* began to supplant them as law students' principal textbooks. These students included Sir Matthew Hale LCJ, Lord Camden (formerly Pratt LCJ), Chatham, and Burke, as well as such American luminaries as James Otis, George Mason, John Adams, John Jay, Alexander Hamilton, and Thomas Jefferson (who were lawyers) and James Madison and George Washington (who were not.)

Thus, *rule of law* or constitutionalism and *liberty* were complementary if not identical terms. Coke defines *libertates* in Magna Carta as meaning, in the first instance, "the Laws of England" or "the Laws of the Realme, in which respect this Charter is called Charta libertatum."[10] And John Phillip Reid recently has insisted on the point as valid for the generation of the American founding:

> Liberty in the age of the American Revolution was not the sum of enumerated rights, the rights to speech, press, security, property or isonomy. It was rather government by the rule of law, government by the customary British constitution. If put in terms of freedom, liberty would . . . be defined . . . as freedom from arbitrary power, from government by will and pleasure, from government by a sovereign, unchecked monarch or from government by a sovereign, unchecked Parliament.[11]

It is on some such understanding as this that Publius in *Federalist No. 38* rhetorically asks, "Is a Bill of Rights essential to liberty?" Relying upon an understanding of human nature as old as Genesis, one theorized by Plato and Aristotle, to undergird the institutional separation and division of powers, and of checks and balances among coordinate branches of government, Publius discloses the "auxiliary precautions" a generally virtuous people can take to avoid arbitrary government. The danger most likely in republics is tyrannical majorities led by demagogues. Publius's purpose is to avoid or control these while, at the same time, fostering justice and liberty in such a compound mixed republic of great extent as the United States. Publius cites Montesquieu and quotes the exemplary Massachusetts Constitution of 1780 as "expressing this fundamental article of liberty. It declares 'that the legislative department shall never exercise the executive and judicial powers, or either of them: The executive shall never exercise the legislative and judicial powers, or either of them: The judicial shall never exercise the legislative and executive powers, or either of them.' This declaration corresponds precisely with the doctrine of Montesquieu."[12]

Publius eventually quotes the preamble to the Constitution, understood by his readers to be the intended "supreme Law of the Land" (article 6) and, so, fundamental law in the United States: "We the People of the United States, [. . .] to secure the blessings of liberty to ourselves and our posterity do *ordain* and *establish* this constitution for the United States of America." And he roundly concludes with the claim, "The truth is . . . that the constitution is itself in every rational sense, and to every useful purpose, a *Bill of Rights*."[13]

Too fine a point, however, need not be put on the dichotomy between *liberty* singular and *liberties* plural. It is indubitably right— and a recovery of a nearly forgotten signification—to stress liberty and just law as coincident in eighteenth-century Anglo-American jurisprudence. This jurisprudential insight is a theoretical insight shared with the religious or pneumatic understanding that "You shall know the truth, and the truth shall make you free," as well with the (classical) philosophical or noetic understanding that the true and free man and just society are the ones in which, respectively, reason and law rule so as to govern the passions in individuals and in society as a whole.[14] The opposite conditions are equated with natural slavery in the individual, its liberty with vulgarian liberty (license), and with tyranny through the rule of base passions in the society.[15]

The particularities of liberty in the singular certainly include— and partly compose—the liberties specified by constitutions and bills of rights. Indeed, for Coke himself the secondary and tertiary meanings of Magna Carta's *libertates* are "the Freedoms, that the Subjects of England have" and "the franchises, and priviledges, which the Subject have of the gift of the King. . . . Generally all monopolies are against this great Charter, because they are against the liberty and freedome of the Subject, and against the Law of the Land."[16]

Lastly, prescriptive *customary law* grounded in the immemorial usages of the ancient constitution and *natural law* comprehending, implying, and securing personal rights (as mentioned) combine to form a matrix of fundamental higher law in Anglo-American jurisprudence, and the two strands can hardly be disentangled. To take a striking illustration from the founding period: in the parliamentary debate over the Declaratory Act (in 1766, after repeal of the Stamp Act) there occurred the remarkable spectacle of Lord Camden, formerly Pratt, lord chief justice of England, powerfully arguing in the House of Lords very much as James Otis in Boston had done in opposing the Writs of Assistance five years earlier. Camden spoke as follows:

> The sovereign authority, the omnipotence of the legislature, my lords, is a favourite doctrine, but there are some things they cannot do. They cannot enact anything against the divine law, and may forfeit their right. They cannot take away any man's private property without making him compensation. They have no right to condemn any man by bill of attainder without hearing. [The Declaratory Bill is] illegal, absolutely illegal, contrary to the fundamental laws of nature, contrary to the fundamental laws of this constitution [which is] a constitution grounded on the eternal and immutable laws of nature; a constitution whose foundation and centre is liberty. . . . [T]axation and representation are inseparably united: God hath united them [and] no British parliament can separate them; to endeavour to do it is to stab our very vitals. [Their union is not only] founded on the laws of nature; it is more, it is an eternal law of nature; for whatever is a man's own is absolutely his own; no man hath a right to take it from him without his consent, either expressed by himself or [his] representative.[17]

The natural and divine law referenced by Lord Camden and elsewhere (as by Jefferson and his associates in the Declaration of

Independence) is that of Western civilization in its Anglo-American articulation as formulated from Aristotle to Cicero to Aquinas to Fortescue to Coke to Locke to Otis, Camden, Jefferson, and Madison (even to include the verbiage of Blackstone in volume 1 of the *Commentaries*)—vital and venerable dimensions of our constitutional and political theory. This is, thus, a tradition—in fact a variety of traditions that we consider together—of generally ascertainable content and experiential specificity. It is not, we must mention, some amorphous mass or blank to be filled with scribbling of equal theoretical cogency or historical efficacy such as the coercive barbarous "natural" law of Nimrod in Genesis or of (say) the Hitlers, Stalins, or Saddam Husseins of the modern world—as some commentators seem prepared to assert.[18]

The confusion between natural law as reason and natural law as passionate indulgence is elucidated by Thomas Aquinas's discussion of the *lex fomitis* and may help to clarify the point. Apparent failure to recognize the distinction vitiates any discussion and puts ostensible adversaries of legal positivism inadvertently right back on a positivist footing, embracing law as merely power, will, or command and "values" as anybody's (supposedly equally untenable) subjective surmises—even while disavowing positivism in the same breath. Some way out of this box must be found, and, in fact, an ample pertinent literature exists. Saint Thomas Aquinas, in *Treatise on Law*, asserts that the rule of passion and brutish inclination "in man . . . has not the nature of law . . . rather is it a deviation from the law of reason. . . . [Such so-called "natural" law in man] is called the 'fomes' in so far as it strays from the order of reason."[19]

4. Religion and the principal terms of higher law. An attitude of openness toward divine reality as higher and hence governing in human affairs was ubiquitous among Americans at the time of the founding, despite the inroads of secularism and the prominence of "Enlightened" statesmen and intellectuals as leading members of that enlightened generation. How may the specifics best be appreciated?

The Americans of that era can best be understood as *Providential Christians*,[20] an attitude we have seen reflected by Shakespeare's Henry V and powerfully affirmed by Benjamin Franklin (himself a major figure of the American Enlightenment) in a speech made at a difficult moment in the Federal Convention. It climaxed with his statement: "I have lived, Sir, a long time, and the longer I live, the more convincing proofs I see of this truth—*that GOD governs in the affairs of men.* And if a sparrow cannot fall to the ground without his notice, is it probable that an empire can rise without his aid?"[21]

These were representative views at the time. As Perry Miller remarked decades ago, the American Revolution was preached as a revival and had the astonishing result of succeeding. A new generation of scholars is concluding that Miller was right. At the center of attitudes lay a kind of consensual Christianity that unified all denominations. It joined with Whig political views to give a resonant core of love of liberty and courageous resistance to tyranny and corruption to a great moral and political cause as the heartbeat of the American community. *Federalist No. 2* reflects this, and it was wonderfully stated by John Adams in a letter to Jefferson late in life. In writing to his fellow "Argonaut" of the American founding in their declining years, Adams stated:

> The *general Principles,* on which the Fathers atchieved Independence, were the only Principles in which that beautiful assembly of young gentlemen [in our army] could unite. . . . And what were these *general Principles*? I answer [John Adams wrote]—the general principles of Christianity, in which all those sects were united: And the *general Principles* of English and American Liberty. . . . Now I will avow, that I then believed, and now believe, that those general Principles of Christianity, are as eternal and immutable, as the Existence and Attributes of God; and those principles of Liberty, as unalterable as human nature and the terrestrial, mundane system.[22]

5. Continuity with classical and medieval higher law. The terms of the higher law embraced by most Americans at the time of the founding were profoundly embedded in the biblical horizon just intimated by John Adams, their most comprehensive and readily accepted frame of reference. John Locke was read that way—as at bottom a Christian and an Aristotelian—and the Declaration of Independence also was understood in that way. As Perry Miller again observed, a cool rationalism such as Jefferson's might have declared the independence of such folk but could never have persuaded them to fight for it. As previously noticed, higher law principles were part and parcel of the tradition of English liberty nurtured by common law Whig jurisprudence and political theory from Sir Edward Coke and the judicious Hooker onward, and by the pervasive dissident Protestant influence whose stress on resistance to tyranny as religious duty and natural right alike animated the invocation of higher law by preachers, citizenry, and statesmen. Nurturing the mind of the founders also were the Greek and Latin classics, this being the "Golden Age of the Classics in America," as Meyer Reinhold and others have demonstrated, where especially Cicero's writings were second nature to educated Americans.[23]

With these perspectives in mind, we may say that higher law is intelligible either from the top down or from the bottom up, so to speak: that is, as objective or subjective. From the top down or macro perspective, there is the biblical Creator and the natural creation with its creatures, nature thus formed and penetrated by divine grace, we should notice. The abiding order of reality is viewed in terms of an ordered cosmos whose being, constancy, and regularities are self-evident and extend not only to materiality but also to the moral and spiritual dimensions of experienced reality. Such a vision is invoked in Genesis as well as in Cicero's famous lines (when read against a biblical background) that

> True law is right reason [*vera lex recta ratio*], harmonious with nature, diffused among all, constant, eternal; a law which calls to duty by its commands and restrains from evil by its prohibitions. . . . It is a sacred obligation not to attempt to legislate in contradiction to this law . . . nor does it require any but ourself to be its expositor or interpreter . . . [it is] one eternal and unchangeable law binding all nations through all time.[24]

This is to equate law and reason as the essential nature of man and hegemonic element, both in society and singly, as Plato and Aristotle taught, and as Cicero summarized for the benefit of subsequent centuries. The "government of laws and not of men" that, in various phrasings, made its way into Harrington's *Oceana* (1656), the Massachusetts Constitution of 1780, and, finally, *Marbury v. Madison* in 1803 began from an original statement by Aristotle in the *Politics* (III.11.3–5 [1187a20–37]) that the rule of law is superior to that of any man. The "law" in question is preeminently customary or higher law, equating with Reason, Justice, and God. This standard lies behind Cicero's and Augustine's maxim that "An unjust law is no law at all" and behind the ready agreement of the founders that "We must obey God rather than men" (Acts 5:29). The American founding was not merely one event among others but a moral cause rooted in the deepest springs of civilization and conscious of being so.

Considered from the bottom up, our micro perspective is that of every individual human person in relationship to God. The sixteenth-century English jurist Christopher Saint Germain summarized the participatory relationship as follows:

> The law of nature . . . is also called the law of reason [and] pertains only to creatures reasonable, that is [to] man wh[o] is created to the image of God. . . . And this is the law which among the learned in English law is called the law of reason, which natural reason has established among all men so that there is a natural instinct present in all men to observe it. . . . [I]t is a sign, possessed naturally, which is indicative of the right reason of God which wills that the human rational creature shall be held or bound to do (or refrain from doing) something, in order to pursue its natural end, which is human happiness *[felicitas]*—be it monastic, domestic or political. . . . Hence the law of reason is nothing else than the *participation* or knowledge of eternal law in a rational creature, revealed to him by the natural light of reason, whereby he has a natural inclination *[naturalem inclinationem]* to act duly, and to a due end. Whence it is said in the Psalm: "The light of thy countenance is signed upon us, O Lord" [4:6?]; that is to say, the light of truth; for the light of God's countenance is truth.[25]

Behind Saint Germain stands Jean Gerson, and behind Gerson, William of Ockham and Thomas Aquinas.

Now it will doubtless alarm a few of you that I think most of the talk about ancient and modern natural law and natural right *in our context* is largely a red herring that puts us off the scent of truth when it comes to understanding the mind of America's founders. The founders, however "enlightened" some of them were, to a man claimed to be Christians, and none of them ever admitted to being a Hobbesian. Even more important, there is no doubt that the society of which they were representative was pervasively religious and pervasively Christian—largely dissenting Protestant

Christian at that—and this determined the tenor of their higher law convictions.

This brings us back to the affinities of the natural law and natural rights thinking reflected in the Declaration of Independence with the medieval Christian understanding of such matters, including that of Thomas Aquinas, the greatest philosopher of that era. To fend off an obvious objection, eighteenth-century Protestantism in America drew substantially on the patristic teachings, and to some extent upon the medieval scholastic ones. Thus, Ralph Barton Perry long ago warned against the "fallacy of difference" in his analysis of American Puritanism, to the end of denying that theologically it was an innovating doctrine or radically different from previous Christian teaching: the similarities and agreements were much more substantive than the dissimilarities and disagreements.[26] Another helpful clue is to remember Presbyterian John Witherspoon's admiration of the "popish divines." Their work was imbibed by young James Madison and seven other members of the Federal Convention who had been his students and were graduates of the College of New Jersey (later Princeton, where Witherspoon was president) as a standard part of their studies.[27] But the substance of the presentation of the key ontological, anthropological, and political issues—the overall understanding of reality, human and divine—shows the *equivalence* in essential respects of the understanding of human nature, natural law, and natural rights advanced in medieval philosophy with that reflected in much of American thought and conviction during the founding.

The matter at this stage can be given a strong formulation: contrary to one vocal school of thought in our midst, "it is just not true that 'the notion of subjective right is logically incompatible with classical natural right,'" nor that "'natural rights and traditional natural law are . . . incompatible,'" as has been alleged. We follow in this judgment the distinguished medievalist Brian Tierney, who flatly rejects these views as "based on a mistaken idea that modern rights theories are derived entirely from Hobbes and on simple ignorance of the history of the concept of *ius naturale* before the seventeenth century." By contrast Tierney demonstrates that "the precepts and prohibitions of natural law [can] readily be seen as implying rights. To say that 'Thou shalt not steal' is a command of natural law is to imply that others have a right to acquire property. . . . In fact one finds natural rights regarded as correlative with natural law at every stage in the history of the doctrine—in the twelfth-century renaissance of law, in the eighteenth-century Enlightenment, and still in twentieth-century discourse"—as, for example, in Jacques Maritain and John Finnis.[28]

6. Aquinas, Algernon Sidney, and the Declaration of Independence. It is just this correlation and reciprocal relationship between the requirements of natural law and implicit natural rights that was decisively important to the founders. It is deserving of emphasis here as a means of reuniting the vision that sustained the Revolution and made the Constitution possible in an America that was not nearly so theoretically shattered and in secularized disarray as some suppose.

To dig a bit deeper into the subject, it will be helpful to consider some of the points advanced by the universally admired and widely read Whig martyr Algernon Sidney (executed in 1683), whose great classic of Liberty, entitled *Discourses Concerning Government*, is a major conduit linking civilizational past and founding era. For Sidney, the complementarity of reason, experience, and revelation (as disclosed in Scripture) in knowing the truth of things is a basic conviction, one shared by the American founding generation. Sidney's self-evident starting point in prudential and political matters is that Good is that at which all things aim. In so holding he is reiterating Western political philosophy, not only back to Aquinas and Augustine but back to Aristotle and Plato as well. In concise summary Sidney writes that

> if governments arise from the consent of men, and are instituted by men according to their own inclinations, they did therein seek their own *good;* for the will is ever drawn by some real good, or the appearance of it. This is that which man seeks by all the regular or irregular motions of his mind. Reason and passion, virtue and vice, do herein concur. . . . A people therefore that sets up [government does it so] . . . that it may be well with themselves and their posterity.[29]

The chief good, therefore, of the social and political order is (ought to be!) the safety and well-being of the people and of every individual among them: *salus populi suprema lex [esto].*[30] Perhaps following John

Selden, then, the supreme well-being of the people is to foster God-given Liberty that, along with Reason, is the specific essence of every human being, each considered to be equal to one another by nature as bearing the mark of their Creator. This, in turn, requires that Justice be the cardinal aim of political and legal administration. Sidney says of the basis or first principle of free government that

> if the safety of the people be the supreme law, and this safety extend to, and consist in the preservation of their liberties, goods, lands and lives, that law must necessarily be the root and beginning, as well as the end and limit of all magistratical power, and all laws must be subservient and subordinate to it. The question will not then be what pleases the king, but what is good for the people . . . what best secures the liberties he is bound to preserve.

As to law, Sidney writes that "we are free-men governed by our own laws, and . . . no man has a power over us, which is not given and regulated by them." The vital connection between the law of nature and natural rights is simply reciprocal. Sidney states that

> if the safety [and well-being] of nations be the end for which governments are instituted, such as take upon them[selves] to govern . . . are by the *law of nature* bound to procure it; and in order to this, to preserve the lives, lands, liberties and goods of every one of their subjects [or citizens]. . . . If all princes are obliged by the law of nature to preserve the lands, goods, lives and liberties of their subjects, those subjects have by the *law of nature a right* to their liberties, lands, goods, &c., and cannot depend upon the will of any man, for that dependence destroys liberty, &c.[31]

Since this reciprocal connection is seldom understood today, I emphasize the point: whatever is required by the law of nature at the same time creates or legitimates a correlative subjective or personal natural right, so that duty and right are mirror images. The law of self-preservation entails the right of defense or the use of such other means as may be essential to preserve one's being, for instance. This correlative connectedness is identifiable in Western theory at least as early as the twelfth century. It is set forth by John Locke, and it is a pivotal argument of the Declaration of Independence.

Liberty itself—to continue with Sidney a little further—is an exemption both from the dominion or will of another as well as from domination by irrational and enslaving passions from within. It "subsists as arising from the nature and being of a man" as God's creature.[32] No man has authority over another except by consent, nor can such authority be continued unless it serves the common good and welfare of the people, which are its raison d'être and ultimate justification.[33] Any power that presumes to usurp or otherwise exercise domination is arbitrary or tyrannical and ought to be resisted: "God helps those who help themselves," Sidney famously writes. And he does not fail to raise the banner of "Christian valor" and to quote from the New Testament, Acts 5:29: "It is better to obey God than man [*sic*]."[34] As for the celebrated teaching of Romans 13 that the "powers that be are ordained of God," Sidney responds much as did the American preachers of the Revolutionary period. "An unjust law is no law at all," Cicero, Augustine, and Aquinas wrote, and Sidney and Americans of the period believed—and still seem to believe, if Martin Luther King's 1963 *Letter from Birmingham Jail* and the "Civil Rights Revolution" it justified are taken as evidence. On this view, only just government, established not for their destruction but for the well-being and preservation of the people, can claim legitimate authority.[35] "All princes therefore that have power are not to be esteemed equally the ministers of God," Sidney states. He continues:

> And tho I am unwilling to advance a proposition that may sound harshly to tender ears, I am inclined to believe, that the same rule, which obliges us to yield obedience to the good magistrate who is the minister of God, and assures us that in obeying him we obey God, does equally oblige us not to obey those who make themselves the ministers of the Devil, lest in obeying them we obey the Devil, whose works they do.[36]

These are views completely consonant with the American argument against the ministry and George III, whose policies are condemned in the Declaration as perverting monarchy into tyranny and thereby rupturing the obligations of allegiance on the part of the colonies. They coincide, also, with the rejection of passive obedience to the powers that be, since American preachers widely agreed that God never intended obedience to tyrants but demanded resistance to evil.

The "fit" of the implicit and explicit American theories with those of Thomas Aquinas's philosophy of human affairs is striking as demonstrating a continuity of civilization and thought, at least in basic principles, over a period of half a millennium and across the vicissitudes of the Protestant Reformation. I can mention here only bare-bones essentials. You will remember that the Declaration asserts the primacy of the laws of nature and of nature's God and seals its claims by invoking "a firm reliance on the protection of Divine Providence" and by pledging the signatories' lives, fortunes, and sacred honor. The Declaration proclaims it to be self-evident truth that all men are created equal and endowed by their Creator with certain indelibly defining characteristics called inalienable rights, included among which are rights to life, liberty, and the pursuit of happiness; governments exist primarily so as to secure these rights to the people individually and collectively, and they draw all of their just authority from the consent of the free men or people who compose the political community governed.

What about Aquinas, who admittedly developed no natural rights doctrine himself? Thomas begins from self-evident truth in setting forth the terms of natural law, which is, in fact, a summary of political no less than legal philosophy. The basic truth that is the self-evident foundation or first principle of all prudential or practical reason, and governs all action, is that all things seek *Good*. This is interpreted as empirically vindicating the Golden Rule as the foundation of all law: the first precept of law is that "good is to be done and ensued, and evil is to be avoided." Thus, "whatever the practical reason naturally apprehends *(naturaliter apprehendit)* as man's good (or evil) belongs to the precepts of the natural law as something to be done or avoided." We should mention that true Good *(bonum verum)* for Thomas is finally validated by cognition, however, not by desire.

Everything else follows from this basic principle, in an account indebted to Aristotle's *Nicomachean Ethics* (1.1.1094a3). Seeking the good is natural to all things. When considered in specifically or properly human terms (as we also saw in Christopher Saint Germain), it is the law of our nature manifested in terms of appetite, tendency, or *inclination (inclinationem)*. These are manifest in three related precepts of natural law as goods to which we are drawn or naturally attracted. As such, in Thomas's terse text, these are ends or objects of pursuit in all human action. The first is the inclination to preserve one's being itself or life, so that whatever tends to the preservation of life or existence and the warding off of its obstacles belongs to natural law. The second is the inclination shared with other animals to reproduce, care for, and protect one's family, educate progeny, and otherwise foster their well-being. The third is the inclination to good according to man's highest faculty of reason, which is proper to him as a being whose specific essence is intelligence: "thus man has a natural inclination to know the truth about God and to live in society; and in this respect, whatever pertains to this inclination belongs to natural law." Thomas later on cites Gratian: " 'the natural law is what is contained in the Law [Torah] and Gospel, . . . by which everyone is commanded to do to others what he would have done to himself [Matt. 7:12], and forbidden to do to others what he would not have done to himself.' "[37]

Our suggestion is merely that the Thomasic account as natural law generally accords with the Declaration's account as natural rights. If we can put labels aside, perhaps we can agree. In any event, we are attempting to explore a fabric of thought shared in substantial degree by a civilization, and it is recognizable in different rhetorical modes in time and place through patently analogous or equivalent articulations of the common reality of human experience. That is the argument. It is far from novel. Locke understood that the medieval constitution was mediated into seventeenth-century English political thought by Richard Hooker in his great work, *Of the Laws of Ecclesiastical Polity;* and Lord Acton was not being wholly facetious in calling Thomas Aquinas the first Whig.[38] Thus, the inalienable right to life corresponds to the law of self-preservation. The right to liberty bears correspondence to the law of freely living so as to propagate and nurture the physical, intellectual, and spiritual well-being of one's self, progeny, and family according to one's own lights and rational inclinations toward the beneficial and good. And the right to "pursue Happiness" corresponds to the desire to know the truth about God and ultimate reality and to live at peace in society. The highest expressions of this quest as proper to the specifically human in man include the desire for earthly flourishing in political and economic communities formed through friendship and like-mindedness and protective of property, peace, and safety. Beyond history and the world itself, the spiritual quest encompasses the hope through love of God of eternal Beatitude.

From Aristotle onward the highest good attainable by action is happiness and blessedness—*eudaimonia* and *makarios* in his words. For Christians it is the *summum Bonum* of union with God, Beatitude, and the satisfactions of a faith-grace relationship formed through love in the here and now in hope of salvation in an eternal beyond. This is experientially to know through participation the presence and truth of God. Such a range of highest goods and their sources clearly fell within the horizon of the American founders' thought as reflected in the Declaration and much more discursively elsewhere at the time.[39] There is, of course, no excluding or minimizing of the lesser goods we seek as contributory to personal happiness in life. The goods whereby we preserve and foster life and well-being, both personally and socially, are both ordained by natural law to human fulfillment, as the rule of our natures, and also presumptive rights that inhere in every person in relation to every other person and to institutional authority of whatever kind.

7. Conclusion. To conclude, then, it can be stressed that both the Declaration and Thomas proffer person-centered teachings. The goods that define inclinations or affections in terms of natural law find their correlates in natural rights to those goods as the just aspirations of every human being considered as all equal and all brothers because each one bears the image and likeness of the Creator, the Christ in every man. The goods essential to human thriving that define what it is to be a man rather than something less are, at the same time, both natural law and natural rights, both the word of the Creator governing life and the just desire of the creature, despite all sin and imperfection. Such a map of human-divine reality as we have limned is a great gift of our civilization in both its medieval and its modern stages. Its vitality continues into the present. Particularly in its political and constitutional aspects, the founders imagined, it may even be civilization's best gift to mankind.

8

The Crisis of Civic Consciousness

Nihilism and Resistance

Nothing exists; if anything exists, it is incomprehensible; if it is comprehensible, it is incommunicable.
—*Gorgias of Leontini*

You shall know the truth, and the truth shall make you free.
—*John 8:32*

I should like us to detach the notion of rationality from that of truth.

In its ideal form, the culture of liberalism would be one which was enlightened, secular, through and through. It would be one in which no trace of divinity remained, either in the form of a divinized world or a divinized self. Such a culture would have no room for the notion that there are nonhuman forces to which human beings should be responsible. It would drop, or drastically reinterpret, not only the idea of holiness but those of "devotion to truth" and of "fulfillment of the deepest needs of the spirit." The process of de-divinization . . . would . . . culminate in our no longer being able to see any use for the notion that finite, mortal, contingently existing human beings might derive the meanings of their lives from anything except other finite, mortal,

121

contingently existing human beings. In such a culture, warnings of "relativism," queries about whether social institutions had become increasingly "rational" in modern times, and doubts about whether the aims of liberal society were "objective moral values" would seem merely quaint.

—*Richard Rorty*

T EACHING POLITICAL SCIENCE ALWAYS has seemed to me to be a noble calling and at times even fun. We political scientists were kept, in some significant degree, from the plunge into the abyss of scientism, positivism, and Marxism that opened under the feet of many of our sociologist colleagues by the fact that we had to teach the Declaration of Independence and the Constitution. We had a block of granite for our cornerstone that gave some stability to our profession that much of the rest of academe lacked. Whether we did it well or poorly, we all were in some degree disciplined and chastened by professional, and thus economic, necessity, compelled to come to terms with our heritage and with the larger tradition of which American government is part. The nobility and fun mainly came through vicarious participation in the high moral fervor of a founding that resisted tyranny in the name of justice and enshrined liberty in a final burst of patriotism by tacking the Bill of Rights on to a Constitution that became the envy of much of mankind. Such stalwarts of our profession as the estimable Charles S. Hyneman admitted to celebrating July Fourth every day of the year.

In heady moments it even seemed plausible to suppose that the profession was, in an odd peripatetic way, carrying out Washington's vision of a national university that would secure the coherence of the American community and instill the principles of free government in rising generations. As Washington believed, "The more homogeneous our citizens can be made in these particulars, the greater will be our prospect of permanent union; and a primary object . . . should be, the education of our youth in the science of government." Thirty years later when the two old argonauts of the founding were designing the University of Virginia to become that national university Congress never would approve, Jefferson wrote to Madison: "In the selection of Law Professor we must be rigorously attentive to his political principles."[1] The principles in mind were those of the

"Whig liberty" concisely distilled in the Declaration as expressive of the consensus of the people and the spirit of '76.

Political science as a school for citizenship is a conception as old as Aristotle's *Nicomachean Ethics* and *Politics* and has had a great run in the United States. But the academy today, and political science with it, is beset by challenges that denigrate every sentiment prized by Washington, Adams, Jefferson, and Madison as constitutive of that cornerstone block of granite and the civilizational tradition it epitomizes. The question is whether the contemporary resurgence of a sound prudential science of human affairs is adequate to resist the challenges that erode civic consciousness and cripple the intellectual life of the nation.

What is the challenge and how might it be overcome? These are questions especially for political scientists to consider. Just a decade ago in his Jefferson Lecture the philosopher Leszek Kolakowski resolutely signaled the path to follow when he said: "However distasteful our civilization might be in some of its vulgar aspects, however enfeebled by its hedonistic indifference, greed, and the decline of civic virtues, however torn by struggles and teeming with social ills, the most powerful reason for its *unconditional* defense (and I am ready to emphasize this adjective) is provided by its alternative."[2] The alternative in view at the time was the triumph of totalitarian Marxism-Leninism through sovietization. The alternative now most evidently in view is more diffuse but of the same order and clearly akin to the horror Kolakowski rejected—namely the triumph of deculturation, social amnesia, and nihilism.[3] Since the root issues are those of mind and spirit and their institutionalization, how is the crisis to be understood and civilization to be defended? Are our philosophers and political scientists up to the task? Perhaps we can at least sketch a few of the issues involved.

1. Civic consciousness. The term *civic consciousness* as used herein means the kind of agreement on fundamentals of association and government that has been evidenced over time in America as a society organized for action in history.

If we take our bearings from the founding, some of the main attributes of America's public mind may be summarized as: an effectively cohesive community that prizes human dignity; the creaturely-Creator relationship (announced in the Declaration) and devotion to liberty under law in the Anglo-American tradition as dimensions of personal character and moral and political identity; a people responsible for the conduct of public affairs through representative state and national institutions with limited powers under civil and higher law. This consensus becomes the foundation of citizenship and civic responsibility in a political order conceived to be natural and resting on consent as befits free men. The general principles governing the founding were articulated by Dr. David Ramsay in 1789 on the last page of his famous *History:* "Remember that there can be no political happiness without liberty; that there can be no liberty without morality; and that there can be no morality without religion."[4]

As stated elsewhere:

> The integrity and virtue of the people must remain the primary force shaping *civic consciousness* as the "first order of reliance." [It] is highly differentiated in the founding period by reason of long self-government and attendant development of an indigenous common law and traditions of governance; the sense of public spirit fostered by pervasive congregationalist church polity; the sense of equality, dignity, and self-reliance generated by social and economic circumstance, and above all, by religious teachings of a Bible-centered faith premised on the priesthood of all believers; and by decades of scrutiny of public policies and officials that engrossed while politically educating Americans as the quarrel with Britain intensified after 1760.[5]

The argument here is that American civic consciousness is moving toward crisis and that this crisis, in principle and intention, goes to the roots of individual and societal existence. The task is to understand the crisis and, then, to seek adequate means to check it.

2. Maladies of free government. At the outset I have to acknowledge that all sorts of ills and crises beset contemporary existence. I have to be selective and deal with only the most basic and virulent. The language of Hippocratic medicine supplied Plato with the useful symbol of the disease *(nosos)* of the soul and polity, and I shall follow this example on the principle that the order and disorders of society reflect the order and disorders of the souls and consciousness of the people who compose it.

Since there are myriad problems of lesser magnitude that it would take a long time just to enumerate, it is by no means to minimize their importance that I pass over most of them here. Americans have taken on a grumpy disposition about themselves and conditions in society. We could trace elements of the crisis of civic consciousness to everything from the chronic divided government of one party dominating Congress with the other holding the presidency, to low election turnout, to the questionable condition of states' rights and the federal system generally, to shrieking demonstrations in the street over the abortion issue. Each suggests at least that all is not well in our republic, and some political candidates for national office are quite prepared to contend that we are engaged in a "culture war" for the soul of America, which is pretty heady language. In fact, there is a new monthly magazine titled *Culture Wars* published in South Bend, Indiana, and preaching "counter-revolution."[6]

My suggestion is of a crisis more profound than any or all of these taken together, although one not unrelated to various other manifestations of malaise and alienation. High on the list of the diseases of American civic consciousness, for example, are statism, economism, and a pervasive social amnesia. Each of these is merely to be mentioned but might concern us at length: the increasing tendency to be married to government and believe it must supply every need; the conservatives' shibboleth that free enterprise economics is the panacea and politics is mostly derivative, secondary, and will take care of itself; and the tendency to dismiss with a contemptuous "that's history" any recollection of the temporal-transcendental dimensions of experience and the formative role that consultation of historical consciousness plays in ordering human existence—this order of "experience" is the sovereign guide to prudential action, the *Federalist* insisted (No. 85). All these are vital elements of the crisis, but I largely set them aside in the present discussion.

Of course, like the frog placed in a pot of lukewarm water that didn't notice the increase in heat until it was too late, we can react to our social deformations and diseases by not reacting or by denying there is anything really amiss. After all, our traditions and institutions are wonderfully resilient and may, like youth itself, be immortal and indestructible. Right? Wrong. Free government is fragile and must be nurtured—by us.

The question is this: how many decades and generations of systematic miseducation can we endure? How much abuse of our heritage through neglect, ignorance, and mendacity can we bear without experiencing disintegration and collapse into some kind of despotic authoritarianism? It continues to be true that eternal vigilance is the price of liberty. The founders sniffed tyranny in the air when Britain levied a three-pence tax on tea, as James Madison admiringly recalled in old age; and they fought the Revolution on the slogan of no taxation without representation. Little clues count in matters of this sort, and the clues are there. So worry! But I must be highly selective and consider only the main thrust of major movements undermining the foundations of the American community.

3. Context of civilizational crisis. Perhaps it might be said that, in a sense, the maladies of American society that endanger free government are the "fault" of nobody in particular. But at the same time, this does not excuse the protagonists of violence of their own responsibility or fundamental obligation to live in truth and to resist evil and the lie. The maladies arise, however, from a complex set of circumstances productive of a climate of opinion—a growth of radical modernity. This is not exclusively American but global in range. What is new is not the lineaments of the disease (which is relatively old and commonplace) but the intensity of its propagation in the United States during the last decade or so, especially since the collapse of the Soviet empire. The syndrome is characterized by pervasive deculturation of society, intensifying secularization to the point of radical immanentization, to the end of defacing if not eradicating culture and personality as they have developed over millennia. The drift, which appears to have accelerated since 1990 into a rush, is toward what can be identified as the horror of Nietzschean nihilism. Generally characterized, this amounts to the desire to find truth by destroying all that ever has been true before and to plunge fearlessly into the primordial abyss of the unbounded. Increasingly, we are cut loose in the uncharted metaphysics of nothingness through a defiant gesture not unlike that of the suicide who hurls himself from the top of the building so he can soar like an eagle. From the perspective of common sense we identify this as madness.

The term is of more than passing interest, and we shall encounter it again in our consideration of the Nietzschean murder of God when the madman seeks the god who will replace the God men have murdered. A parallel is to be seen in the young Karl Marx's quotation of Prometheus from Aeschylus' *Prometheus Bound* (line 975), which he took as the motto of his doctoral dissertation. "Philosophy makes no secret of it," Marx wrote. "The confession of Prometheus, '*In a word, I hate all the gods,'* is its own confession, its own verdict against all gods heavenly and earthly who do not acknowledge human self-consciousness as the supreme deity. There shall be none beside it." But Marx omits the context, for in Aeschylus, Hermes the messenger of the gods rebukes Prometheus for his defiant statement with the reply: "It appears you have been stricken with no small madness [*nosos*]." The term translated as madness means, as mentioned earlier, "bodily or mental sickness. In the sense of a disease of the spirit [*pneumopathology*] it can mean hatred of the gods or simply being dominated by one's passions."[7]

As any adequate sketch of the ground of the American founding will attest, to the extent that America stands for a coherent idea or vision of reality, it is rooted in the classical and Christian philosophy of being, as filtered through the Enlightenment, which magnifies the individual human person as possessed of certain inalienable rights and properties that are God-given in an indelibly defining creaturely-Creator relationship.[8] The human being is *imago Dei*. The political and ethical order is, thus, surmounted by a metaphysical process-structure anchored in an order of truth reaching back to Moses and the prophets in Israel and to Plato, Aristotle, and the Stoics in Hellas and Rome. Not merely the rationalistic aspects of the American idea, as (say) proclaimed in the Declaration of Independence, but also its representative habits and customs or historicity partake of this general understanding of human existence: its origin and destiny generally reflect this same vision of reality and truth. The coherence and resilience of this vision that is representatively American and in significant degree merges with the universal vision of what it is to be a human being living in truth under God have shaped American civic consciousness. The evocative power of this vision has heretofore made it substantially immune to the most radical aspects of ideological or gnostic politics. Its general acceptance by the public and academy alike has supplied the groundwork of an identifiable consensus in political and social matters productive of a stable community based on a morality of liberty and justice beyond merely utilitarian interests and claims. Even the greatest breach of American history through the War between the States or Civil War, as one prefers, revolved around contradictory interpretations of this consensus and its meaning.[9]

Avant-garde intellectuals loathe and despise all of this. To trace this hatred would require a separate study. But it seems that such militantly secular intellectuals never have forgiven America that in 1776 they were not able to conduct our revolution as they did in 1789 the French Revolution. On the contrary, our revolution was instead conducted mainly by the "black regiment" of the clergy and by lawyers and other political leaders. It was neither antireligious nor antiproperty but the very opposite. At any rate, these intellectuals' condemnation and repudiation of the Christian and classical truth of reality is broadly characteristic of the trendy "isms" that continue to float on the surface of political discourse and antiphilosophy—above all in the scientistic accents of Freudianism, positivism, and Marxism, their amalgam and derivatives. These now are streamlined and vulgarized into burgeoning "new" totalitarian movements loudly and boringly familiar to everyone in academe as political correctness, radical feminism, critical legal studies, multiculturalism, and deconstructionism. The nature of the crisis of civic consciousness therewith becomes more clearly apparent. It centers in an attack on America's constitutive historical understanding of itself and the truths fundamental to the American idea or vision of reality as part and parcel of an unlimited rebellion against the order of being itself and most directly against reality's divine Ground in theory and institutions.

4. Specific focus of attack. The "God Is Dead" movement is the heart of the matter. Edmund Burke carefully diagnosed the fact in his valedictory *Letters on a Regicide Peace* (1796), there identifying the comprehensive destructive intentions of the revolution in terms of *Regicide, Deicide,* and *Jacobinism*.[10] But Burke had himself been anticipated (with a cheer!) by the Marquis de Sade in *Français, encore un effort si vous voulez être républicains!* (1792) where the author advocates regicide, deicide, homicide, and suicide.[11] The illustrious founder, litany, and rancid headwaters of radical modernity therewith appear.

While it is only a little less lurid (and not overtly pornographic), it may be more instructive for present purposes to savor the hatred of being, and rebellion against its truth, as that came to crystal clarity in nineteenth-century German thought or antiphilosophy. This is because, for complex reasons, many members of the American academy have inherited this legacy and actively propagate its message as central to their vocations, especially it seems at our premier institutions. Friedrich Nietzsche (1844–1900) diagnosed this state of mind with extraordinary insight. It must also be acknowledged that he promoted and participated in the tragic rebellion himself until, for the final decade of his life, he broke psychologically and became irretrievably insane.

Nietzsche concentrated negation of long-prevailing truth in the name of truth in the symbol *nihilism,* which he called that "uncanniest *[unheimlichste]* of all guests," and "a pathological transitional stage."[12] Only a few central points can be noticed here. What is vital as providing the key with which to understand our present situation is this: the chief object of rejection, repudiation, and annihilation is God and the morality of Christianity. Thus: " 'To become as God,' 'to be absorbed into God'—for thousands of years these were the most naive and convincing desiderata" (*WP,* 15). The nihilist is the liberated one who has concluded that the world of ordinary experience or of

> becoming has no goal and that underneath all becoming there is no grand unity in which the individual could immerse himself completely as in an element of supreme value, [but] an escape remains: to pass sentence on this whole world of becoming as a deception and to invent a world beyond it, a *true* world. . . . [T]he last form of nihilism comes into Being: it includes disbelief in any metaphysical world [whatever] and forbids itself any belief in a *true* world. Having reached this standpoint, one grants the reality of becoming as the *only* reality, forbids oneself every kind of clandestine access to afterworlds and false divinities. (*WP,* 13)

But this stance is ultimately unendurable even if it may reflect truth. Human beings must worship God or idols, Luther once remarked. In a later passage Nietzsche writes: "War against the Christian ideal, against the doctrine of 'blessedness' and 'salvation' as the goal of life, against the supremacy of the simple, the pure in heart, the suffering and unfortunate. What does God, faith in God, matter to us any longer? 'God' today [is] merely a faded word, not even a concept any longer! But as Voltaire says on his deathbed: 'only don't speak of that man there!' When and where has any man of consequence resembled the Christian ideal?" (*WP*, 127–28, note incorporated).

The antagonism equally extends to Greek philosophy, which must be obliterated: "The appearance of the Greek philosophers from Socrates onwards is a symptom of decadence; the anti-Hellenic instincts come to the top. . . . *In summa:* the mischief has already reached its climax in Plato. . . . [T]he consequence of the denaturalization of moral values was the creation of a degenerate type of man—'the good man,' 'the happy man,' 'the wise man.' Socrates represents a moment of the profoundest perversity in the history of values" (*WP*, 221, 235).

In *The Gay Science*, Nietzsche writes of "*The Madman.*"

> Have you not heard of that madman who lit a lantern in the bright morning hours, ran to the market place, and cried incessantly, "I seek God! I seek God!" Since many of those who do not believe in God were standing around just then, he provoked much laughter. . . . "Whither is God" he cried. "I shall tell you. *We have killed him*—you and I. All of us are his murderers. . . . God is dead. God remains dead. And we have killed him. How shall we, the murderers of all murderers, comfort ourselves? What was holiest and most powerful of all that the world has yet owned has bled to death under our knives. Who will wipe this blood off us?. . . . There has never been a greater deed; and whoever will be born after us—for the sake of this deed he will be part of a higher history than all history hitherto."

> *The background of our cheerfulness.* The greatest recent event—that "God is dead," that the belief in the Christian God has ceased to be believable—is even now beginning to cast its first shadows over Europe. . . . [Only the very few will understand] what has really happened here, and what must collapse now that this belief has been undermined—all that was built upon it, leaned on it, grew into it: for example, our whole European morality. . . . [W]e philosophers and "free spirits" feel as if a new dawn were shining on us when we receive the tidings that "the old god is dead"; our heart overflows with gratitude, amazement, anticipation, expectation.[13]

The deification of Man at last is at hand, but even Nietzsche finds the possibility dubious: "*if* there were gods, how could I endure not to be a god! *Hence* there are no gods. Though I drew this conclusion, now it draws me. God is a conjecture. . . . God is a thought that makes crooked all that is straight" (*PN*, 198). The solution approaches from the future:

> *Dionysian wisdom.* Joy in the destruction of the most noble and at the sight of its progressive ruin: in reality joy in what is coming and lies in the future, which triumphs over existing things, however good. *Dionysian:* temporary identification with the principle of life (including the voluptuousness of the martyr). . . . Thereupon I advanced further down the road of disintegration. . . . We have to be destroyers! . . . To the paralyzing sense of general disintegration and incompleteness I opposed the *eternal recurrence*. (*WP*, sec. 417, 224)

At the end of *The Antichrist*, Nietzsche draws his conclusion: "I *condemn* Christianity. . . . The Christian church has left nothing untouched by its corruption; it has turned every value into an unvalue, every truth into a lie, every integrity into a vileness of the soul. . . . I call Christianity the one great curse, the one great innermost corruption, the one great instinct of revenge, for which no means is poisonous, stealthy, subterranean, *small* enough—I call it the one immortal blemish of mankind" (*PN*, 655–56; sec. 62). Hatred, derision, contempt, and will to power are reflected in Nietzsche's attitude by turns, and he finds the final solution for the faithful in self-apotheosis: "Love yourself through grace, then you are no longer in need of your God, and you can act the whole drama of Fall and Redemption to its end in yourself."[14]

5. Anatomy of crisis. I do not pretend to supply a detailed analysis of Nietzsche on this occasion.[15] But the tenor of his thought is evident. An understanding of it at its most fundamental level—that is, as it is relied upon by contemporary radical ideologues of every stripe, whatever mystics may find in it—is important if we are to comprehend the inspiration of a climate of opinion well represented in the academy. It is obvious that in Nietzsche we are very far—indeed, eons—away from the temper and frame of mind of the American founders and the consciousness they engendered as authoritative for the American ethos and institutional order. It is plain enough also that we are far away from the commonsense understanding of reality of the general citizenry today. That Nietzschean nihilism in the specific senses limned here should form the basis, virtually provide the script, for assault in George Washington's America on civic consciousness by American intellectuals is astonishing, even breathtaking. The chickens have come home to roost through alienated intellectuals. As one commentator observes, they must now dutifully shoulder (with a sigh) the dreadful burden of "the modern project, as a radical manifestation of the will to power. . . . The great creator must also be a great destroyer; in destroying or accelerating the natural decadence of the past, he also destroys his own historical consciousness and becomes like a child, freed from loyalty to and vengeance against the old world, able to create new values in the innocence of his playful strength."[16] The earnest purpose of such playful malevolent intoxication, however, is the destruction of America and the civilization of which it is an integral part.

In vivid terms, we thereby glimpse what Eric Voegelin identifies as *egophanic revolt*. Its key aspect is hatred of divine Being as emblematized in the murder of God. From this embrace of Cain there follows the murders of kings and millions of men in the name of humanity for Autonomous Man, or the Great Being Man, or the Superman as actually encountered in various guises in our own century. Egophany inverts and expunges wherever it can the great theophanies of Judaism (Yahweh), Christianity (Christ), and philosophy (*Nous*) that have structured human existence throughout history and into the present. Egophany's most noteworthy marks are systems, the prohibition against the asking of questions, and complicity in the murder of God as the sine qua non act of closure.[17]

To the degree that the reward for America in winning the Cold War is to inherit radical modernity as "education" through the conduit of its leading universities and public discourse more generally, we glimpse the rudiments of that odious legacy by means of the diagnosis of Nietzsche. The onslaught has been and remains massive. In Lionel Trilling's characterization, such education (including civic education, if that is not an oxymoron), even when undertaken so as to illustrate the grotesque, often actually results seductively and inadvertently in "the socialization of the anti-social, or the acculturation of the anti-cultural, or the legitimization of the subversive."[18]

There is irony in this strange recent passage of events. The hideous exemplars of Autonomous Man as formed by Nazi Germany and Soviet Russia lie slain and shattered in the dust of remembered history. Or is social amnesia so pervasive that already that, too, has been forgotten? The ideological antipolitics of the nihilistic second realities has been defeated theoretically, politically, economically, and by all the facts of human existence. Yet unremitting assault continues on the American and generally Western heritage in the name of enlightenment and social progress by the ghosts of the very politics of atrocity whose true monuments are the Nazi death camps and the Soviet gulag. Its protagonists, unable to cope with reason and experience, resort to brute force tending toward the lethal. Shouting and abusive proponents of the new totalitarianism in the academy will have conveyed to common experience this characteristic feature on almost any occasion where opposition or contrary viewpoints come under consideration. This is the spirit of the S.S., representing the onset of the New Holocaust in the name of liberation and progress; the fact should not be mistaken.

In his most poetic work, *Thus Spake Zarathustra*, Nietzsche wrote: "Man is a rope stretched between the animal and the Superman—a rope over an abyss. A dangerous across, a dangerous on-the-way, a dangerous looking-back, a dangerous shuddering and stopping" (*PN*, 126; sec. 4).

This image, however, perverts both philosophy and faith and falsifies the fundamental experiences of reality. The vertical tension experienced by man toward transcendent divine reality in the faith-grace relationship—or in the erotic mania and noetic tension symbolized in the philosopher's ascent to Good and Beauty—is no bridge from the brute to the superman whose imaginary parousia approaches mankind by a horizontal transcendence from the future. Moreover, man is an end and not a mere means or transition. Man experiences as the core of his humanity the immanent and the divine polarities of existence in the tensional In-Between (Plato's *metaxy*) of preeminently human existence. As self-reflective participants aware of their communion with God, human beings also are conscious of their inherent ineradicable worth and dignity. By contrast, the imaginative pretense to the superman experientially means a fall into the abyss of narcissistic self-salvation. If psychic deformation through such pneumopathology remains isolated in individuals, the result may be various psychoses or outright insanity. If the disease of the soul becomes socially prevalent through ideology, the manipulation of mass communication, and other means of institutionalization, then it demonstrably can create the hell on earth familiar to us as *totalitarianism*. To succumb to *libido dominandi* is, in effect, to reverse the *periagoge* (*Republic* 515c–d) of Plato or the Christian's conversion (*metanoia*, Luke 15:7). The movement can be described as the soul's turning away from openness to the divine through contraction into the closed self. This is rebellion against the uncertain truth of faith so as to embrace the certain untruth of gnostic ideology.[19]

6. Politics of resistance. The reasonable response by the unafflicted to perverse education is resistance—now as in antiquity when the philosophers resisted the sophists, themselves a glib and fashionable lot. We are obliged to become our own physicians through the therapy of common sense and a steady appeal to the givens of common reality as experienced in the concrete consciousness of everyman and accumulated in the evidentiary treasury of history. History constantly recollected exhibits the collaborative way of God with his sometimes responsive, sometimes rebellious creature, man. Since experience shows that the vanguard of perversion and pneumopathology is the debauchery of language so fashionable now in the forefront of the political-correctness onslaught, it is important to recall the insight conveyed by George Orwell in a memorable sentence: "The purpose of Newspeak," he wrote, "was not only to provide a medium of expression for the world-view and mental habits proper to the devotees of Ingsoc, but to make all other modes of thought impossible."[20] Those who control your language will control your thoughts. The result is to make the asking of inconvenient questions impossible, socially irrelevant, or ludicrous—and thus de facto prohibited within the new orthodoxy of closure and deformed souls.

To live in truth requires at all times resolute resistance to untruth and tyranny as the first courageous step. Behind the novel and unheard-of truths of the insistent ideologue hides the artful lover of power who as incipient *uebermensch* seeks to engender Leviathan. As a friend of the eighteenth-century Americans we admire as founding fathers may have said: "All that is necessary for evil to triumph is for good men to do nothing."

Unless the game already is up and—as I recently heard proposed —we are meekly to surrender the educational and other basic ordering institutions of this country to the minions of vacuity and second reality; or to be content simply to drift and hope it all turns out well; or in surrendering to withdraw (as a last desperate resort) into enclaves or oases protective of truth as a besieged remnant— then the order of the day can be only to resist! These exhaust the available choices, unless we, too, decide to join the nihilists in disdaining truth. Resistance, of course, is far from novel in a nation we used to salute as the land of the free, the home of the brave. While it may mean nothing to apocalyptic dreamers and purveyors of second realities, it means a lot to common sense to remember that the evidence of experience is on the side of those resolute enough to resist.

7. Epilogue. Last, the character of effective resistance itself demands brief explanation in a time of terrorism and street demonstrations teetering on the edge of violence. Polarization of American society has proceeded so far through the influences of socialism, Marxism, multiculturism, and the welfare state's collision with traditional attitudes (among other factors) that the World Trade Center and Oklahoma City catastrophes suggest the possibility, however remote, of a slide toward sedition and civil strife on a scale perhaps not seen in America in the century since the end of Reconstruction in the South.

The primary mode of resistance envisaged in the present context— it must therefore be stressed—is intellectual and spiritual resistance to untruth, conducted by reason and persuasion. It is resistance in the name of liberty and truth to revolutionaries who are succeeding in wresting major universities, academic professional associations, and much of public discourse into radical control. It is important to show the theoretical (as well as prudential) shortcomings of such developments. The connection with the Murder of God movement as the revolutionaries' common ground must be repeatedly demonstrated as inspiring their onslaughts. The consequences must then be shown for the destruction of American society as it has existed historically and claimed respect as the last best hope of mankind. The ethic of resistance is the ethic of hope.

Mere conservatism and staunch appeal to tradition ultimately are not in themselves enough and aggravate the general problem of dogmatic closure to truth—even if the essential starting point of resistance is to accept the American founding as the ground of a renaissance of our traditions, patriotism, and civic consciousness. And, to be sure, a muting or omission of the glories and triumphs of American history as part of civic education in the name of pedagogical "standards" is patently an attack on the soul of the country as historically constituted—one rightly condemned by Lynne V. Cheney and others as such and justifiably resisted. The sternest of warnings have repeatedly been given by Samuel Huntington, who sees Christianity at the core of our society and civilization. The insight is not original. Toynbee elaborated it a half century ago, and well before that Theodore Roosevelt observed: "the one absolutely certain way of bringing this nation to ruin, of preventing all possibility of its continuing as a nation at all, would be to permit it to become a tangle of squabbling nationalities." Huntington bluntly comments: "In the 1990s, however, the leaders of the United States have not only permitted that but assiduously promoted the diversity rather than the unity of the people they govern."

> The American multiculturists . . . reject their country's cultural heritage. Instead of identifying the United States with another civilization, however, they wish to create a country of many civilizations, which is to say a country not belonging to any civilization and lacking a cultural core. History shows that no country so constituted can long endure as a coherent society. A multicivizational United States will not be the United States; it will be the United Nations. . . . Rejection of the Creed of Western civilization means the end of the United States of America as we have known it. It also means the end of Western civilization.[21]

In this high-stakes game, invoking tradition is not enough. Resistance requires recovery of the philosophical and spiritual ground itself, in the academy and churches as well as in public discourse in the country at large. And this means finding the profoundest sources of truth in the meditative life of our civilization and recovering these as living presence through the educative processes. Back to the books! Judaism and Christianity are founded on the Bible, and that book lay at the center of American consciousness at the time of the founding. It is not merely one among other books. The philosophical and religious life of the country can *only* be reinvigorated by recourse to the great works of the great minds of the ages, from Plato to Augustine to Shakespeare.

Education itself is no monolith, however, and person-peripheral scientific and mathematical education does little to restore the understanding of uniquely human reality. Rather, taken alone, it does the very opposite and helps make human beings an endangered species through obfuscation. Both Nazism and Marxism-Leninism evoke natural science as their paradigm, we remember. Natural science, a great boon to human existence in most respects, is not itself the core problem, of course. The problem is science's perversion into scientism and positivism and, thereby, into methodological and other assumptions about knowledge and reality that fallaciously presume to supply the sovereign, even the sole, road to truth. Systematic reductionism and deformation of reality inevitably result.

The question remains whether contemporary philosophers and political scientists (many of them hardened in the orthodoxies of Marxism, positivism, and behavioralism and in varying degrees part of the problem) are up to the challenge. The situation is not entirely hopeful, and the answer at best doubtful. As one astute commentator discerned thirty years ago: "The 'givenness' of American life can no longer be taken for granted, and neither can it be rescued by an intellectually empty citizenship training, nor by the attempted reduction of liberalism to scientism. . . . [I]t is no longer plausible to view the American civilization either as a closed or happily isolated society . . . or as *the* society where a fixed system of natural rights had first been established and could then be generalized universally."[22]

What seems requisite seems also to be uncertain if not improbable. For if we are to preserve and revitalize free government in America and the world, we are obliged to look to the deepest sources that from Abraham and Aristotle to Thomas Jefferson and John Adams persuasively grounded the self-evident truths that this country is founded on and strives to live by. These sources are to be found in reason and experience concretely disclosed through the historical events of revelation and philosophy in Israel and Hellas and the life of mind uniquely cultivated since antiquity on that foundation in the Christian West. By recovering the vital past, its implications, illuminations, and vision of reality, we lay groundwork that can help assure the essentially unknowable future. The unconditional defense of civilization is, therefore, the essential posture that makes possible the life of mind and spirit whose thriving crowns historical existence. The alternative is to choose a descent into barbarism.

A final caveat and an implication may be mentioned. No institutional order is immortal, however well contrived or prudentially nurtured, and this includes the American republic no less than Western civilization. Experience remains our best guide. And, while Wittgenstein may have been correct in saying that an attempt to prop up a faltering tradition is like trying to repair a cobweb with your bare hands, there is a venerable school of thought that argues the efficacy of just action by individuals abiding in truth: "A little leaven leaveneth the whole lump."[23]

9

Eric Voegelin a Conservative?

ERIC VOEGELIN WAS REGULARLY identified as "a conservative," a designation he himself politely declined. On one such occasion, an interlocutor responded with, "Well, you must be a liberal then!" To which Voegelin retorted: "Just because I'm not a conservative does not mean I'm so stupid as to be a liberal!"[1]

So, what's the point? Voegelin had his political preferences like everybody else. But Voegelin the scholar—and he was a scholar to the soles of his shoes—was a philosopher and political scientist, not a political activist, policy advocate, or polemicist. His thought and almost all of his work move at several removes from the level of political debate we vaguely reference with our conservative/liberal labels and dichotomy. If we consider that the terms themselves are highly indeterminate—after all, the old Communists in eastern Europe now are called "conservatives"—there is good reason to apply them with caution. Voegelin for his part found it amusing that, at one time or another, he had been accused in print of being everything from a gnostic, a fascist, and a communist to a liberal, a Hegelian, a Jew (by Nazi writers), a Christian, and even a follower of Huey Long.

If we stress that Voegelin was in fact and by his own insistence a genuinely independent thinker who was not anyone's man but his own, we scarcely comprehend the statement. Such personalities are rare. The unique is baffling. The point is not unrelated to the deeper notion that, in Voegelin's estimate, the great historical exemplars of the contemplative life that he himself sought to follow not only stood apart from their societies in a critical posture but achieved little theoretical continuity with one another. Their chief insights were unsusceptible of institutionalization as schools or movements. He roundly denied that there was such a thing as the history of political theory—and partly for that reason abandoned his own monumental study of political ideas in favor of his study of the engendering experiences in *Order and History.* He also was taken with T. S. Eliot's insight into the character of philosophizing, that "the only method is to be very intelligent." By contrast, the positivists think that, like sausage making, it merely requires use of the right method to produce the deposit called science.

Even if it is not conservative, there is rightly enough something strongly conserving about Voegelin's work. The range of subject matter itself leads one to the conclusion. There is the vast and meticulous survey of human intellection from Israel and Hellas, through the Christian centuries, into the Renaissance, the Enlightenment, down to the present—not to omit the recently published translation of his first book (originally published in 1928), *On the Form of the American Mind.*[2] The burden of this uncommon effort is the elevation of the worth and dignity of the individual human person in the face of collectivisms left and right. This affirmation is accompanied by a theoretically acute reinterpretation of the core of human nature itself as consciousness of man's tension toward the divine ground of being— by his analysis the primary meaning of reason *(Nous),* man's specific nature or essence in traditional philosophy.

While Voegelin's analysis often is demanding, his style is powerful and remarkably lucid. His reliance on common sense and his appeal to ordinary experience are markedly American and pervade his work. The revival of classical and Christian thought that he effects is a major achievement and one that is immediately clarifying for existence in our time of crisis. He summarized this point on one occasion as follows:

> The language of the classics has become the general language of Western civilization, especially the Anglo-Saxon (that is, English, American, and everywhere that influence has spread). In the eighteenth century—that was the great good luck—before the ideologies really got developed and under way, you had the commonsense philosophers of Scotland: Reid, Herbert, Stewart,

and so on. Commonsense philosophy is the real, fundamental, common language in which, thank God, we still speak in Anglo-Saxon civilizations. Here is an optimum situation for rationalization because these Scottish philosophers absorbed Plato and Aristotle if not directly at least in Ciceronian form, which was not too bad a deformation. . . . Scottish commonsense philosophy is an Aristotelian ethics and politics minus the metaphysics. . . . The whole classic pattern of rationality is preserved to an enormous extent (and more so than on the European continent) in England and America. That is a great cultural advantage. . . . One must never forget that all classic philosophy is built on common sense, while no ideology is built on common sense—not the positivism of Comte or Marx, not Hegelianism. Realizing that is the great breakthrough.[3]

Voegelin's reaffirmation and experiential reauthentication of reality as presented in Greek philosophy and the Bible—capped by the divine and tensionally structured through man's participation in the divine-human encounter—powerfully serve to revitalize both faith and reason in the rediscovered mode of classical "noesis." The habitual "traditions" and institutions struggling to uphold our civilization are thereby strengthened, but not by the sound of one more voice in the choir. Rather, a fresh philosophical analysis emerges that lays the ax of critical intelligence to dominant modern ideologies. At the same time, it persuasively revives and reinterprets the experiences that, underlying the dogmas, are basic to the truths men live by.

At this point the conserving efforts of Voegelin merge with a movement of radical critique and constructive philosophizing. Dogmas, doctrines, and traditions that roll trippingly off the tongue are themselves, Voegelin insists, secondary ideologies that are deadening to the living spirit of faith no less than to the living tension of the philosopher's contemplative (noetic) quest. If conservatives rejoice that belief in God is vindicated in the thought of a contemporary thinker of rank, that the meditative life of religion and theory are rescued from the dustbin of history and from the derision of nihilist manipulators in our midst, their sense of complacency and relief may be short-lived. The crisis of consciousness that has propelled alienated intellectuals' assault on all that our most venerable traditions hold dear and true cannot be met merely by reasserting dogmas even more loudly than before. Rather, something more is needed. And that something more depends principally upon loving recovery of restorative communion in the souls of men with the divine ground of being and its rational articulation as the foundation of civilizational order.

By Voegelin's account, then, the rightness of what always has been right must be not only reaffirmed but also recaptured in the hearts of men and as the living truth of a science of human affairs fit for the postmodern world. This can only be done, Voegelin repeatedly stressed, in the concrete consciousness of concrete persons whose experiences of order might then spread to form new communities and reinvigorate old ones. In the details of what is involved there is something distinctly revolutionary in this, all the while conserving though it is. But in their various ways faith and philosophy always are revolutionary, if one credits the historical evidence.

Voegelin's well-known scathing critique of modern gnosticism and sundry related deformations of reality that—whether armed or unarmed—have claimed privileged positions in the contemporary world extends to all of the "isms." In his later work these are classified under the general rubric of *egophanic revolt*, the libidinous assertion of Autonomous Man's unrestrained power over some imaginary "Second Reality" of his own devising. Appearing in many varieties (Freudianism, Marxism-Leninism, and National Socialism, for instance), all are characterized by a reductionist account of human life and existence, and especially by occlusion against divine Being— as in the "God Is Dead" movement. It would be egregious error to relegate resistance to untruth to an episode of the past, especially now that the so-called Cold War is "over" and we can get back to much-rumored "normalcy." In the face of such gnosticism and apocalypticism, Voegelin refused to fall for one more tempting second reality and, instead, asserted the stable structure of being. The human condition is not over, nor has it been nor can it be transfigured through human initiative, however many ends of history may be proclaimed hither, thither, and yon by whatever chorus of false prophets and magicians.

Resistance to untruth was a hallmark of the maturation of philosophy in Hellas two and a half millennia ago, if one considers Socrates' and Plato's well-documented opposition to the sophists. What was at stake in ancient Athens still remains at stake today, namely the truth of human existence—within the finite capacities of men to know it given the mystery of divine disclosure. For philosophy by Voegelin's account must ever be the love of wisdom and never its systematic possession. Like the Apostle Paul, in the now of historical existence, we see as through a glass darkly. The human pilgrimage through time in partnership with God is permanently emblematized as faith in search of understanding—the Anselmian image of *fides quaerens intellectum*.

Thus, such philosophical *truth* as we attain is always perspectival, not because it is merely relativistic opinion *(doxa)*, but because even critical knowledge *(episteme)* of reality experienced can only be the cognitive grasp of reality through reflective consciousness as that arises within the ineluctable participatory perspective available to human beings. The limit of cognition, then, is truth representative of the Truth beyond representation. Even this, however, Voegelin often stressed, is not something one can possess or sit on and protect like a thing. Rather, it is the living truth whose embodiment by conscious-ness in tension—in the lives of persons and communities—is to be won and lost and perchance won again in the loving process of open quest called *philosophy* that extends indefinitely into an unknowable future. The dynamics of politics and history, in a meditative pro-cess so conceived, can best be symbolized by recalling the undying struggle, Plato's *mache athanatos*, whose temporal fulfillment is ever imperfect and whose happy ending lies in the hope of eschatological fulfillment.

10

Voegelin's Philosophy of History and Human Affairs

ERIC VOEGELIN'S MASTERWORK IS *Order and History*. It appeared over a period of three decades with the fifth and final volume published posthumously in 1987.[1] While the focus here is on the first of these volumes, *Israel and Revelation*, that book is only a part of the larger enterprise. Thus, a few words on the range of Voegelin's thought may be helpful in order to suggest something of the context of discussion.[2]

By the time Voegelin came to the book before us, he had researched and written the sprawling "History of Political Ideas," running well over four thousand pages in typescript, published five books in German and dozens of articles in German and English, and achieved a degree of celebrity in America through the publication of *The New Science of Politics*, whose thesis that gnosticism is the essence of modernity evoked *Time* magazine's feature story, "Journalism and Joachim's Children," for its thirtieth-anniversary issue.[3] The two succeeding volumes of *Order and History*, titled *The World of the Polis* and *Plato and Aristotle*, actually already had been written, apart from prefatory and introductory materials, so that *Israel and Revelation* can properly be read as their intellectual sequel.[4] At age fifty-five and the height of his powers, Voegelin by this time had at his disposition a remarkable range of philological and scholarly capacities and a distinctive philosophical perspective on major theoretical and historical issues. But he had practical purposes in mind, too, in writing *Israel and Revelation,* as he explained in 1954 to an editor at Macmillan, which had first intended to publish Voegelin's studies. The work on Israel and especially on Moses, Voegelin enthusiastically wrote, "will make [the book] a 'must' in theological seminaries and for reverends, because (though that may sound almost unbelievable) no book on the political ideas of Israel has ever been written at all. Besides the part on Israel is particularly well written and should, therefore, appeal to a general public that is interested in Jewish history."[5]

1. Scope of the philosophy of human affairs. In his mature work, Voegelin constantly invokes the participation of man in all the spheres of reality identified from Aristotle onward in the hierarchy of being and, most especially, in transcendent divine Being whose consideration is ineluctable and central to philosophy as engendered by the ancient Greeks, and now energetically resumed by Voegelin. The restoration of wholeness in human affairs—in personal, social, and historical dimensions—is radically dependent upon the scholarly recovery of the facts of human experience as they register through time the participatory dimension that defines the human condition. The inquiry in its several (overlapping) stages is conducted in terms of a philosophical anthropology that gives way, in turn, to a theory of politics, a philosophy of history, a philosophy of experience-symbolism (or of symbolic forms), and a theory of consciousness that is fundamental to the entire enterprise. Voegelin's method is the critical method, by which is meant that he writes on the basis of a mastery of all of the chief philosophical and meditative writers from the pre-Socratics to Anselm to Husserl, Bergson, and Whitehead—and of the principal secondary literature—critically adapting and modifying the analyses in the light of their cogency as accounts of reality experienced and of his own command of the sources of knowledge. Thus there is the constant silent asking of the Socratic question: look and see, is this not the case? The form of the inquiry is primarily a search of the historiographic record as the available evidentiary material of human experience over the five thousand years of civilized existence. As explained in the preface to *Plato and Aristotle:*

> *Order and History* is a philosophical inquiry concerning the principal types of order of human existence in society and history as

well as the corresponding symbolic forms. The oldest civilizational societies were the empires of the ancient Near East in the
form of the cosmological myth. And from this oldest stratum
of order emerged, through the Mosaic and Sinaitic revelations,
the Chosen People with its historical form in the present under
God. . . . In the Aegean area emerged, from the stratum of order
in cosmological form, the Hellenic polis with the symbolic form
of philosophy. (*OH3*, ix)

As will have become clear, the *empiricism* of Voegelin's philosophy and philosophical (noetic-pneumatic) science of politics (or
human affairs) insists on an accounting of the entire range of human
experience-symbolization, with the accent falling on the highest
reaches of reality as formative of the distinctively human reality. The
problem of transcendent Being, of the divine Ground of being, is the
central problem of all philosophy from the time of the pre-Socratics
into the present, in his view. Philosophy itself is defined as "the love
of being through the love of divine Being as the source of its order"
(*OH1*, xiv). The love of Being and resistance to untruth take shape as
a struggle against pervasive "climates of opinion" that tend to form a
veritable iron curtain of the soul in the modern world, enforcing spiritual blindness through massive control of communication and action
(see *OH3*, 79). The truth to be recovered in openness to reality, then,
embraces personal, social, historical, and ontological dimensions as
disclosed through the most differentiating experiences-symbolisms
left as the trail of the human pilgrimage through time with God.
This is the record of participatory reality in the In-Between of divine-
human encounter (Plato's *metaxy*) given in events and artifacts from
the Neolithic Age onward. The search requires great respect for all
relevant testimony. It also requires a redefinition of *empiricism*—
and of *science* itself—so as to include cardinal modes of nonsen-
sory experience fundamental to moral, religious, aesthetic, mystical,
and noetic life and representation. In result, it can be said that
comprehensive reality becomes intelligible in terms of apperceptive
experiences central to a philosophical science that seeks adequately
to account for the heights and depths of human existence. Polarities
traditionally identified as religion-science and faith-reason tend to
blur and almost to disappear as they find redefinition as noetic-
pneumatic experiences-symbolizations in the course of meditative

analysis, especially in such capital late essays as "Reason: The Classic Experience" and "The Beginning and the Beyond: A Meditation on Truth" and the final volume of *Order and History*.[6]

2. Resistance and balance. The vast effort whose monument is *Order and History* is an act of resistance aimed especially against the contemporary ideological enterprise first identified in antiquity in the prophets' excess as "metastatic faith" (*OH1*, 452–58), that is, the attempt magically to transform reality through divine intervention— and in its modern forms the transformation of the world through human volition and coercion by this or that gnostic revolutionary movement. Such attempts involve the ideologues' mutilation of philosophy, which merely seeks to interpret the world in various ways: first by undertaking to change the world, thus perverting philosophy into comprehensive knowledge through various systems; then by proclaiming Autonomous Man (meaning this or that libidinous elite) master of reality—often with lethal consequences for millions of human beings. Voegelin's resistance and therapeutic purpose is the recovery of truth and reality as far as philosophy (ever the *love* of wisdom, not its definitive possession) permits.[7] Further, he urges it as a *duty* that the massive social means deployed in deformation and corruption of our common human reality be resisted by everyone to the limits of each person's capacities: "No one is obliged to take part in the spiritual crisis of a society; on the contrary, everyone is obliged to avoid this folly and live his life in order."[8]

Thus the center of resistance arises in the evocation of the inviolable integrity of the individual human person qua participant in the ever-mysterious transcendent divine Ground, whose reflective mind and conscience lie tensionally at the core of society and history—and of reality experienced, in its ontic and knowable dimensions. The social "amnesia," or forgetfulness of what ought to be remembered (*OH1*, ix), that obscures the recollection and understanding of reality historically attained over centuries, and woven into representations of true order reflective of the struggle of existence, is dispersed in the act of recovering differentiated truth from the historical record. This work of resistance to socially enforced forgetfulness and the reconstitution of philosophy as the noetic-pneumatic means of critically ascertaining the truth of being yield consequences for political and social order.

Certain of these consequences can be stated as *Postulates of Balance*, as follows.[9]

a. The unspeakable depth of the Mystery of being must not be allowed to overwhelm the truth of being critically ascertained through the philosophers' noetic-pneumatic inquiry: that is, we know only what we know! That vision and knowledge (modest as they sometimes seem to be) are to be prized, nurtured, and refined against all opining, skepticism, fanciful imagining, and (today) nihilistic disdain of deconstructionists and other power-intoxicated predators.[10]

b. Human reality is persuasively represented as the stratified participatory reality of the In-Between (Plato's *metaxy*), each level of which, from material to divine reality, possesses its dignity, worth, and rightful claim. Thus, man is neither God nor brute; and human reality is both hierarchically structured (from *apeiron* to divine Nous, founded from the "bottom" up, formed from the "top" down through the individual man's participation in transcendence)[11] as well as directionally oriented toward eschatological fulfillment, a suspense of time-space in the mysterious eternity called God. *Reality*—comprised experientially of *Thing-reality* and the comprehensive divine *It-reality*, in later work[12]—thus manifests itself as "a recognizably structured process that is recognizably moving beyond its structure" (*OH4*, 227).

c. The philosophical or noetic science of human affairs rests upon a triadic structure historically evinced as: (a) spiritual outbursts, the leaps in being or flashes of eternity into time, whereby universal divine transcendent Being is apperceived in a variety of modalities, especially pneumatically in Israel and Christianity and noetically in Hellenic philosophy (although that distinction sharply narrows in Voegelin's late work); (b) historiography, whereby the before-and-after of the divine irruption is articulated as a recognizable epoch under the particularities of culture and ethnicity in time, space, and place, thus creating history; and (c) power constellations, such as the ecumenic empires, recognizable as social and political entities organized for action in history and expressive of the concupiscential or passionate dimension of existence, including especially man's *libido dominandi*. These aspects ramify variously through the reality spheres termed *Person*, *Society*, and *History*—with the strict understanding that the individual person constitutes core human reality.

d. Human reality with horizontal (time-space) and vertical (ontological) dimensions is always recognizably human as in tension toward the Ground and thereby so structured as incipiently to constitute history and historical existence itself.

In compact form, human reality arises in an indeterminate distant past (twenty to fifty thousand years ago) and moves directionally toward an indefinite and uncertain future open to its horizon. The structure-process of reality ranges from compact to differentiated through stages identifiable as cosmological, anthropological, and soteriological (*NSP*, 76–77). These stages (if they may be so termed, in light of post-1974 work when unilinear development is sharply qualified or rejected) in the movement from compactness to differentiation present complicated problems. They are understood to be cumulative rather than discrete, so that earlier insights retain their truth. But they are subject to reversal and deformation, and they do not necessarily lie along any time line at all. Rather, they open into a complex pluralistic field of historical development, one concretely characterized by reversal, rebellion, loss of clarity, and decline as much as by advance and greater luminosity (*OH4*, 1–11). Finally, the noetic-pneumatic dimension always appears concretely in the context of material reality, that is, in the life experiences of a human person in bodily existence, in the form of specific historical configurations, and in tension with concupiscential demands as well as in attraction to the Good. The steely cords of passion are no less real than the golden cord of *Nous*. All are pulled by the divine Puppet Master, to remember Plato.[13]

3. Consequences of the leap in being. The convictions regarding the process and structure of history and the nature of man that emerge in *Israel and Revelation* are permanent gains to Voegelin's understanding of these vast issues, as reflected in the foregoing comments. He took stock of matters in the introduction to *The World of the Polis*, entitled "Mankind and History":

> The leap in being, the epochal event that breaks the compactness of the early cosmological myth and establishes the order of man in his immediacy under God—it must be recognized—occurs twice in the history of mankind, at roughly the same time, . . . and the two experiences differ so profoundly in content that they

become articulate in the two different symbolisms of Revelation and Philosophy. . . .

The primary field of order is the single society of human beings, organized for action to maintain itself in existence. If, however, the human species were nothing but a manifold of such agglomerations, all of them displaying the same type of order under the compulsion of instinct as do insect societies, there would be no history. Human existence in society has history because it has a dimension of spirit and freedom beyond mere animal existence, because social order is an attunement of man with the order of being, and because this order can be understood by man and realized in society with increasing approximations to its truth. Every society is organized for survival in the world and, at the same time, for partnership in the order of being that has its origin in world-transcendent divine Being; it has to cope with the problems of its pragmatic existence and, at the same time, it is concerned with the truth of its order. This struggle for the truth of order is the very substance of history; and in so far as advances toward the truth are achieved by the societies indeed as they succeed one another in time, the single society transcends itself and becomes a partner in the common endeavor of mankind. Beyond the primary field of order there extends a secondary field, open toward the future, in which mankind is constituted as the subject of order in history. (*OH2*, 1–2)

The emergence of the truth of order in the present under God as experienced in revelation and symbolized in the paradigmatic history of the Old Testament is the primary concern of *Israel and Revelation*. The strength of the study is the power and care with which Voegelin delineates the meaning of the familiar account in terms of spiritual experiences. Herein lies the vital thread of revelation through the response of Israel by its representative personalities and by Israel as the chosen representative of mankind in the passage of history from Abram and Moses to the Suffering Servant of Deutero-Isaiah. Accordingly, it will be useful to organize the further presentation by attempting to clarify briefly with respect to Israel the experiences symbolized, the truth of order, the meaning of history and the problem of universality, and the enduring significance of Exodus as emblematic of the human quest.

4. Experiences symbolized. The core of the experience is a break with the myth of the divine cosmos as deficient truth or outright untruth through discovery of the truth of divine Being beyond all cosmic representation by the leap in being. This concretely occurs especially in the drama of Exodus as symbolized in the *berith* or Covenant between God (Yahweh) and his Chosen People of Israel as this unfolds at the Burning Bush through Moses and on Sinai with the People and their acceptance of the Decalogue. The reality of experience-symbol thereby is differentiated by the polarities of immanent and transcendent divine being. The experiences are presented as a passion of being chosen and of responding to the commands of the divine partner in reality as the means of securing more perfect attunement through existence in truth.

> They entered into a covenant with [God], and thereby became his people. As a new type of people, formed by God, Israel conquered the promised land. The memory of Israel preserved the otherwise unimportant story, because the irruption of the spirit transfigured the pragmatic event into a drama of the soul and acts of the drama into symbols of divine liberation.
>
> The events of the Exodus, the sojourn at Kadesh, and the conquest of Canaan became symbols because they were animated by a new spirit. Through the illumination of the spirit the house of institutional bondage became a house of spiritual death. Egypt was the realm of the dead, the Sheol, in more than one respect. . . . When the spirit bloweth, society in cosmological form becomes Sheol, the realm of death; but when we undertake the Exodus and wander into the world, in order to found a new society elsewhere, we discover the world as the Desert. . . . When the world has become Desert, man is at last in the solitude in which he can hear thunderingly the voice of the spirit that with its urgent whispering has already driven and rescued him from Sheol. In the Desert God spoke to the leader and his tribes; in the Desert, by listening to the voice, by accepting its offer, and by submitting to its command, they at last reached life and became the people chosen by God. (*OH1*, 112–13)

Voegelin explores the texture of the experiences with care. To begin with, the condition of revelation is the human response, and if there is no response there is no revelation (*OH1*, 417). But, as with Moses, to hear the voice means to have become a servant of Yahweh, for the command could be rejected only by one who could not hear it: "the man who can hear cannot reject, because he has ontologically entered the will of God, just as the will of God has entered him. When the consciousness of the divine will has reached the clarity of revelation, the historical action has begun" (*OH1*, 407). The symbolism continues through various permutations throughout subsequent time. The call of the past and the call of the present blend in prophetic consciousness as parts of "the continuum of revelation, which creates historical form when it meets with the continuum of the people's response" (*OH1*, 429). The attunement to the timeless revelation of the eternal God must be preserved as a constant tension of existence in the concrete community of the people to prevent a fall from historical form under God into the Sheol of civilizations from which they had been delivered. This dynamic is expressed in the prophetic effort as the people are exhorted to do justice and seek truth, and "listen!" becomes a fundamental command in Jeremiah (*OH1*, 434). The inability of the people to maintain this tension moves the symbolism of chosen people toward the symbol of the chosen man in Jeremiah and the Suffering Servant, a mark of increasing spiritualization and a breaking of the collective experience by differentiation of the individual human personality in the present under God. Spiritual autobiography emerges as a new symbolism, and prophetic existence is experienced as "participation in the suffering of God" (*OH1*, 485–88).

   5. Truth of order. Differentiation of the truth of order in Israel through the leap in being achieving existence in the presence under God in historical form places the divine Ground in a beyond of the cosmos. Yahweh is experienced-symbolized as Creator and sustainer of the world and its order. The order of Israel becomes therewith historical, and its exodus from Egypt marks a liberation from the death of existence in the compact cosmological order. Israel experiences itself as living in an emphatic partnership with Yahweh as a peculiar people, the carrier of a new truth in history through attunement with transcendent Being. The record of this relationship is the content of the Old Testament understood as paradigmatic history. "Israel alone constituted itself by recording its own genesis as a people as an event with a special meaning in history" (*OH1*, 124). The content of the truth of order is given especially in the Decalogue and other aspects of the Sinaitic Covenant. And the truth experienced and symbolically elaborated is sensed not merely as parochial truth for Israel alone but also as truth for a mankind that Israel has been divinely chosen to represent, even if the universalist components are long in differentiating fully.

But the problem Voegelin first emphasizes in the introduction to his study has a place in this aspect of our discussion, namely that the leap in being is not a leap out of existence (*OH1*, 11, 452). Thus, the differentiation of the truth of being that marks the emergence of existence in historical form leaves untouched the large range of reality not directly related to divine truth. This raises the question of the relationship between pragmatic and paradigmatic history— or profane and sacred history—in a consideration of the historical form. In terms of the truth of existence it is observed that the order of Israel as a practical matter denotes the history of a society with a core of ethnic identity that is formed through living memory of the Sinai Covenant. The shortcomings as an order fit for action in the world came to a crisis with the desire to have a king like the other nations and the Davidic Covenant. For the Berith "provided for the right relation between God and man, as well as for the relations between the members of the Chosen People, but made no provision whatsoever for a governmental organization that would secure the existence of the people in the power field of pragmatic history. This gap was now filled by the organization of David's conquest in the wake of the Philistine wars" (*OH1*, 300). This brings to attention the fact that the vacuum is filled at the time of David with the cosmological symbolisms that attend to the basic problems of existence in the world quite satisfactorily and remain of permanent validity even after the differentiation of transcendent Being.

The interaction with the historical form, however, also effects a differentiation of the old cosmological symbols themselves. And in this connection two developments are noted. One is the immanentization of the transcendent symbols of Israel in certain respects, as reflected in what Voegelin terms "the imperial symbolism." For example, the opening of Psalm 93 (*Yahweh malak*), "The Lord reigneth!" in the King James Version,[14] has the original meaning of "Yahweh has become King!"—"right here and now in the cult of Yahweh's enthronement which the faithful in the time of the monarch attended. . . . And . . . nobody can say with certainty at which point in the history of Israel the *Yahweh malak* in the sense of a present rule of the God over his

Chosen People has begun to taste bitter on the tongue of the singer who suffered the misfortunes of Judaite history, and out of despair arose the hope that someday Yahweh would be really the king of his people in a perfect realm of peace. That would be the point at which the ritual renewal of Yahweh's rule in the cosmological sense began to shift into the eschatological hope of a restoration of order, never in need of renewal, at the end of time." "When the revelation of the transcendent God has become the experiential center of order and symbolization," Voegelin concludes, "the transcendental implications of the compact symbols are set free; and correspondingly the volume of meaning in the symbols shrinks until the ritual renewal of order in time becomes a prefiguration of its ultimate restoration in eternity" (*OH1*, 302–3).

The other, related development is the prophets' attempt to distend the terms of the Covenant to cover pragmatic exigencies, which eventually derails the revelatory experience into the excesses Voegelin calls *metastasis* and *metastatic faith*, as previously mentioned. At that juncture, Voegelin the spiritual realist steps forth to write two of the most arresting pages in a great book and, in so doing, touches on "the fundamentals of a philosophy of history."

> The prophets had no doubts about the ontological presuppositions of their problem of order: Without the God who "knows" his people and the prophet who "knows" God, there would be no Chosen People, no defection from the commandments, no breaking of the Covenant, no crisis of Israel, no prophetic call to return, and no suspense between destruction and salvation. Existence in historical form presupposes the existence of the world-transcendent God, as well as the historical fact of his revelation. . . . For the prophets lived concretely as members of a people called Israel, which experienced its order, in historical continuity, as constituted by the Sinaitic revelation. While they anticipated disasters for the empirical humanity surrounding them, they never doubted for a moment that the dispensation of history created by the Message would continue, whatever "remnant" of Israel or "offshoot" from the House of Jesse would be its empirical carrier in the future. History, once it has become ontologically real through revelation, carries with it the irreversible direction from compact existence in cosmological form toward the Kingdom of God. "Israel" is not the empirical human beings who may or may not keep the Covenant, but the expansion of divine creation into the order of man and society.

No amount of empirical defections can touch the constitution of being as it unfolds in the light of revelation. Man can close the eye of his soul to its light; and he can engage in the futility of rebellion; but he cannot abolish the order by which his conduct will be judged. . . . In the surrounding darkness of Israel's defection and impending political destruction—darker perhaps than the contemporary earth wide revolt against God—the prophets were burdened with the mystery of how the promises of the Message could prevail in the turmoil. They were burdened with this mystery by their faith; and history continued indeed by the word of God spoken through the prophets. There are times when the divinely willed order is humanly realized nowhere but in the faith of solitary sufferers. (*OH1*, 464–65)

In this blazing affirmation of the truth of being inspired by his meditation on the plight of the prophets, even as they are driven to the excess of trusting in divine intervention to salvage the physical well-being of Israel, Voegelin's own faith shines through as a matter of more than mere reflection.

The primordial quaternarian structure of being—experienced-symbolized as God, man, world, and society (*OH1*, 1)—differentiates historically through revelation and philosophy. The differentiation yields the truth of reality in human consciousness. Noetic-pneumatic consciousness of the participatory tension toward the Ground is the constitutive presence that cognitively defines the specific nature of man as Reason (*Nous*), in the philosophical language of Plato and Aristotle. It is cherished as the prize of personal existence in prophetic and in Christian experiences, to the limits of divine disclosure variously symbolized as *Ruach*, Logos, or *Nous*:

the Deutero-Isaianic drama moves from the compact revelation from Sinai toward the Logos of God. From Aeschylus the movement goes toward the Platonic Vision of the Agathon; from Deutero-Isaiah it goes toward the Incarnation of the Logos. When man is in search of God, as in Hellas, the wisdom gained remains generically human; when God is in search of man, as in Israel, the responsive recipient of revelation becomes historically unique. (*OH1*, 496)

Thus, "the substance of the creative action is the 'word.'"

From the Beginning, reality is the divine word speaking in succession the evolution of being from matter through plant to animal life, until it speaks man who, in the persons of patriarchs and prophets, responds by his word to the word spoken by god in history. . . . In the Hellenic context, the sense of close relationship between reality and the word that renders it truly engenders the meaning of *aletheia* as both reality and truth; in the Israelite context, the relationship is traced back to its source in the divinely creative word-reality. The word of man when he articulates his consciousness of reality emerges from the reality that is the word of god. (*OH4*, 13; cf. *OH1*, 222; *OH5*, 18)

With respect to the core meaning of *reason*, then, Voegelin summarizes matters from the philosophers' perspective in the following remarkable language:

"Reason" did not exist in language in the history of mankind until it was formulated in the Greek fifth century [B.C.] as a word denoting the tension between man as a human being and the Divine ground of his existence of which he is in search. The consciousness of being caused by the Divine ground and being in search of the Divine ground—that is reason. Period. That is the meaning of the word *reason*. That is why I always insist on speaking of "noetic" and use the term *nous:* in order not to get into the problems of the ideological concept of reason of the eighteenth century. The word *nous* is applied by Plato and Aristotle to the consciousness of being in search of the ground of one's existence, of the meaning of one's existence—the search, the *zetesis*. One is in the state of ignorance, of *agnoia;* one asks questions, the *aporein;* and the answer is that the Divine *Nous* is the cause that moves me into the search. . . . It is a divine pull that pulls you. It is not a [merely] natural movement.[15]

6. Meaning of history and universality. While history as a whole has no identifiable essence and no knowable meaning as extending into an indefinite future and being thereby inexperientiable as a noetic matter (*NSP*, 120), the philosophical impediment does not wholly hinder the prophets' pneumatic experience of history as the movement through time in partnership with God toward an eschatological fulfillment in Canaan, the Kingdom of God (cf. *OH1*, 345n). The limitations of philosophy give rise to paradox in Voegelin's work. "The fact of revelation is its content"(*NSP*, 78). "Philosophy can touch no more than the being of the substance whose order flows through the world" (*OH1*, 411). And the paradox is expressed in the late work where Voegelin, in reflecting again on the tetragrammatic God of Thomas Aquinas, writes: "The God who is experienced as concretely present remains the God beyond his presence. The language of the gods, thus, is fraught with the problem of symbolizing the experience of a not-experientiable divine reality. . . . Not the Beyond but its Parousia in the bodily located consciousness of questioning man, the experience of the not-experientiable divine reality has history: the history of truth emerging from the quest for truth" (*OH5*, 68; cf. 103). While Voegelin freely acknowledges the importance of pragmatic history, it is history as the "inner form" of Israel's existence that is his concern, as it is the concern of the prophets who struggle to maintain attunement to the intended order of the people under God against the inroads of actual disorder (*OH1*, 355, 409). The work of the prophets is most especially "to clarify the meaning of existence in historical form." The universalist implications emerged in the reliving of the Berith drama by "solitary spiritualists tortured by the destiny of the Chosen People" (*OH1*, 430). One urgent question was whether the Kingdom of God had to take the form of a political Israel, or a political society at all, where constitutionalism, legalism, and dogmatism transform the living faith into spiritually deadening ritual conformity of action, both political and religious. Moses therewith becomes no longer the author of his people but merely the author of a book. The conflict between the mundane and divine orders as exemplified in the drama of Jeremiah and his trial is seen in parallel to the conflict in Athens two centuries later with the trial and condemnation of Socrates that also yields mutual death sentences to the man and to the corrupt society (*OH1*, 436). "From the middle of the eighth century BC to the fall of Jerusalem, the historical order under a universal God is the constant concern of the prophets. . . . The order of society and history participates in the order of God only in as much as the universal, transcendent God is experienced as such in the faith of men who order their existence in the light of their faith" (*OH1*, 471–72).

The prize of existence and the pulse of historical form is the living faith of individual persons under God, and this experience is at the heart of prophetic existence and their call to the community to return to the life of salvation. Anything less is defection from truth. Thus Voegelin interprets the prophetic effort as "a struggle against the Law," as a deadening of the spirit of Yahweh (*OH1*, 447n). Admittedly, their attitude seemed to contradict common sense and the pragmatic need for effective community action based on political and religious cohesion. The prophets' point in their exhortations, rejections, and demands is to overcome externalization and the superficial in life by disengaging the existential from the theopolitical merging of divine and human, and by rejecting the mundane order. Even absent philosophy and its symbolization of the order of the immortal *psyche* developed in Hellas, the prophets nonetheless "recognized the formation of the soul through knowledge (Hosea) and fear (Isaiah)." They were not only unable to see, but "not even interested in finding, a way from the formation of the soul to institutions and customs they could consider compatible with the knowledge and fear of God" (*OH1*, 446–47). This rejection of institutional order on principle, which marks the prophetic attitude and defies common sense, "adds up to an ontological denial of the conditions of existence in the world" (*OH1*, 455). At the heart of the attitude is the metastatic yearning of the prophets for a new world so that "the constitution of being is transfigured into a state of perfection" to be achieved through "a divine act of grace that will bestow ultimate order on the world." The real issue is to reorder existence through knowledge (*da'ath*) of God, and, at least in Hosea, this is not a disturbing factor but an effort to "bring the Kingdom of God in the souls of men forth from its theopolitical matrix" (*OH1*, 456). The prophetic effort's insistent spiritualization leads toward the insight in Jeremiah "that the order from eternity is not incarnate in a people and its rulers in pragmatic history." It also leads to the contraction of the Chosen People into the existence of the chosen man who has to act out the fate of Israel in his own life.

The prophet has become the City of God, the sole representative of divine order (*OH1*, 466–67, 490). The authority in existence has shifted from king to prophet. The stages of prophetism pass through the institutional (Amos and Hosea), the metastatic (Isaiah), and the existential (Jeremiah). Behind the problem of metastasis lie the problems of balance and faith. To repeat: "the order of society and history participates in the order of God only in as much as the universal, transcendent God is experienced as such in the faith of men who order their existence in the light of their faith and thereby become the representative center of society and history" (*OH1*, 472, 474). Metastasis is explored to its end in Isaiah, who envisions the spirit of God filling a glorified world so that "the wolf shall dwell with the lamb, and the leopard shall lie down with kid" (Isa. 11:3–5). The vision of transfigured Israel grows into a vision of world peace with God the judge of nations: " 'they will beat their swords into plowshares' and learn no more the art of war. Governmental institutions and their human incumbents are no longer mentioned" (*OH1*, 480, quoting Isa. 2:4). Metastatic faith, thus, precludes any sort of fulfillment through pragmatic action, and one could only wait for the miracle to happen (*OH1*, 481). The balance can be recovered only when divine presence is rescued from futurism and recognized as the tension of existence at once ontologically present and eschatologically directed.

7. Exodus as enduring symbol. The Exodus of Israel from itself forms the final act of the drama as it is resolved in the eschatological hope of the Suffering Servant of Deutero-Isaiah. There is a "terrible truth" to be glimpsed from the prophets' suffering participation in the divine suffering. This is that no concrete society of any sort whatever can resolve the problem of order in history or serve as the chosen vessel or People and center of the true order of mankind.

> When Abram emigrated from Ur of the Chaldeans, the Exodus from imperial civilization had begun. When Israel was brought forth from Egypt, by Yahweh and Moses his servant, and constituted as the people under God, the Exodus had reached the form of a people's theopolitical existence in rivalry with the cosmological form. With Isaiah's and Jeremiah's movement away from the concrete Israel begins the anguish of the third procreative act of divine order in history: The Exodus of Israel from itself. (*OH1*, 491)

The present as lived in the experience of the Servant as a participation in divine suffering becomes the experience of redemption in the here and now, thereby completing the last act in the drama of Exodus in the movement "from the order of a concrete society toward the order of redemption" (*OH1*, 501). But the meaning of *completion* must be clarified. "It means that the order of being has revealed its mystery of redemption as the flower of suffering. It does not mean, however, that the vision of the mystery is the reality of redemption in history: The participation of man in divine suffering has yet to encounter the participation of God in human suffering" (*OH1*, 501). The Exodus from the cosmological order of empires is completed in the Servant, and the history of Israel as "the people under God consummated in the vision of the unknown genius, for as the representative sufferer Israel has gone beyond itself and become the light of salvation to mankind" (*OH1*, 515). The revelation is not a transfiguration of the order of the world but "a revelation of God as Redeemer" (*OH1*, 499).

Last, the force of the Exodus motif in Voegelin's philosophy of man and history is an enduring symbolism of the mystery of history with its open horizon, and of the quest of man as ever unfulfilled. It is this aspect of his work that I would particularly stress for its pivotal significance and wonderful nobility. It is a motif, sounded in the opening pages of *Israel and Revelation*, that recurs in many passages as abiding insight, one indicative of the man and his work, but also emblematic of the human condition itself and of the quest of faith in search of understanding that binds together prophets, philosophers, saints, and sages from Abraham onward. From the philosopher's perspective:

> It means that the quest for truth is ultimately penultimate. In the quest, reality is experienced as the mysterious movement of an It-reality through thing-reality toward a Beyond of things. . . . For the questioner has to tell the story of his struggle for the unflawed order from his position in the flawed order of thingly existence; and he can tell it, therefore, only in the flawed language that speaks of non-things in the mode of things. . . . When the paradoxic experience of not-experientiable reality becomes conscious in reflective distance, the questioner's language reveals itself as the paradoxic event of the ineffable becoming effable. This tension of effable-ineffable is the paradox in the structure in meditative language. (*OH5*, 102–3)

The sense of quest and penultimacy in tension toward the Ground and its transformative pull is reflected in Voegelin's fondness for a passage in *Enarrationes in Psalmos* 64.2. It illustrates the understanding that the tension of faith is not a Christian monopoly but a trait of human nature, and that the structure-process of history is the same as that of personal existence. As exemplified in the cited passage, Augustine

> lets the historical symbols of exodus and of Babylon express the movement of the soul when it is drawn by the love of God:
>
> > Incipit exire qui incipit amare.
> > Exeunt enim multi latenter,
> > et exeuntium pedes sunt cordis affectus:
> > exeunt autem de Babylonia.
>
> > He begins to leave who begins to love.
> > Many the leaving who know it not,
> > for the feet of those leaving are affections of the heart:
> > and yet, they are leaving Babylon.
>
> His conception of history as a tale of two cities, intermingling from the beginning of mankind to its end, conceives it as a tale of man's personal exodus written large. . . . History is Christ written large. This last formulation is not in conflict with the Platonic "man written large."[16]

With these reflections, we touch the meaning of Voegelin's steadfast insistence that the soul is the sensorium of transcendence and that the experience of transcendence is inseparable from the understanding of man as human—whether in his individual and personal or social and historical existence—fundamentals of the philosophy of history and human affairs.

8. Conclusion. In terms of genre, *Israel and Revelation* must be seen in the context of Voegelin's study of order in history and as a part of his philosophy of history. The concern with the biblical sources is primarily directed toward discerning and analyzing the revelatory experiences symbolized therein. The thrust of the study, therefore, is to clarify the order of being beyond the primordial experience of cosmic divinity as this is articulated in Israel's leap in being. The ethical order as it finds primary expression in the response of Moses and of Israel for mankind in the Sinaitic Covenant and the Ten Commandments clearly is derivative *from* the revelation of Yahweh and grounded in the attunement to the truth of Being glimpsed in these indelible experiences and constantly recurred to in subsequent generations, centuries, and millennia into the present as the heart of the living faith. An ungrounded ethical order is a dogmatic derailment and a deformative externalization of faith akin to legalism, by Voegelin's analysis. The same principle applies in philosophy in the Hellenic horizon where he is equally insistent that the formation of character through the experience of transcendence lies at the core of elaborations of order as consequences in the ethical and political spheres. An ungrounded ethics or politics constitutes a derailment of both Yahwism and philosophy.

The cardinal ethical principle that emerges, then, is the obligation of each person to resist corruption and disorder so as, thereby, to live in accord with the truth of the divine Ground. In the horizon of revelatory experience this requires the nurture of living faith of the kind Voegelin discerns in the tenacious effort of prophets to "listen" to the Word of God and bring with them the community of Israel they represent. This would seem to be a position wholly consistent with the resolute proclamation of the *Shema* and with its reiteration as the Great Commandment by Jesus (Deut. 6:4–5; Matt. 22:37; Mark 12:29–30; Luke 10:27). The basis for this stress by Voegelin is the emphasis in the sources themselves and in the perceived tendency of those who defect from truth to assert various false grounds to justify their deformation and disorder. Occlusion against the Ground is the abiding fallacy and mutilation of reality against which Voegelin contends as the root of evil, to the extent that it implies the sufficiency of man to himself as autonomous.

While there is an affirmation of the constancy and resiliency of being and its order as coming from the hand of God, there is also a sense of direction and pilgrimage in the process of history and the Whole in Voegelin's attention to the experiences-symbolizations of order. We have touched on this aspect of his account in terms of the experience of permanent exodus in recalling the passage from Augustine. The structure of reality is not a rigidly inflexible fixity but a structure in process of moving beyond itself. This is to say that history has ontological dimensions and eschatological direction.[17] These attributes also register in Voegelin's philosophy as he constantly revises and finds now one, then another figure or symbol to express in meditative discourse the experiences he tries to illuminate. The point is captured in many places but perhaps nowhere better than in the closing paragraph of *The Ecumenic Age:*

Once the fallacies are removed, the hierarchy of being comes into view, not as a number of strata one piled on top of the other, but as [the] movement of reality from the apeirontic depth up to man, through as many levels of the hierarchy as can be discerned empirically, and as the countermovement of creative organization from the divine height down, with the Metaxy of man's consciousness as the site where the movement of the Whole becomes luminous for its eschatological direction. When the historical dimension of humanity has differentiated, the Question thus turns back to the process of the Whole as it becomes luminous for its directional movement in the process of history. The Mystery of the historical process is inseparable from the Mystery of a reality which brings forth the universe and the earth, plant and animal life on earth, and ultimately man and his consciousness. Such reflections are definitely not new, but they express, in differentiated form . . . the mode of questioning engendered in the contemporary situation by a philosopher's resistance to the distortion and destruction of humanity committed by the "stop-history" Systems. They are an act of open participation in the process of both history and the Whole. (*OH4*, 335)

9. Epilogue. A few additional words may be of value for locating Voegelin's thought in the landscape of contemporary scholarship as it bears on some of the questions he himself addressed. Nothing but the barest hints can be given, and the rather paradoxical reasons for this need to be made clear at the outset. To begin with, and on several counts, Voegelin was something of a one-man band. William C. Havard (quoting Gregor Sebba) explains matters this way:

Two things have prevented the appropriate recognition of the emergence of [a] new theory of politics. . . . the first is that the advancement of that theory "is largely the work of one independent thinker, Eric Voegelin, who published his first book four decades ago . . . and is still forging ahead at a pace which leaves his best readers behind." The second is the "enormous demand" which the Voegelinian achievement makes on the "newcomer to such studies." Not only must the reader be able to follow abstract reasoning at its highest level; he must also know the history of ideas, philosophy (in all its dimensions), theology, the full sweep of history from prehistory to modernity, and the present development of scholarship in fields as widely separated as anthropology, biblical criticism, comparative literature, and psychology. . . . "all of this is very far from the concerns of the practicing political scientist today."[18]

Sebba, who was a friend and colleague of Voegelin's in Vienna, from the 1930s prior to the Nazi *Anschluss* and until the end of his life, engagingly writes elsewhere:

> The philosopher Eric Voegelin has the distinction of being kept unread in [the philosophers'] storage basement, presumably as a contemporary fossil. Or perhaps they mistake him for a political scientist, as the political scientists do.
>
> Voegelin has always defied departmentalization. . . . One could almost speak of three Voegelins, in reverse chronological order. First comes the author of *Order and History* (1956–1987). Then there is the Voegelin of *The New Science of Politics* (1952), still a focus of fruitless controversy among political scientists. (Is he a kind of Saint Francis preaching to the birds in a positivistic aviary? A dangerous but happily unreadable reactionary? An irrelevant unscientific dilettante?) Finally, there is the virtually unknown Voegelin of the period from 1922 to 1938, the author of five books and nearly forty papers on topics from the Federal Reserve System to the Sun Hymn of Akhenaton. I took him at that time for a young sociologist of the Max Weber, Georg Simmel, and Max Scheler type, a born theoretician with an insatiable intellectual appetite, whose work was very hard to understand.[19]

Preaching to the birds in a positivistic aviary is both useful and colorful as a metaphor to describe Voegelin's relationship to so-called mainstream political science. This does not alter the fact, however, of Voegelin's lifelong self-identification as a political scientist, nor of his ambition from the beginning of his academic career to develop a viable science of politics that might more adequately reflect human reality and permit its more precise scientific investigation. From the standpoint of the discipline and profession it is not too much to say that this is, indeed, the core of Voegelin's work as a revolutionary thinker. It would seem that not even Sebba understands this fully. What is entailed by the achievement passes over the heads of most other readers as well; so it is worth emphasizing that there is, indeed, a new philosophical science of politics awaiting more general discovery in Voegelin's work.[20]

Voegelin's singularity is further suggested by his employment of the previously mentioned technique of analysis variously called the "critical method" or "Aristotelian procedure" or "unoriginal thinking."[21] This has two aspects. The first is the spirit of comparative analysis that he admired in Max Weber and that involves the pursuit of questions on the basis of a mastery of the pertinent literature in all relevant languages to the point that the state of scholarly understanding can be assayed and, where possible, the issues then analytically penetrated a step or two further. This method is well displayed in *Israel and Revelation*. The fact was noticed by Bernhard Anderson, the distinguished Old Testament scholar and theologian, who commented: "It is refreshing to read the work of a philosophical 'layman' in the field who has taken it upon himself to master the original sources and the secondary literature up to the time of his writing. . . . This is one of the few books on the Old Testament which has so engrossed my interest that I have eagerly wondered what would be on the next page." In 1997 Anderson commented: "Revisiting Voegelin's *Israel and Revelation* after a quarter of a century is intellectually exhilarating. . . . Essentially I stand by what I wrote then."[22] Fittingly, Voegelin's appointment at the University of Munich in 1958 was to the chair of political science conveniently left vacant for the momentous three decades after the death of its previous incumbent—Max Weber.[23]

The other aspect of Voegelin's critical method is the leveling of much conventional thought because of its ideological, deformed, or dogmatic character. Such doctrinaire thinking falls before the Weberian principle of intellectual honesty ("intellectuelle Rechtschaffenheit"),[24] and it is enduringly symbolized on the model of the relationship between Socrates-Plato and Athens. It is biographically rooted in Voegelin's long effort to extricate himself from the methodological morass of neo-Kantian positivism as a young academic, and in his personal and professional face-to-face confrontation with ideologues of left and right in the intellectual and political brawl that first climaxed in Nazi hegemony in central Europe and persisted in various forms thereafter.[25] But it amounts to more than this, for a principle is involved: the philosopher qua philosopher, if true to the calling, inevitably stands in tension with—in some degree of critical opposition to—all received and conventional truth of any kind whatsoever, a message of the Allegory of the Cave. This is Voegelin's stance as a scholar who refuses to be bound by anybody's orthodoxies, friend or foe—not as a fetish, pose, or eccentricity but as the indispensable condition of what he takes to be requisite for the true servant of science, philosophy, and truth. He pulls no punches. This is not the Dale Carnegie School prescription for how to win friends and influence people, of course, and the truth-sayers of history typically have been notorious outcasts.

The attitude appears often enough in Voegelin's writings to be taken as paradigmatic. A good example that hits close to home and is, therefore, of particular interest considers "The Oxford Political Philosophers." This essay consists of a critique of Liberal theory (specifically as found in writings by A. D. Lindsay, R. G. Collingwood, J. D. Mabbott, E. F. Carritt, G. R. G. Mure, C. H. Wilson, R. B. McCallum, J. W. Gough, Max Beloff, W. Harrison, and A. P. d'Entrèves), which after praising only Mure's "brilliant lecture" *The Organic State*, ends with the following paragraph:

> I shall conclude on an Aristotelian point. . . . The polis offers the opportunity for full actualization of human nature. The fully actualized man is the *spoudaios,* the mature man, who has developed his dianoetic excellences and whose life is orientated by his noetic self. This is the decisive issue in a philosophy of politics, the issue which the distinguished authors whose work we have discussed studiously avoid. Under pretext of respect for the freedom of conscience they ignore the fact that conscience, however "good" it may be putatively, can only be as good as the man who has it. A theory of conscience that shies away from ontology, and in particular from a theory of the nature of man, is empty; it is a parlor game in which one can indulge as long as the surrounding society contains enough Christian substance to make at least the worst sort of good consciences socially ineffective; but even under such favorable conditions (as they still exist in England) this nihilistic theory of conscience contributes to the intellectual and moral confusion which paves the way for the best of all consciences, *viz.,* that of the totalitarian killers. All men are equal, to be sure, or they would not be individuals of one species; but sometimes it is forgotten that the point in which they most certainly are equal is their capacity for evil. Enough of that evil is rampant; and this is no time to pat the viciously ignorant on the back for being "sincere," or abiding

by their "conscience." This is a time for the philosopher to be aware of his authority, and to assert it, even if that brings him into conflict with an environment infested by dubious ideologies and political theologies—so that the word of Marcus Aurelius will apply to him: "The philosopher—the priest and servant of the Gods."[26]

Thus the "paradox" of a thinker (seen as something of a loner) who took his vocation with utmost seriousness and expected his colleagues to do the same; ransacked the sources in every field his inquiry led him into; conducted an enormous correspondence with scholars throughout the world on a vast array of subjects; constantly rejoiced in the collaborative achievements of the historical and theoretical sciences in the twentieth century, even while condemning radical modernity's gnosticism; roundly rejected the characterization of himself as a solitary thinker, embracing in its place the image of a cosmopolitan scholar in touch with experts in every field; eagerly insisted that his own work be as completely informed as possible with all the latest scientific results. Voegelin's is not so much the loneliness of a Saint Francis preaching to the birds (even though his "ism"-ridden aviary is a hostile environment, to be sure), but that of the personality for whom Diogenes long before lit a candle at midday.

If one considers the range of topics—dimensions of reality— Voegelin addresses and looks for connecting links and organizing centers among them in his writing and thought, the very top of the list belongs to his steadfast devotion to the integrity of the individual human being as *imago Dei*[27] and as the justification for the entire constellation of historical, social, and intellectual activities and arrangements associated with civilization per se. The theory of human nature is central to that of community, political, and social order and to the philosophy of history or historicity, symbolization, and consciousness.[28] In a great variety of ways this emphasis and direction of inquiry are present from early writings onward. In the abandoned "Herrschaftslehre" "the person . . . is the intersection of divine eternity and human temporality."[29] Man is more than merely biological or social and shares in the entire hierarchy of being from material reality to the spiritual and divine, Voegelin vociferously and repeatedly argues against the Nazi race "theorists" in his two 1933 books, *Race and State* and *The History of the Race Idea*.[30] He looks for a place to stand in addressing the crisis of modernity, and that place is development of a differentiated understanding of what it is to be a human being—this he calls a theory of human nature, a philosophical and political anthropology as part of a general ontology, to use the language of the *New Science of Politics* and of the initial volumes of *Order and History*. But what is the *differentia specifica* of man in his humanity if not his soul or consciousness?—to maintain the continuity with classical and Christian philosophy, while at the same time basing analysis indubitably in empirical or experiential, self-evident fact.

The theory of consciousness, noticed earlier, dominates the work of the final years and is seen to underlie all of the work from the 1940s onward, as the correspondence with Alfred Schütz about Edmund Husserl and phenomenology indicates.[31] The introduction to the American edition of *Anamnesis*, "Remembrance of Things Past" (1978), is the key document, and what is perhaps the key sentence there reads: "What I had discovered was consciousness in the concrete, in personal, social, and historical existence of man, as the specifically human mode of participation in reality."[32] The anamnetic exploration of consciousness as the center of a critical philosophy of human affairs in palpable continuity with that of Plato and Aristotle animated all of the remaining work.

There are important qualifications, however. The unfolding of the potential of human nature is not given in full actualization immediately, either in individuals or in mankind as a whole, but develops (or atrophies) biographically in each person's lifetime and in exuberant diversity historically in multiple civilizational, religious, and other communities of the one mankind down to the present.[33] This pivotal point is stated—with a warning against obsessive "intellectualism"—in the early *History of Political Ideas* in the chapter on Dante, as follows:

> Our modern [philosophical] anthropology is enriched by insight into the historical structure of the human mind. It is no longer possible to identify the essence of man with ahistoric intellect. . . . The unity of mankind is not intellectually static; it is an open field in which the possibilities of the human mind unfold historically and manifest themselves in the sequence of

civilizations and of nations. To stop history at any point of time, and to elevate a civilizational crosscut, or more frequently a fragment of the crosscut, to the rank of an absolute and to call it the nature of man has become impossible. With this insight into the historicity of the mind, the idea falls that [any] static "organization" can be the political answer to the idea of man. The drama of human history can not be caught in a governmental power organization, imperial or otherwise.[34]

Voegelin adds later on, apropos Nicholas of Cusa:

> The reception of the Aristotelian ranks [of human types] of the free *sapientes* and the slavish *insipientes* created a formidable problem, for the Hellenic idea of a natural slave is incompatible with the Christian idea of the spiritually free man. . . . The principal obstacle to an integration of Hellenic political theory into the Christian is formed by the Hellenic idea of nature: *Hellenic nature is nature without grace.* The differentiation of types [of man] is a brute fact. . . . In a Christian system, nature itself has to be penetrated spiritually in order to make natural differences psychologically bearable and systematically compatible with the fundamental idea of spiritual freedom.[35]

When we concluded the body of the present essay with a suggestion of the open horizon of human and historical endeavor by remembering Augustine's experience of the translation of time into eternity and subtly striking an eschatological note, we found a fitting symbol for Voegelin's own open quest and search for order in exodus. Complementing it are such further clues and insights as the Question that is more important than the answers found; the knowing questions and the questioning knowledge that structure inquiry; the Socratic and Anselmian awareness of their ultimate ignorance before the abysmal mystery of being as faith seeks understanding; and recognition that the "temptation to fall from uncertain truth into certain untruth is stronger in the clarity of Christian faith than in other spiritual structures."[36] These are some of the hallmarks of Voegelin's meditative science and theoretical achievement.[37]

Notes

Essay 1. The Politics of Poetry

1. I have not sought to update the perspectives of 1990, when this essay was originally written.

2. Leon Aron, "The Soviet Union on the Brink: An Introductory Essay," *Foreign Affairs* 152 (summer 1989): 3.

3. Dimitri Simes, "The Specter of Bloody Chaos," *Washington Post,* as reprinted in the *Baton Rouge Morning Advocate,* October 27, 1990, p. 11B.

4. See Eric Voegelin, *The New Science of Politics: An Introduction* (Chicago: University of Chicago Press, 1952), chap. 4.

5. A. I. Solzhenitsyn, "How Are We to Structure Russia?—A Modest Contribution," *Literaturnaya Gazeta,* no. 38 (September 18, 1990): 3–6; English translation quoted from *Foreign Broadcast Information Service FBIS-SOV-90-187* (September 26, 1990): 37–58 at 42; hereafter cited as *FBIS.* Gorbachev commented that he found Solzhenitsyn's views "disrespectful" and continued: "[His views] are alien to me. . . . He is all in the past, the Russia of old, the czarist monarchy. This is not acceptable to me. I consider myself a democrat, moreover a democrat who is inclined toward radical views both for the present and the future" (quoted from *Washington Post,* September 26, 1990). It is good to learn that Comrade Mikhail is a *democrat!*

There is, however, nothing in Solzhenitsyn's text that suggests a return to the czarist monarchy, raising the question of how carefully Gorbachev (as quoted in our press) read the article. Solzhenitsyn, in fact, supports Gorbachev's new version of the strong Soviet presidency (*FBIS,* 46), reluctantly embraces democracy as the only practicable kind of government (*FBIS,* 49), and enters into a long disquisition on elections, representation, and parties in democracies with particular attention to Russia and such "grassroots" institutions as the *zemstvos* as a native growth to be revitalized (*FBIS,* 50–58).

Neither the *Post* nor the *New York Times* (see issue of September 19, 1990, pp. A1, A4 [mail edition]) published more than brief excerpts from the Solzhenitsyn article, although the latter did print the KGB passage quoted herein in a slightly different translation.

6. Jack F. Matlock Jr., "Literature and Politics: The Impact of Fyodor Dostoevsky," *Political Science Reviewer* 9 (fall 1979): 39–60, at 47–48, citing in support Vladimir Bukovsky, *To Build a Castle—My Life as a Dissenter* (New York: Viking Press, 1978). In the quotation, the last sentence of the second paragraph (beginning [Such] . . .) has been interpolated from Matlock's footnote. Cf. Ellis Sandoz, *Political Apocalypse: A Study of Dostoevsky's "Grand Inquisitor"* (Baton Rouge: Louisiana State University Press, 1971), chap. 9 (2d ed. Wilmington, Del.: Intercollegiate Studies Institute, forthcoming).

7. Eric Voegelin, *Autobiographical Reflections,* ed. Ellis Sandoz (1989; available Columbia: University of Missouri Press, 1999), 107, in chap. 22: "Why Philosophize? To Recapture Reality!"

8. Aleksandr I. Solzhenitsyn, *The First Circle,* trans. Thomas P. Whitney (1949; New York: Bantam Books, 1969), 415. See the reflections on this and related matters in Marion Montgomery, *The Men I Have Chosen for Fathers: Literary and Philosophical Passages* (Columbia: University of Missouri Press, 1990), 136.

9. See Julien Benda, *La trahison des clercs* (Paris: B. Grasse, 1927), and the fine analysis by Lewis P. Simpson, "Voegelin and the Story of the Clerks," in *Eric Voegelin's Significance for the Modern Mind,* ed. Ellis Sandoz (Baton Rouge: Louisiana State University Press, 1991), 71–110.

10. Václav Havel, *The Power of the Powerless: Citizens against the State in Central-Eastern Europe,* intro. Steven Lukes, ed. John Keane (London: Hutchinson, 1985), 34–35; see also Václav Havel, *The Art of the Impossible: Politics as Morality in Practice; Speeches and Writings, 1990–1996* (New York: A. A. Knopf, 1997).

11. President Václav Havel's address to the U.S. Congress as printed in the *Washington Post,* February 22, 1990, p. A28; rpt. in Havel, *Art of the Impossible,* 10–20.

12. See Lech Walesa, *A Way of Hope* (New York: H. Holt, 1987), esp. 142–44.

13. Roger Scruton, "A Catacomb Culture," *Times Literary Supplement,* February 16–22, 1990, pp. 170, 176.

14. Josiah Lee Auspitz, "Where Philosophy Matters," *Commentary* 87 (June 1989): 54, 56.

15. Eric Voegelin, *Order and History,* vol. 3, *Plato and Aristotle* (1957; available Columbia: University of Missouri Press, 1999), 67–68, quoting Plato's *Republic* 382a–b.

16. Aleksandr I. Solzhenitsyn, *A World Split Apart: Commencement Address Delivered at Harvard University, June 8, 1978,* trans. Irina Ilovayskaya Alberti (New York: Harper and Row, 1978), 51. For commentary see Ronald Berman, ed., *Solzhenitsyn at Harvard: The Address, Twelve Early Responses, and Six Later Reflections* (Washington, D.C.: Ethics and Public Policy Center of Georgetown University, 1980), esp. 105–13 (by Harold J. Berman).

17. Václav Havel, *Disturbing the Peace: A Conversation with Karel Hvízdala,* trans. Paul Wilson (New York: A. A. Knopf, 1990), 11–12.

18. A disciple of Edmund Husserl and one of three founding spokesmen for Charter 77, Patočka died after relentless interrogation and hounding by the police in 1977. The quotation is taken from Havel, *Power of the Powerless,* 48–49.

19. Solzhenitsyn, "How Are We to Structure Russia?" *FBIS,* 49.

20. Ibid., 47.

Essay 2. Liberty and Rule of Law in Czechoslovakia and East-Central Europe

1. This previously unpublished paper was written in the fall of 1991, after my first trip since the Velvet Revolution to east-central Europe (where, in May, I had been honored to address the Federal Parliament in Prague), and in the wake of a conference in Charlottesville at the University of Virginia School of Law on problems and prospects for constitutionalism and free government in the newly independent states of the old Soviet empire. I have made no attempt herein to eliminate my perspective of the time on the historic events associated with the Velvet Revolution of late 1989 and the related subjects I discuss. It may be borne in mind, however, that the country peacefully split into the Czech Republic and Slovakia on January 1, 1993, and that Václav Havel was elected president of the Czech Republic on January 26—an office he continues to hold in 1998. In July 1997, NATO invited the Czech Republic to become a full member by 1999.

2. See Chief Justice John Marshall's opinion in *McCulloch v. Maryland* (4 Wheat. 316, 4 L. Ed. 579, 1819).

3. A Czech-language translation of *The Federalist Papers* emerged from this conference: *Listy federalistů,* trans. Jan Jařab and Ivan Ryčovský, ed. Josef Jařab (Olomouc: Palacky University Press and Baton Rouge: Eric Voegelin Institute, 1994).

4. Franklin J. Havlicek, "Let's Give East Europe Democracy First," *Washington Post,* reprinted in the *Baton Rouge Morning Advocate,* August 4, 1991. Of course, "we" cannot "give" democracy (whatever the term may mean) to anyone else.

5. Cf. Ellis Sandoz, *A Government of Laws: Political Theory, Religion, and the American Founding* (Baton Rouge: Louisiana State University Press, 1990), 170–74.

6. Melor Sturua in *Parade Magazine,* July 28, 1991, p. 7.

7. Thucydides, *The Peloponnesian War* II.6.40, trans. Richard Crawley, intro. Joseph Gavorse, Modern Library Ed. (New York: Random House, 1951), 105.

8. The expression *liber homo* occurs in the crucial arts. 14 and 29 of the authoritative statutory 1225 version (arts. 20 and 39 in the 1215 original); it occurs in the plural (*omnibus liberis hominibus regni nostri . . .*) in art. 1. For the

text see *The Roots of Liberty: Magna Carta, Ancient Constitution, and the Anglo-American Tradition of Rule of Law,* ed. Ellis Sandoz (Columbia: University of Missouri Press, 1993), appendix, 253–66, 323.

9. Quoted from Stephen Mansfield, *Never Give In: The Extraordinary Character of Winston Churchill,* 2d ed. (Elkton, Md.: Highland Books, 1995), 210.

10. See J. L. Talmon, *Political Messianism: The Romantic Phase* (1960; New York: Frederick A. Praeger, 1968) and his related *The Origins of Totalitarian Democracy* (New York: Frederick A. Praeger, 1960) and *The Myth of the Nation and Vision of Revolution: Ideological Polarization in the Twentieth Century,* intro. Irving Louis Horowitz (1981; rpt. New Brunswick, N.J.: Transaction, 1991). What "gnostic" perversion of politics consists of is theoretically explored in Eric Voegelin's important writings, especially the *New Science of Politics* and *Science, Politics, and Gnosticism: Two Essays,* trans. William J. Fitzpatrick, intro. Ellis Sandoz, Gateway Edition (1968; Washington, D.C.: Regnery Publishing Co., 1997), and *From Enlightenment to Revolution,* ed. John H. Hallowell (Durham: Duke University Press, 1975). For a new edition of the material in Hallowell's volume see *The Collected Works of Eric Voegelin,* vol. 26, *History of Political Ideas,* vol. VIII, *Crisis and the Apocalypse of Man,* ed. David Walsh (Columbia: University of Missouri Press, 1999). How to fit democratic rule to the ancient traditions of Russia (with implications for central and eastern European lands as well) is perceptively argued by Aleksandr Solzhenitsyn in the widely ignored "How Are We to Structure Russia—A Modest Contribution," *Literaturnaya Gazeta,* no. 38 (September 18, 1990): 3–6.

11. Richard Hooker, *Of the Laws of Ecclesiastical Polity: Preface, Book I, Book VIII,* ed. Arthur Stephen McGrade (Cambridge: Cambridge University Press, 1989), 49 (preface 9.1).

12. Keith C. Burris, "Conformity's Newest Guise," *Christian Science Monitor,* July 29, 1991; Václav Klaus quoted in *National Review,* December 16, 1991, p. 8.

13. See *Prognosis,* June 1991; *Christian Science Monitor,* July 2, 1991, p. 18.

14. *New York Times,* June 10, 1991.

15. Quoted from Roland Prinz, Associated Press dispatch datelined Ceske Budejovice, *Baton Rouge Morning Advocate,* July 6, 1991.

16. Cf. R. W. Seton-Watson, *A History of the Czechs and Slovaks* (1943; rpt. Hamden, Conn.: Archon Books, 1965), chap. 10.

17. Sir Dudley Digges quoted from *Proceedings in Parliament, 1628 . . . ,* ed. Robert C. Johnson et al., 6 vols. (New Haven: Yale University Press, 1977–1983), 2:334.

18. *Works of the Reverend John Witherspoon,* 4 vols. (Philadelphia: William Woodward, 1800–1801), 3:37; Aristotle, *Politics* 2.1–2.

19. Lloyd Cutler and Herman Schwartz, "Constitutional Reform in Czechoslovakia: *E Duobus Unum?*" *University of Chicago Law Review* 58 (1991): 511–53 at 522, 523.

20. Alexis de Tocqueville, *Democracy in America*, ed. J. P. Mayer, trans. George Lawrence, 2 vols. in 1 (Garden City, N.Y.: Doubleday Anchor Books, 1969), 1:270–86, 727–30.

Essay 3. The Politics of Truth

1. These remarks are published here in English for the first time. They were made as my response upon the conferral of the degree Philosophiae Doctorem Honoris Causa at Palacky University, Olomouc, Czech Republic, on May 17, 1995.

2. George J. Kovtun, ed., *The Spirit of Thomas G. Masaryk (1850–1937): An Anthology* (New York: St. Martin's Press, 1990), 71 (excerpted from *Česká otázka*).

3. Ibid., 95 (quoted as the last lines from Masaryk's speech of July 1910 on Jan Hus).

Essay 4. Philosophical and Religious Dimensions of the American Founding

1. Alexander Pope, *Essay on Man*, in *English Poetry, vol. I: Chaucer to Gray*, ed. Charles W. Eliot, Harvard Classics XL (New York: P. F. Collier and Son, 1910), 417–18. That Pope's *Essay on Man* was favorite reading is stated by Forrest McDonald, *Novus Ordo Seclorum: The Intellectual Origins of the Constitution* (Lawrence: University Press of Kansas, 1985), 164n.

2. Pope, *Essay on Man*, 424, 425. Cf. discussion and literature cited in Ellis Sandoz, *A Government of Laws: Political Theory, Religion, and the American Founding* (Baton Rouge: Louisiana State University Press, 1990), 223–25.

3. John Jay, Alexander Hamilton, James Madison, *The Federalist*, ed. Jacob E. Cooke (Middletown, Conn.: Wesleyan University Press, 1961), 349; emphasis added.

4. *Records of the Federal Convention of 1787*, ed. Max Farrand, 4 vols. (1911; rev. ed. 1937; rpt. New Haven: Yale University Press, 1966), 2:278.

5. Cf. J. C. D. Clark, *The Language of Liberty, 1660–1832: Political Discourse and Social Dynamics in the Anglo-American World* (Cambridge: Cambridge University Press, 1994), 296–391.

6. *The Federalist*, ed. Cooke, 32, 96, 128, 355, 489; emphasis added.

7. The large question of Autonomous Man is discussed from a range of perspectives in Essays 1, 3, and 10 herein; with respect to Hume in Donald W. Livingston, *Hume's Philosophy of Common Life* (Chicago: University of Chicago Press, 1984), esp. 20–33, "Notes and Discussions: A Sellarsian Hume?" *Journal of the History of Philosophy* 29 (April 1991): 281–90, and *Philosophical Melancholy and Delirium: Hume's Pathology of Philosophy* (Chicago: University

of Chicago Press, 1998); with respect to socialism in F. A. Hayek, *The Collected Works of F. A. Hayek*, vol. I, *The Fatal Conceit: The Errors of Socialism*, ed. W. W. Bartley III (Chicago: University of Chicago Press, 1988), 21–28, 66–88; and broadly with respect to modern political and economic liberalism in John Gray, *Beyond the New Right: Markets, Government, and the Common Environment* (London: Routledge, 1993), esp. 66–123. Peter J. Stanlis's interpretation of Edmund Burke centers on this subject in his *Edmund Burke and the Natural Law* (Lafayette, La.: Huntington House, 1986), esp. 160–94. Last, the wisdom of experience as it forms the virtue of right action or "prudence" *(phronesis)* in Aristotle's sense of the term and one of his two best human types, called *phronimos* (equivalent to Cicero's "optimate")—and exhibited in the American founders—is trenchantly analyzed by Eric Voegelin, "What Is Right by Nature?" in *Anamnesis,* ed. and trans. Gerhart Niemeyer (1978; Columbia: University of Missouri Press, 1990), 61–70.

8. From "The Rise of the Arts and Sciences" as quoted by Publius in *The Federalist,* ed. Cooke, 594; emphasis as in original. Cf. David Hume, *Essays Moral, Political, and Literary,* ed. Eugene F. Miller (Indianapolis: Liberty Fund, 1985), 124. On the range of skepticism with its representative of millennial importance being Pyrrho of Elis with influence from antiquity down to Montaigne, Joseph Glanvil, and Hume see the discussion in Eric Voegelin, *Order and History,* vol. 3, *Plato and Aristotle* (1957; available Columbia: University of Missouri Press, 1999), 368–72, and the literature cited therein.

9. The preceding four paragraphs are drawn from my "Philosophical Foundations of Our Democratic Heritage: A Recollection," *Presidential Studies Quarterly* 24 (summer 1994): 669–73.

10. Harry P. Kerr, "The Election Sermon: Primer for Revolutionaries," *Speech Monographs* 29 (March 1962): 18. Quoted from Mark A. Noll, *Christians in the American Revolution* (Washington, D.C.: Christian University Press, 1977), 152.

11. Robert M. Calhoon, "The Evangelical Persuasion," in *Religion in a Revolutionary Age,* ed. Ronald Hoffman and Peter J. Albert (Charlottesville: University Press of Virginia, 1994), 156–83 at 176. Calhoon thus generally confirms the much earlier interpretation of the influence of religion on the politics of the South provided by Alice M. Baldwin, "Sowers of Sedition: The Political Theories of Some of the New Light Presbyterian Clergy of Virginia and North Carolina," *William and Mary Quarterly,* 3d ser., 5 (1948): 52–76. Calhoon, in fact, dates Baldwin's essay from "1921 or 1922" (162n13), explaining that it began as a seminar paper at the University of Chicago. Basic to any study of religion in the American founding remains Alice M. Baldwin, *The New England Clergy and the American Revolution* (Durham: Duke University Press, 1928). See also Robert M. Calhoon, *Dominion and Liberty: Ideology in the Anglo-American World, 1660–1801* (Arlington Heights, Ill.: Harlan Davidson, 1994).

12. Alexis de Tocqueville, *Democracy in America*, ed. J. P. Mayer, trans. George Lawrence, 2 vols. in 1 (Garden City, N.Y.: Doubleday Anchor Books, 1969), 432, cf. 46–47, 288–91; Edmund Burke, "Speech on Moving His Resolutions for Conciliation with the Colonies, March 22, 1775," in Burke, *Selected Writings and Speeches*, ed. Peter J. Stanlis (Chicago: Henry Regnery, 1963), 147–85 esp. 158–60; Sidney E. Mead, *The Nation with the Soul of a Church* (1975; rpt. Macon: Mercer University Press, 1985); Sacvan Bercovitch, *The American Jeremiad* (Madison: University of Wisconsin Press, 1978), esp. 176–210. The quotation is from Carl Bridenbaugh, *Spirit of '76: The Growth of American Patriotism before Independence, 1607–1776* (New York: Oxford University Press, 1975), 117. This section of the present essay draws upon the author's foreword in *Political Sermons of the American Founding Era, 1730–1805*, ed. Ellis Sandoz (Indianapolis: Liberty Fund, 1991).

13. Perry Miller, "From the Covenant to the Revival," in *Religion in American Life*, ed. J. W. Smith and A. L. Jamison, 4 vols. (Princeton: Princeton University Press, 1961), 1:336n.

14. Cf. Voegelin, *Order and History*, vol. 1, *Israel and Revelation* (1956; available Columbia: University of Missouri Press, 1999), 1, for this "primordial community" and its "quaternarian structure," which were clearly intact in the American eighteenth century, as the documents demonstrate. See Essay 10 for further analysis.

15. Stephen A. Marini, "Religion, Politics, and Ratification," in *Religion in a Revolutionary Age*, ed. Hoffman and Albert, 184–217 at 196; emphasis added.

16. The "law of liberty" or "perfect law of freedom *(nomon teleion eleutherias)*" of James 1:25 (cf. James 2:12 and 1 Pet. 2:16) echoes the Johannine Christ: "Ye shall know the truth, and the truth shall make [set] you free *(eleutheroosei)*" as given in John 8:32 and reiterated in subsequent verses (8:33, 36) culminating in the great declaration: "If the Son therefore shall make you free, ye shall be free indeed."

17. For the bold account of the distinction between love of self and love of God *(amor sui, amor Dei)*, symbols of the radical reorientation in reality marked by a person's conversion, see the classic passage in Saint Augustine, *The City of God*, trans. Marcus Dods, intro. Thomas Merton (New York: Modern Library, 1950), 477 (bk. XIV, chap. 28). The term *like-minded*, or those who are united in Christ through faith in him, in the English of the King James Version, renders the *isopsuchos* of Paul's Letter to the Philippians (2:20); the English word occurs in two other places in the New Testament: Rom. 15:5, where it translates *auto phronein*, and Phil. 2:2, 5: "Fulfil my joy, that ye be like-minded *(to auto phronete)*, having the same love, *being* of one accord, of one mind.... Let this mind be in you which was also in Christ Jesus." The equivalent symbols in classical philosophy are *homonoia* in Aristotle and *concordia* in the Latin literature; cf. Voegelin, *Plato and Aristotle*, 321, 357, 364.

18. Ralph Barton Perry, *Puritanism and Democracy* (New York: Vanguard Press, 1944), 82–83; cf. Sandoz, *A Government of Laws*, 98–101.

19. Perry Miller, *The New England Mind: From Colony to Province* (1953; rpt. Boston: Beacon Press, 1961), 464.

20. See Alan Heimert and Perry Miller, eds., *The Great Awakening: Documents Illustrating the Crisis and Its Consequences* (Indianapolis: Bobbs-Merrill, 1967), xiii. From a large and valuable literature see especially Harry S. Stout, *The New England Soul: Preaching and Religious Culture in Colonial New England* (New York: Oxford University Press, 1986), chap. 10; Patricia U. Bonomi, *Under the Cope of Heaven: Religion, Society, and Politics in Colonial America* (New York: Oxford University Press, 1986), 131–222; Nathan O. Hatch, *The Democratization of American Christianity* (New Haven: Yale University Press, 1989). A generally contrasting perspective to that of Miller, Heimert, Marini, Stout, Bonomi, Hatch, and the present essay is given in Jon Butler, *Awash in a Sea of Faith: Christianizing the American People* (Cambridge: Harvard University Press, 1990) and his more recent "Coercion, Miracle, Reason: Rethinking the American Religious Experience in the Revolutionary Age," in *Religion in a Revolutionary Age*, ed. Hoffman and Albert, 1–30. Valuable for its canvass of some of the historiographic perspectives at issue here is the review of Clark's *Language of Liberty* by Jack P. Greene, "Why Did They Rebel?" *Times Literary Supplement*, June 10, 1994, pp. 3–6.

21. Heimert and Miller, eds., *The Great Awakening*, xiv; cf. Perry Miller, "The Great Awakening from 1740 to 1750," *Encounter* (Divinity School, Duke University, Durham, N.C., March 1956), 5–9; also Herbert L. Osgood, *American Colonies in the Eighteenth Century*, 4 vols. (1924; rpt. Gloucester, Mass.: Peter Smith, 1958), 3:407–90; and Carl Bridenbaugh, *Cities in Revolt: Urban Life in America, 1743–1776* (New York: Knopf, 1955), 64, 150–56, 404. Cf. Rhys Isaac, *The Transformation of Virginia, 1740–1790* (Chapel Hill: University of North Carolina Press, 1982): "The interpretation of the Virginia patriot movement offered here is aligned with others that stress the importance of the Great Awakening as a crisis of authority that prepared the way for the Revolution among both colonial elites and lower orders" (266n).

22. See the biographical notes and sermons 4, 13, 14, and 18 in *Political Sermons of the American Founding*, ed. Sandoz. On the Gin Age see W. E. H. Lecky, *A History of England in the Eighteenth Century*, Cabinet Edition, 7 vols. (London: D. Appleton and Co., 1892), 2:chap. 5; also M. Dorothy George, *London Life in the Eighteenth Century* (1925; rpt. New York: Harper and Row, 1964), esp. 27–37; more entertainingly see the first modern novels, Fielding's *Tom Jones* (1749) and, especially, *Amelia* (1751). For Hogarth see *The Harlot's Progress, The Rake's Progress, Marriage à la Mode, Industry and Idleness, Beer Street, Gin Lane*, which appeared between 1732 and 1751. Cf. Richard E. Moore, *Hogarth's Literary Relationships* (Minneapolis: University of Minnesota Press, 1948).

23. For a fine concise account of the relationship of the Great Awakening to political developments see William G. McLoughlin, " 'Enthusiasm for Liberty': The Great Awakening as the Key to the Revolution," in *Preachers and Politicians: Two Essays on the Origins of the American Revolution*, by Jack P. Greene and William G. McLoughlin (Worcester, Mass.: American Antiquarian Society, 1977), 47–73; see also Donald Weber, *Rhetoric and History in Revolutionary New England* (New York: Oxford University Press, 1988).

24. Marini, "Religion, Politics, and Ratification," 188, 193. Perry Miller, "From the Covenant to the Revival," in *Religion in American History: Interpretive Essays*, ed. John M. Mulder and John F. Wilson (Englewood Cliffs: Prentice-Hall, 1978), 145–61 at 157. Patricia U. Bonomi, "Religious Dissent and the Case for American Exceptionalism," in *Religion in a Revolutionary Age*, ed. Hoffman and Albert, 31–51; for her rejection of some of Jon Butler's arguments, see 37n. The earlier writings indicated are Patricia U. Bonomi and Peter R. Eisenstadt, "Church Adherence in the Eighteenth-Century British American Colonies," *William and Mary Quarterly*, 3d ser., 39 (1982): 245–76, and Bonomi, *Under the Cope of Heaven*.

25. James Downey, *The Eighteenth Century Pulpit: A Study of the Sermons of Butler, Berkeley, Secker, Sterne, Whitefield, and Wesley* (Oxford: Oxford University Press, 1969), 155, 157, internal quote cited from J. Gillies, ed., *Works of Whitefield*, 6 vols. (London, 1771–1772), 5:161.

26. *The Confessions of St. Augustine*, trans. E. B. Pusey, foreword by A. H. Armstrong, Everyman Edition (London: J. M. Dent and Sons, 1907), 132–34 (bk. 7, chap. 10, sec. 16); cf. 219–27 (bk. 10, chaps. 17–26). The *It* of Augustine's meditation receives powerful development in Eric Voegelin's late writings when he speaks of the *It-reality*: "To denote the reality that comprehends the partners in being, *i.e.*, God and the world, man and society, no technical term has been developed, as far as I know, by anybody. However, I notice that philosophers, when they run into this structure incidentally in their exploration of other subject matters, have a habit of referring to it by a neutral 'it.' The It referred to is the mysterious 'it' that also occurs in everyday language in such phrases as 'it rains.' I shall call it therefore the It-reality, as distinguished from the thing-reality [apprehended through sensory perception]" (*Order and History*, vol. 5, *In Search of Order* [1987; available Columbia: University of Missouri Press, 1999], 16).

27. The spiritual depth of American religion generally is so often passed over in favor of defining the various doctrinal beliefs and disputes that emphasis must be placed on it here, even if it cannot be widely illustrated. Whether New Light or Old Light, the eighteenth-century clergy (and their audiences) imbibed Scripture with great thoroughness and profundity. They widely read such meditative literature as Augustine's *Confessions*, whose spiritual discipline they took to heart and practiced day and night. Among other "popish divines," Blaise Pascal was a favorite author of the Scottish Presbyterian John Witherspoon at Princeton, for instance; and Ezra Stiles at

Yale was reading Pseudo-Dionysius as much as he was the New Testament at the end of his life, he said. Jonathan Edwards the Elder, the greatest American mind of the age and a leading New Light, was himself a mystic. On Edwards's mysticism see Eric Voegelin, *The Collected Works of Eric Voegelin*, vol. 1, *On the Form of the American Mind*, trans. Ruth Hein, ed. Jürgen Gebhardt and Barry Cooper (1995; available Columbia: University of Missouri Press, 1999), 126–43. Cf. Sandoz, *A Government of Laws*, 179–83; *Political Sermons of the American Founding*, ed. Sandoz, 529–58, for Witherspoon's *The Dominion of Providence over the Passions of Men* (1776); and Edmund S. Morgan, *Gentle Puritan: A Life of Ezra Stiles* (New Haven: Yale University Press, 1962), 447; Nathan O. Hatch and Harry S. Stout, eds., *Jonathan Edwards and the American Experience* (New York: Oxford University Press, 1988), esp. chaps. 7 and 11. See also Glenn Tinder, *The Political Meaning of Christianity: An Interpretation* (Baton Rouge: Louisiana State University Press, 1989).

28. The Virginian Edward Baptist and the John Corbly Memorial Baptist Church "Declaration of Faith in Practice, Being a Covenant, . . . November 7, 1773," quoted by Calhoon, "Evangelical Persuasion," 157.

29. Lemuel Burkitt and Jesse Read, *A Concise History of the Kehukee Baptist Association* (Halifax, N.C., 1803) as quoted in Marini, "Religion, Politics, Ratification," 211; Calhoon, "The Evangelical Persuasion," 160, quoting George Whitefield, *The Indwelling of the Spirit, the Common Privilege of All Believers* (London, 1739), 1–2; Marini, "Religion, Politics, and Ratification," 215 (internal quote unattributed).

30. *The Autobiography of Benjamin Franklin*, intro. R. Jackson Wilson (New York: Modern Library, 1981), 132.

31. Noah Webster as excerpted in Verna May Hall, ed., *The Christian History of the American Revolution* (San Francisco: Foundation for American Christian Education, 1976), 21; Noah Webster, preface to *The Webster Bible* (New Haven: Durrie and Peck, 1833; facsimile rpt. Grand Rapids, Mich.: Baker Book House, 1987), v; emphasis as in original. See also the biographical note and reprinted address by Webster entitled *The Revolution in France* [1794], in *Political Sermons of the American Founding*, ed. Sandoz, 1235–99.

32. Gen. 1:31. This, and Ps. 119:134 (quoted below), were the texts for the Gad Hitchcock's Plymouth Anniversary Sermon; this sermon is the principal source of the summary in the following three paragraphs of the text. It is reprinted in Hall, ed., *Christian History of the American Revolution*, 30–43.

33. Benjamin Franklin in *Records of the Federal Convention*, ed. Farrand, 1:451.

34. Calhoon, "Evangelical Persuasion," 159, 162–63. Hatch is quoted from his "In Pursuit of Religious Freedom: Church, State, and People in the New Republic," in *The American Revolution: Its Character and Limits*, ed. Jack P. Greene (New York: New York University Press, 1987), 391.

35. Hatch, *Democratization of American Christianity*, 5.

36. John Leland's 1790 and 1791 statements, principally from *The Rights of Conscience Inalienable . . . or, the High-flying Churchman, Stripped of his Legal Robe, Appears a Yaho* (New London: Charles Holt, 1791), 8, 15–16, as quoted in Hatch, *Democratization of American Christianity*, 98. For the full text of Leland's pamphlet see *Political Sermons of the American Founding*, ed. Sandoz, 1079–99.

37. Wycliffe's Bible was the first complete English version, a translation from the Latin Vulgate completed around 1384, the year of his death, and another version followed in 1388; both were largely the work of his pupils, Nicholas of Hereford and probably John Purvey, who did the revision. But the first complete printing of Wycliffe's Bible occurred only in 1850 in the edition by Josiah Forshall and Sir Frederic Madden, which distinguished between the original and revised versions and was based on some 170 manuscript copies. The quotation is taken from the prologue to *The Holy Bible, containing the Old and New Testaments, with the Apocryphal Books, in the earliest English Versions made from the Latin Vulgate by John Wycliffe and his Followers*, ed. Forshall and Madden, 4 vols. (Oxford: Oxford University Press, 1850), 1:2, 3. Wycliffe's teachings inspired certain aspects of the later Reformers' efforts and political theory; they are suggestive, also, of themes of the New Light preachers of the eighteenth century. He was condemned and his bones were exhumed and burned in 1428. Cf. K. B. McFarlane, *John Wycliffe and the Beginnings of English Nonconformity* (London: English Universities Press, 1952); and L. J. Daly, S.J., *The Political Theory of John Wyclif* (Chicago: Loyola University Press, 1962). Wycliffe's manuscripts after ca. 1380 were so thoroughly destroyed as often to survive only in Czech versions; he was a major influence on Czech scholars and reformers, especially on the reformer and Czech national hero Jan Hus, who was betrayed and burned at the stake in 1415 following the Council of Constance, which also finally condemned Wycliffe's doctrine. The mere mention of Jan Hus as "a good Catholic priest" by Pope John Paul II to a gathering of high officials in the Spanish Hall of Prague Castle during his first visit to Czechoslovakia, on April 21, 1990, evoked a twenty-minute ovation (eyewitness account, privately communicated to the author; cf. Clyde Haberman, "John Paul Visits a New Prague," *New York Times*, April 21, 1990, p. 4, which passes over the incident without mention; *New York Times*, April 22, 1991, p. 10.) For scholarly analysis of the complexities of the subject and bibliography see Sven L. Fristedt, *The Wycliffe Bible . . .* , Stockholm Studies in English, 3 vols. (Stockhlom: Almqvist and Wiksells, 1953–1973).

38. Cf. Teresa Toulouse, *The Art of Prophesying: New England Sermons and the Shaping of Belief* (Macon, Ga.: Mercer University Press, 1987), chap. 1.

39. Trevelyan as quoted by H. Richard Niebuhr, "The Idea of Covenant and American Democracy," *Church History* 23 (1954): 126–35 at 130. Cf. Henning Graf Reventlow, *The Authority of the Bible and the Rise of the Modern World*, trans. John Bowden (Philadelphia: Fortress Press, 1985), 211–14.

40. Baldwin, "Sowers of Sedition," 76. Cf. her *New England Clergy and the American Revolution*, 168–72.

41. Bonomi, "Dissent and Exceptionalism," 50–51.

42. Clark, *Language of Liberty*, 36, 384.

43. Sandoz, *A Government of Laws*, 160–61. The internal quote is from Patrick Riley, *Will and Political Legitimacy: A Critical Exposition of Social Contract Theory in Hobbes, Locke, Rousseau, Kant, and Hegel* (Cambridge: Harvard University Press, 1982), 5.

44. Harold J. Berman, "The Origins of Historical Jurisprudence: Coke, Selden, Hale," *Yale Law Journal* 103 (May 1994): 1651–1738 at 1722. The ellipsis omits the word *England*, but the sense equally applies to America as heir to English historical jurisprudence and common law.

Essay 5. Religious Liberty and Religion in the American Founding

1. Quoted from Nicholas von Hoffman, "God Was Present at the Founding," *Civilization: The Magazine of the Library of Congress* 5:2 (April/May 1998): 39. From Thomas Jefferson's presidency until well after the end of the Civil War, church services were conducted regularly in the chamber of the U.S. House of Representatives, often with the president and members of the cabinet in attendance. President Jefferson secured the newly formed U.S. Marine Corps Band to play for divine worship on occasion. When the band's playing proved not to be the best, the president connived with the director and commandant to recruit some eighteen Italian musicians into the corps to improve its quality. Cf. Anson P. Stokes, *Church and State in the United States*, 3 vols. (New York: Harper and Brothers, 1950), 1:499–507; Helen Cripe, *Thomas Jefferson and Music* (Charlottesville: University Press of Virginia, 1974), 24–26. According to his biographer, Jefferson "was going to great pains to attend divine services in the House of Congress. One Federalist observer . . . believed that it went far to prove that 'the idea of bearing down and overturning' the religious institutions of the country, which in his opinion had been 'a favorite object,' had been given up. Jefferson did not need to give up that object since he had never had it" (Dumas Malone, *Jefferson and His Time*, vol. 4, *Jefferson the President: First Term, 1801–1805* [Boston: Little, Brown, and Co., 1970], 199). On Jefferson's religion more fully see Dixon W. Adams, ed., *Jefferson's Extracts from the Gospels: "The Philosophy of Jesus" and "The Life and Morals of Jesus"* (Princeton: Princeton University Press, 1983), esp. 14–25. For a sermon preached in the Capitol by a minister invited for the purpose at Jefferson's suggestion, see John Hargrove, *A Sermon on the Second Coming of Christ, and on the Last Judgment. Delivered the 25th December, 1804, Before both houses of Congress at the Capitol in the City of Washington,* in *Political Sermons of the American Founding Era,*

1730–1805, ed. Ellis Sandoz (Indianapolis: Liberty Fund, 1991), 1573–96. On President Jefferson's presence for a sermon delivered by his fiery Baptist supporter the Elder John Leland in 1802 see Malone, *Jefferson the President: First Term*, 106–9.

2. Carl Bridenbaugh, *Spirit of '76: The Growth of American Patriotism before Independence, 1607–1776* (New York: Oxford University Press, 1975), 118. Church membership in America in 1780 is estimated at 59 percent of the population with a surge of increase after the onset of the Second Great Awakening in 1790; see Patricia U. Bonomi and Peter R. Eisenstadt, "Church Adherence in the Eighteenth-Century British American Colonies," *William and Mary Quarterly*, 3d ser., 39 (1982): 245–76 at 274. "American Christianity became a mass enterprise. The eighteen hundred Christian ministers serving in 1775 swelled to nearly forty thousand in 1845. The number of preachers per capita more than tripled; the colonial legacy of one minister per fifteen hundred inhabitants became one per five hundred. . . . The Congregationalists, which had twice the clergy of any other American church in 1775, could not muster one-tenth the preaching force of the Methodists in 1845" (Nathan O. Hatch, *The Democratization of American Christianity* [New Haven: Yale University Press, 1989], 4).

In terms of demographics, at the end of the colonial period America had fewer than three million people, of whom about one-sixth were slaves. There were some 3,005 religious congregations or churches, of which all but 50 were Protestant, with the largest number being Congregationalist (658), Presbyterian (543), Baptist (498), Anglican/Episcopalian, including the Methodists (480), Quakers (298), German and Dutch Reformed (251), followed by Lutheran (151), miscellaneous minor groups (76), and the 50 Roman Catholic congregations, located mainly in large eastern towns and in Maryland. There were fewer than 2,000 Jews, concentrated in New York, Philadelphia, Newport, Charleston, and Savannah. Nine of the thirteen colonies had established churches at the beginning of the Revolution. When the Federal Convention met in Philadelphia in 1787, all of the New England states but Rhode Island retained their virtually established Congregational churches; Maryland and South Carolina retained the Anglican/Episcopalian establishment, a connection given up by Virginia, North Carolina, and Georgia; New York and New Jersey retained only vestiges of their earlier connections with the Episcopal and Dutch Reformed churches; Rhode Island, Pennsylvania, and Delaware never had established churches. Establishment continued in America long after ratification of the Constitution and the Bill of Rights, lasting until 1833 in Massachusetts, despite all the earlier efforts of Isaac Backus and the Baptists. Anson P. Stokes, *Church and State in the United States*, 1:273–74.

3. Quoted from Steven G. Gey, "Why Is Religion Special? Reconsidering the Accommodation of Religion under the Religion Clauses of the First Amendment," *University of Pittsburgh Law Review* 52 (1990): 75, citations omitted.

4. Friedrich Nietzsche, *Thus Spake Zarathustra* (New York: Modern Library, 1970), 5; quoted by Michael W. McConnell, "'God Is Dead and We have Killed Him!' Freedom of Religion in the Post-Modern Age," *Brigham Young University Law Review*, 1993, no. 1, 163–88 at 163, 188 (citations omitted).

5. Harold J. Berman, *Faith and Order: The Reconciliation of Law and Religion* (Atlanta: Scholars Press, 1993), 219.

6. Gey, "Why Is Religion Special?" 167, following Stanley Ingber, "Religion or Ideology: A Needed Clarification of the Religion Clauses," *Stanford Law Review* 41 (1989): 233, 285.

7. For a general discussion of the problem see Jack P. Greene, *The Intellectual Constitution of America: Exceptionalism and Identity from 1492 to 1800* (Chapel Hill: University of North Carolina Press, 1993), esp. 141–42, 148–49, 170–72, 182–83, and 196; Ruth H. Bloch, *Visionary Republic: Millennial Themes in American Thought, 1756–1800* (Cambridge: Cambridge University Press, 1965). America's exceptionalism, including religious uniqueness, is a theme of David Ramsay's 1789 *The History of the American Revolution*, ed. Lester H. Cohen, 2 vols. (Indianapolis: Liberty Fund, 1990), whose final sentence reads: "May the Almighty Ruler of the Universe, who has raised you to Independence, and given you a place among the nations of the earth, make the American Revolution an Era in the history of the world, remarkable for the progressive increase of human happiness" (2:667).

8. Cf. Thomas Jefferson to James Madison, February 17, 1826, in *Thomas Jefferson: Writings*, ed. Merrill D. Peterson (New York: Library of America, 1984), 1512–15; also John Phillip Reid, "The Jurisprudence of Liberty: The Ancient Constitution in the Legal Historiography of the Seventeenth and Eighteenth Centuries," in *The Roots of Liberty: Magna Carta, Ancient Constitution, and the Anglo-American Tradition of Rule of Law*, ed. Ellis Sandoz (Columbia: University of Missouri Press, 1993), 147–231, 292–320; and James R. Stoner Jr., *Common Law and Liberal Theory: Coke, Hobbes, and the Origins of American Constitutionalism* (Lawrence: University Press of Kansas, 1992), esp. 13–68. On Whig versus Jacobin liberty see J. G. A. Pocock in "*The Machiavellian Moment* Revisited: A Study in History and Ideology," *Journal of Modern History* 53 (1981): 49–72 at 72. See also Harold J. Berman, "The Origins of Historical Jurisprudence: Coke, Selden, Hale," *Yale Law Journal* 103 (May 1994): 1651.

9. John Adams to Thomas Jefferson, June 28, 1813, in *The Adams-Jefferson Letters: The Complete Correspondence between Thomas Jefferson and Abigail and John Adams*, ed. Lester J. Cappon, 2 vols. in 1 (1959; rpt. New York: Simon and Schuster, 1971), 2:339–40. In two preceding paragraphs (summarized by the inserted bracketed passage) Adams had written as follows:

> Who composed that Army of fine young Fellows that was then before my Eyes? There were among them, Roman Catholicks, English Episcopalians, Scotch and American Presbyterians, Methodists, Moravians, Anababtists,

German Lutherans, German Calvinists, Universalists, Arians, Priestleyans, Socinians, Independents, Congregationalists, Horse Protestants, House Protestants, Deists and Atheists; and 'Protestans qui ne croyent rien ['Protestants who believe nothing'].' Very few however of several of these Species. Never the less all Educated in the *general Principles* of Christianity: and the general Principles of English and American Liberty.

Could my Answer be understood, by any candid Reader or Hearer, to recommend, to all the others, the general Principles, Institutions or Systems of Education of the Roman Catholicks? Or those of the Quakers? Or those of the Presbyterians? Or those of the Menonists? Or those of the Methodists? or those of the Moravians? Or those of the Universalists? or those of the Philosophers? No. (2:339; spelling, capitalization and punctuation as in the original)

10. Thus Gey argues that "since Immanuel Kant's publication of the *Critique of Pure Reason*, theistic forms of religion have been unable to rely upon the traditional logical proofs of God's existence. This transformation in the nature of theistic religion rendered God unknowable and placed theistic religion on the same foundation with nontheistic religion—a manifestation of human faith alone." A. J. Ayer, Bertrand Russell, and (of course) Sigmund Freud are cited in support (Gey, "Why Is Religion Special?" 168–69, 186–87). Is this seriously asserted, or is the author putting us on? Whatever the case (and I hope it is the latter), the critique of neo-Kantian positivism as a satisfactory instrument for philosophizing generally and for exploring human reality theoretically has been conducted from a number of perspectives that radically discount the sweeping assertions made by Gey. Cf. Eric Voegelin, *The New Science of Politics: An Introduction* (Chicago: University of Chicago Press, 1952), 1–26; and Leszek Kolakowski, *The Alienation of Reason: A History of Positivist Thought*, trans. N. Guterman (Garden City, N.Y.: Doubleday Anchor Books, 1968). Generally, the so-called philosophical proofs of the existence of God are intended to be epideictic, not apodictic. They are never the central justification of the truth of faith that rests upon apperceptive experience. For this class of experience see, for example, Saint Augustine's *Confessions*, trans. H. Chadwick (Oxford: Oxford University Press, 1991), 179–220 (bk. 10). As Stephen F. Brown explains in analyzing Christian mysticism (a pertinent context) by quoting Bonaventure:

> *"Behold, if you can, this most pure Being"* From all that has been said about the theory of illumination . . . and the indubitability of the existence of God . . . , it is obvious that the 'reasons' or proofs which Saint Bonaventure offers for the existence of God, insofar as they imply the existence of God, are not considered by him as proofs or reasons which first make known the existence of God, since the existence of God is evident in itself and is immediately known in the proposition 'God exists.' Hence, the reasons taken from the exterior world, although not denied by Saint Bonaventure, are not of primary importance; they are rather stimuli inducing us to think and to become aware of the immediacy of our cognition of God. The being perceived in any created being cannot be perceived in its ultimate meaning without the knowledge

of the Being which is God. Neither can any absolute and final and evident truth be known with certitude without the divine light shining through the objects and ideas. This light is always there; we have but to pay full attention to it. When we bring to full awareness the content of our first idea, it is impossible for us to think that God does not exist. . . . [T]he existence of God is included in the notion of God. We may deny His existence, but the denial is not evident and cannot be evident. We may believe that we do not know God, because we are ignorant of the meaning of the term 'God,' but if we go to the bottom of our knowledge and conceive God as 'being itself,' there is no possibility of giving our assent to the denial of His existence. See Étienne Gilson, *The Philosophy of Saint Bonaventure*, [trans. Illtye Trethowan (London: Sheed and Ward, 1938] chap. 3: "The Evidence for God's Existence," 107–26. (Bonaventure, *The Journey of the Mind to God*, trans. Philotheus Boehner, ed. Stephen F. Brown [Indianapolis: Hackett, 1993], 67–68n151)

As Gilson elsewhere remarks, seriously to consider Kant's view of religious philosophy we must break "the habit of identifying him with the *Critique of Pure Reason* and of forgetting the existence of the *Critique of Practical Reason* altogether" (*The Spirit of Medieval Philosophy*, trans. A. H. C. Downes [New York: Charles Scribner's Sons, 1936], 16–17). The phrase *transcendental moonshine* is used by A. E. Taylor, *Aristotle*, rev. ed. (New York: Dover, 1955), 30. For an informed discussion of the nature of faith and related matters, see Wilfred C. Smith, *Faith and Belief* (Princeton: Princeton University Press, 1979).

The rational desert Gey imagines for religion is not so desolate after all, as we see, and as can further be seen from Eric Voegelin's late writings, such as the essays "Immortality," "The Gospel and Culture," "Reason," and "Quod Deus Dicitur," in *The Collected Works of Eric Voegelin*, vol. 12, *Published Essays, 1966–1985*, ed. Ellis Sandoz (1990; available Columbia: University of Missouri Press, 1999), 52–94, 172–212, 265–91, 376–94. The entertaining page on the "God Is Dead" movement is to the point of the discussion herein:

But the movement has also its comic touch: The God who is declared dead is alive enough to have kept his undertakers nervously busy by now for three centuries. Yet the life he is leading, before and after his death, is troubled and complicated. When interrogated by eminent thinkers, he does not seem to be sure whether he is a substance or a subject (Spinoza/Hegel), or perhaps both, or whether he perhaps does not exist at all, whether he is personal or impersonal, whether conscious or unconscious, whether rational or irrational, whether spirit only or matter too (Spinoza), whether he is perhaps only a regulative idea (Kant), whether he is identical with himself or not, or whether he is something entirely different (Heidegger). What is absolute in this ambiguous debate about the Absolute is its deadly seriousness. The only one permitted to laugh in the situation appears to be God. (Eric Voegelin, *Order and History*, vol. 5, *In Search of Order* [1987; available Columbia: University of Missouri Press, 1999], 67)

11. Perry Miller, "From the Covenant to the Revival," in *Religion in American History: Interpretive Essays*, ed. John M. Mulder and John F. Wilson (Englewood Cliffs: Prentice-Hall, 1978), 145–61 at 160.

12. It is doubtless a sign of the widespread dismay and resentment of the American people in matters religious that both houses of Congress overwhelmingly voted for and President William J. Clinton promptly signed into law in November 1993 P.L. 103–141, entitled the Religious Freedom Restoration Act of 1993, characterized in the press "as one of the most important measures affecting religious liberty since the Bill of Rights was ratified in 1791" (*Baton Rouge Advocate*, November 6, 1993, 2E). This statute (known as RFRA) reached the U.S. Supreme Court in 1996 and was declared unconstitutional in the case *City of Boerne v. Flores*, 117 S. Ct. 2157 (1997). See Roger Clegg, "*City of Boerne v. Flores:* An Overview," in *Nexus: A Journal of Opinion* 2 (fall 1997): 5–19; the entire issue is devoted to this case.

13. This was a theme of Sir Edward Coke and John Selden in the debate over the Petition of Right; see Selden's words in retort to Coke's quotation of the maxim (in which he added "et libertas popula summa salus populi" [and the people's liberty is their supreme well-being]) in *Proceedings in Parliament, 1628 . . .* , ed. Robert C. Johnson et al., 6 vols. (New Haven: Yale University Press, 1977–1983), 2:183; cf. 2:173–74.

14. Marvin Myers, ed., *The Mind of the Founder: Sources of the Political Thought of James Madison* (Indianapolis: Bobbs-Merrill, 1973), 408. Drew R. McCoy quotes Myers and analyzes the implications in a manner pertinent to our general argument here in *The Last of the Fathers: James Madison and the Republican Legacy* (Cambridge: Cambridge University Press, 1989), 137–40. Madison in April 1787 wrote that "the fundamental principle of republican Government [is] that the majority who rule in such Governments, are the safest Guardians both of public Good and of private rights" ("Vices of the Political System of the United States," in *The Papers of James Madison*, ed. William T. Hutchinson et al., 17 vols. to date [Chicago: University of Chicago Press; Charlottesville: University of Virginia Press, 1962–], 9:345–58 at 354). The Constitution as defended in *The Federalist Papers* is calculated to remedy the worst evils of majoritarian rule without destroying liberty and republicanism in the process, justice under rule of law being their objective. Thus, *Federalist No. 22:* "that fundamental maxim of republican government, which requires that the sense of the majority should prevail"; *Federalist No. 58:* "In all cases where justice or the general good might require new laws to be passed . . . the fundamental principle of free government would be reversed. It would no longer be the majority that would rule"; and *Federalist No. 78:* "that fundamental principle of republican government, which admits the right of the people to alter or abolish the established constitution whenever they find it inconsistent with their happiness" (*The Federalist*, ed. Jacob E. Cooke [Middletown, Conn.: Wesleyan University Press, 1961], 139, 397, 527).

15. *Federalist No. 2*, in *The Federalist*, ed. Cooke, 8–10.

16. John Locke, the putative father of modern constitutionalism, stoutly maintained that all governments begun in peace "had their beginning laid on that foundation, and were *made by the Consent of the People.*" Moreover, "That the *beginning of Politick Society* depends upon the consent of the Individuals, to joyn into and make one Society; who, when they are thus incorporated, might set up what form of Government they thought fit" (*The Second Treatise of Government*, §104, §106, in *Two Treatises of Government; A Critical Edition with an Introduction and Apparatus Criticus*, ed. Peter Laslett [Cambridge: Cambridge University Press, 1963], 354, 355; see also §§95–96).

17. Cited from Smith's *De Republica Anglorum*, ed. L. Alston, preface by F. W. Maitland (Cambridge: Cambridge University Press, 1906), bk. 2, chap. 1, in F. W. Maitland, *The Constitutional History of England: A Course of Lectures* (Cambridge: Cambridge University Press, 1926), 255. Also Sir Francis Bacon: "in an Act of Parliament every man's consent is included"; "The Constitution had institutionalized methods of expressing and redressing grievances; Congress was no local parliament, representing only part of an empire, but was the legitimate embodiment of the whole people" (*New Abridgement of the Law*, in James H. Kettner, *The Development of American Citizenship, 1608–1870* [Chapel Hill: University of North Carolina Press, 1978], 32, 340).

18. Henry J. Abraham, *Freedom and the Court: Civil Rights and Liberties in the United States*, 5th ed. (New York: Oxford University Press, 1988), 238n170 (for "celebrated warning"); *Terminiello v. City of Chicago*, 337 U.S. 1, 37 (1949), Jackson, J., dissenting; cf. Chief Justice Warren Burger's majority opinion in *Haig v. Agee*, 453 U.S. 280 (1981).

19. Matt. 22:21; John 18:36 (King James Version). Thus, Madison commended "a system which, by a due distinction, to which the genius and courage of *Luther* led the way, between what is due to Caesar and what is due God, best promotes the discharge of *both* obligations. . . . A mutual independence is found most friendly to practical religion, to social harmony, and to political prosperity" (Madison to Rev. F. L. Schaeffer, December 3, 1821, in *The Writings of Thomas Jefferson*, ed. Henry A. Washington, 9 vols., Congress ed. [Washington, D.C., 1853–1854], 3:242). In writing of the debate in the Virginia General Assembly in 1786 over enactment of Thomas Jefferson's Statute for Religious Liberty, Madison remarks that the members recoiled at inserting the words *Jesus Christ* into the preamble when it was successfully argued "that the better proof of reverence for that holy name wd be not to profane it by making it a topic of legisl. discussion, & particularly by making his religion the means of abridging the natural and equal rights of all men, in defiance of his own declaration that his *Kingdom was not of this world*" (Elizabeth Fleet, ed., "Madison's 'Detached Memoranda,' " *William and Mary Quarterly*, 3d ser., 3 [1946]: 534–68 at 556; emphasis added).

This document is undated; Fleet believes it probably was written soon after Madison's retirement from the presidency in 1817.

20. Michael W. McConnell, "The Origins and Historical Understanding of Free Exercise of Religion," *Harvard Law Review* 103 (1990): 1409, 1497; emphasis as in original.

21. Sir Edward Coke, *Second Part of the Institutes of the Laws of England . . .* (1641; London: M. Flesher and R. Young, 1642), 47.

22. Plato, *Republic* 435ff., 571b–578e; *Laws* 689a–e; Aristotle, *Politics* 1254b5–1255a2, 1287a18–35; Hobbes, *Leviathan,* chaps. 5, 6, 11, 15. Notice that the philosophical anthropology of Plato and Aristotle finds its substantive equivalent in the hierarchical conception of human nature adopted by James Madison, where it is (perhaps) derivative mainly from Scottish Enlightenment writings, especially those of Francis Hutcheson and the common sense school as mediated by John Witherspoon at the College of New Jersey (Princeton). Thus, Madison deals with the springs of human action in terms of a psychological model of man that places virtue at the top, in preference to rational self-interest, which is to be preferred to the passions. As in classical philosophy, the order of worth is inversely proportional to the order of innate power. Hence, the triumph of virtue in the individual—justice and the public good in society—or even of rational self-interest requires auxiliary assistance from institutions and from historically ingrained habit ("prejudices") in a carefully constructed social system. The pattern will be familiar from *The Federalist Papers* (Nos. 10, 49, and 51). See the discussion in McCoy, *The Last of the Fathers,* esp. 39–83, where he stresses the importance of David Hume for Madison's thought (42–44). There are hints of the equivalent of Socrates' anthropological principle from the *Republic* (368d–e) as McCoy reflects on "the character of the good statesman" and "the character of the good republic" (9, 39). "The struggles to maintain the supremacy of reason over passion and of public virtue over narrow self-interest run through this work like recurring themes in a symphony," wrote Daniel Walker Howe in reviewing McCoy's book in *William and Mary Quarterly,* 3d ser., 47 (1990): 140–42 at 142.

23. John 14:6; James 1:25. Cf. James 2:12; 1 John 2:7–8, 15–17; Gal. 6:2; 2 John 5. For a counterpoint to the argument that the American founders were Christian see John M. Murrin, "Religion and Politics in America from the First Settlements to the Civil War," in *Religion and American Politics: From the Colonial Period to the 1980s,* ed. Mark A. Noll (New York: Oxford University Press, 1990), 19–43. But even Murrin must acknowledge that "Jefferson and Madison along with George Washington, John Adams, Benjamin Franklin, and nearly all of the Founding Fathers claimed to be Christians"—all the while insisting that "hardly any of them was" (29); "the Founding Fathers all claimed to be 'Christians' " (35). This is very curious argumentation. The founders are famous for their veracity and sense of honor; they *said* (thus, presumably *thought*) they were "Christians" in some defensible sense of the

term. Contemporary historians seem to understand them better than they understood themselves, oddly enough.

24. James Madison, "Memorial and Remonstrance," in *Papers of Madison,* ed. Hutchinson et al., 8:298–304 at 302 (para. 11); Richard Hooker, *Of the Laws of Ecclesiastical Polity: Preface, Book I, Book VIII,* ed. Arthur Stephen McGrade (Cambridge: Cambridge University Press, 1989), 49 (preface, 9.1).

25. Cf. Thomas Lindsay, "James Madison on Religion and Politics: Rhetoric and Reality," *American Political Science Review* 85 (1991): 1321–37. This Spinozistic analysis of "Madison's deepest intentions" (1322) finds the Enlightenment subversion to be his true "project" (1329, 1330, 1332, 1333), which is "hostile, in key respects, to religion" (1323), to the end that "religion would be gagged by its own liberty" (1334, final words of the article). The most astonishing thing about this breathtaking performance is that the main thesis hangs on Lindsay's reading, with no evidence to back him, of a single clause in *Federalist No. 10,* "persons of other descriptions" (1324), as a code meaning "Moses, Christ, and Muhammed" (1324), "the world's great religious figures" (1334, 1325). They are, thus, secretly and slyly condemned by Madison as the real villains of history, the culprits who are "destructive of their followers' abilities to 'cooperate for the common good' " (1324, citing *The Federalist,* ed. Clinton Rossiter [New York: New American Library, 1961], 79). This is the wildest surmise and sensationalism. Our most celebrated founders (did Madison act alone? or was there a conspiracy?) are portrayed as accomplices in a diabolical plot to dupe gullible religious Americans into surrendering their birthright. But perhaps this is merely a case of hunch intoxication.

26. Alexis de Tocqueville, *Democracy in America,* ed. J. P. Mayer, trans. George Lawrence, 2 vols. in 1 (Garden City, N.Y.: Doubleday Anchor Books, 1969), 1:46–47, 288–91, 2:432.

27. Benjamin Rush, *A Plan for the Establishment of Schools . . .* (Philadelphia: Thomas Dobson, 1786), rpt. in *American Political Writing during the Founding Era, 1760–1805,* ed. Charles S. Hyneman and Donald S. Lutz, 2 vols. (Indianapolis: Liberty Fund, 1983), 1:682. For discussion see Sandoz, *A Government of Laws,* esp. 132–33, and Barry Alan Shain, *The Myth of American Individualism: The Protestant Origins of American Political Thought* (Princeton: Princeton University Press, 1994), esp. 96–97.

28. James Lord Bryce, *The American Commonwealth,* new ed., 2 vols. (New York: Macmillan, 1922), 2:676–69, 874. A document published in observation of the centenary of the Constitution had this to say about religion, America's providential destiny, and the actual operation of separation of church and state:

> [I]t has worked well in practice. It has stood the test of experience. It has the advantages of the union of church and state without its disadvantages. . . . The tendency to division and split is inherent in Protestantism, and it must be allowed free scope until every legitimate type of Christianity is developed and matured. The work of history is not in vain. But division is only a means

to a higher unity than the world has yet seen. . . . God has great surprises in store. The Reformation is not by any means the last word He has spoken. We may confidently look and hope for something better than Romanism and Protestantism. And free America, where all the churches are commingling and rivalling with each other, may become the chief theater of such a reunion of Christendom as will preserve every truly Christian and valuable element. . . . The denominational discords will be solved at last in the concord of Christ, the Lord and Savior of all that love, worship, and follow Him. (Philip Schaff, *Church and State in the United States; Or, The American Idea of Religious Liberty and Its Practical Effects, with Official Documents,* Papers of the American Historical Association, vol. 2, no. 4 [New York: C. Scribner, 1888], 2:389–565 at 460–65 [also paged as a separate publication, quoting from 78–83])

The sentiments Schaff expressed in 1888 accord well with those Ezra Stiles expressed a century earlier in the Connecticut election sermon of 1783: "It may have been of the Lord that Christianity is to be found in such great purity in this church exiled into the wilderness of America; and that its purest body should be evidently advancing forward, by an augmented natural increase and spiritual edification, into a singular superiority—with the ultimate subserviency to the glory of God, in converting the world" (Stiles, *The United States Elevated to Glory and Honour,* quoted as given in excerpted form in *God's New Israel: Religious Interpretations of American Destiny,* ed. Conrad Cherry [Englewood Cliffs: Prentice-Hall, 1971], 82–92 at 92. For the complete text see John Wingate Thornton, ed., *The Pulpit of the American Revolution: or, the Political Sermons of the Period of 1776* [1860; rpt., New York: B. Franklin, 1970]).

29. Perry Miller, "The Contribution of the Protestant Churches to Religious Liberty in Colonial America," *Church History* 4 (March 1935): 55–66.

30. William G. McLoughlin, *New England Dissent, 1630–1833: The Baptists and the Separation of Church and State,* 2 vols. (Cambridge: Harvard University Press, 1971), 1:xv. I rely upon McLoughlin in the next paragraph. See also his *Soul Liberty: The Baptists' Struggle in New England, 1630–1833* (Hanover: University Press of New England, 1991).

31. *Soul Liberty,* 260.

32. See the account in Hatch, *Democratization of American Christianity,* 49–192; also Gordon S. Wood, *The Radicalism of the American Revolution* (New York: A. A. Knopf, 1993), 229–369.

33. McLoughlin, *New England Dissent,* 1:xx–xxi. See also Isaac Backus, *An Appeal to the Public for Religious Liberty* [Boston, 1773], in *Political Sermons of the American Founding,* ed. Sandoz, 327–68. On America's providential destiny see Stiles, *The United States Elevated;* analyzed in Sandoz, *A Government of Laws,* 109–11.

34. Cf. E. Benjamin Andrews's address of 1893 in Joseph M. Dawson, *Baptists and the American Republic* (Nashville: Broadman Press, 1956), 67.

35. McConnell, "Origins of Free Exercise of Religion," 1438–39. On John

Leland see *Political Sermons of the American Founding*, ed. Sandoz, 1079–1100, which reprints his famous tract *The Rights of Conscience Inalienable* (New London: T. Green and Son, 1791).

36. Madison to William Bradford, January 24, 1774, in *Papers of Madison*, ed. Hutchinson et al., 1:106–7. Madison was born on March 16, 1751 (March 5, 1750 Old Style), and died June 28, 1836. See Ralph Ketcham, *James Madison: A Biography* (New York: Macmillan, 1971), 8–9n. (Great Britain's calendar reform adopting the Gregorian for the Julian calendar came in 1752 and required an eleven-day addition to Old Style dates; it also changed the beginning of the year from March 25 to January 1. When Madison was born, toward midnight, the calendar on the wall would have read March 5, 1750.) The standard account of the persecution of the Baptists in Virginia is Lewis Peyton Little, *Imprisoned Preachers and Religious Liberty in Virginia* (Lynchburg, Va.: J. P. Bell Co., 1938.)

37. Henry F. May, *The Heart Divided: Essays on Protestantism and the Enlightenment in America* (New York: Oxford University Press, 1991), 172.

38. Ketcham, *James Madison*, 165, 167–68. See also Ralph L. Ketcham, "James Madison and Religion: A New Hypothesis," in *James Madison on Religious Liberty*, ed. Robert S. Alley (1960; rpt. Buffalo, N.Y.: Prometheus Books, 1985), 175–96; Paul Finkelman, "James Madison and the Bill of Rights: A Reluctant Paternity," *The 1990 Supreme Court Review* (Chicago: University of Chicago Press, 1991), 301–47; and Daniel L. Dreisbach, "A New Perspective on Jefferson's Views on Church-State Relations: The Virginia Statute for Establishing Religious Freedom in Its Legislative Context," *American Journal of Legal History* 35 (1991): 172–204, and "In Search of a Christian Commonwealth: An Examination of Selected Nineteenth-Century Commentaries on References to God and the Christian Religion in the United States Constitution," *Baylor Law Review* 48 (1996): 927–1000.

39. Virginia Declaration of Rights of 1776 as given in Bernard Schwartz, ed., *The Bill of Rights: A Documentary History*, 2 vols. (New York: Chelsea House, 1971), 1:231–43 at 236. Mason's original draft read: " . . . violence; and, therefore, *that* all men *should enjoy the fullest toleration in* [are equally entitled to] the [free] exercise of religion, according to the dictates of conscience,[;] *unpunished and unrestrained by the magistrate, unless, under color of religion, any man disturb the peace, the happiness or the safety of society*.[;] [a]nd. . . ." The italicized words were deleted in the final draft and the bracketed changes made (ibid., 239).

40. James Madison's *Autobiography*, quoted ibid., 250. Not dated precisely, but probably written after August 1833, according to Irving Brant (quoted ibid., 249n).

41. Isaac Backus quoted from McLoughlin, "Isaac Backus and Thomas Jefferson," in *Soul Liberty*, 260. In *Isaac Backus on Church, State, and Calvinism: Pamphlets, 1754–1789* (Cambridge: Belknap Press of Harvard University, 1968), McLoughlin remarks that Backus "was the most forceful and effective writer America produced on behalf of the pietistic or evangelical theory of

separation of church and state" (1). Backus doubtless had in hand Mason's intermediate draft version, which had been given preliminary emendation by the committee (printed on May 27, 1776) and which his own language tracks to some degree. This preliminary text was republished far and wide, including Massachusetts, where John Adams made use of it in 1776 and 1780, and it was everywhere taken as the finished document. The final version, containing Madison's emendations, was "not published outside of Virginia for about a half-century"; he therefore received little credit for his important accomplishment until much later. "Editorial Note," in *Papers of Madison*, ed. Hutchinson et al., 1:171.

42. Thus, Madison remarked of the four Executive proclamations for days of fasting and thanksgiving that he issued during his presidency: "I was always careful to make the Proclamations absolutely indiscriminate, and merely recommendatory; or rather mere *designations* of a day, on which all who thought proper might *unite* in consecrating it to religious purposes, according to their own faith & forms" (Madison to Edward Livingston, July 10, 1822, in *The Writings of James Madison*, ed. Gaillard Hunt, 9 vols. [New York: G. P. Putnam's Sons, 1900–1910], 9:101). Elsewhere Madison states of these proclamations: "a form & language were employed, which were meant to deaden as much as possible any claim of political right to enjoin religious observances" (Fleet, ed., "Madison's 'Detached Memoranda,'" 562); proclamations in response to Congress's requests were issued by President Madison on July 9, 1812; July 23, 1813; November 16, 1814; and March 4, 1815 (562n54.)

43. "Memorial and Remonstrance," in *Papers of Madison*, ed. Hutchinson et al., 8:298–302.

44. Madison to Jefferson, January 22, 1786, in ibid., 8:474.

45. See the account in Sandoz, *A Government of Laws*, 203–17; and Helen E. Veit et al., eds., *Creating the Bill of Rights: The Documentary Record from the First Federal Congress* (Baltimore: Johns Hopkins University Press, 1991).

46. Madison to Edward Everett, March 19, 1823, in *Writings of Madison*, ed. Hunt, 9:126–27; spelling, capitalization, and emphasis as in original.

47. McConnell, "Origins of Free Exercise of Religion," 1513.

48. This large subject is canvassed from related perspectives in Edward S. Corwin, *The "Higher Law" Background of American Constitutional Law* (1928, 1929; rpt. Ithaca: Cornell University Press, 1955); Sandoz, *A Government of Laws*, 163–240; Ralph Ketcham, *Framed for Posterity: The Enduring Philosophy of the Constitution* (Lawrence: University Press of Kansas, 1993), esp. 6–10. See also Essay 7 herein.

49. Ketcham, *Framed for Posterity*, 163–64. This is the language of *The Federalist* as well, as can be seen in this passage by Publius [Alexander Hamilton]: "A constitution is in fact, and must be, regarded by the judges as a fundamental law. . . . where the will of the legislature declared in its statutes, stands in opposition to that of the people declared in the constitution, the

judges ought to be governed by the latter, rather than the former. They ought to regulate their decisions by the fundamental laws, rather than by those which are not fundamental" (*Federalist No. 78*, in *The Federalist*, ed. Cooke, 525).

50. Harold J. Berman, "The Rule of Law and the Law-Based State *(Rechts-staat):* With Special Reference to the Soviet Union" (1991), in *Toward the "Rule of Law" in Russia? Political and Legal Reform in the Transition Period*, ed. Donald D. Barry (Armonk, N.Y.: M. E. Sharpe, 1992), 45–46. The higher law appeal as given in the language of the Declaration of Independence also is echoed in *The Federalist*, which finds James Madison (as Publius) affirming "the transcendent law of nature and of nature's God, which declares that the safety and happiness of society are the objects at which all political institutions aim, and to which all such institutions must be sacrificed" (*Federalist No. 43* in *The Federalist*, ed. Cooke, 297).

51. Martin Luther King Jr., *Letter from Birmingham Jail*, April 16, 1963, in *God's New Israel*, ed. Cherry, 347–60 at 351–52. King's allusions to Augustine and Thomas Aquinas rest on passages in the latter's *Treatise on Law* in *Summa Theologiae I–II [First Part of the Second Part], Questions 90–108*, esp. quest. 91, art. 2: "[A]ll things subject to divine providence are ruled and measured by the eternal law. . . . Now among all others the rational creature [Man] is subject to divine providence in the most excellent way. . . . Wherefore it has a share of the eternal reason, whereby it has a natural inclination to its proper act and end: and this participation of the eternal law in the rational creature is called the natural law." Quest. 95, art. 2: "As Augustine says, 'that which is not just seems to be no law at all' *[De libero arbitrio* i.5.]; wherefore the force of a [human or positive] law depends on the extent of its justice. Now in human affairs a thing is said to be just from being right according to the rule of reason. But the first rule of reason is the law of nature, as is clear from what has been stated above (Quest. 91, Art. 2. *ad* 2). Consequently, every human law has just so much of the nature of law as it is derived from the law of nature. But if in any point it deflects from the law of nature, it is no longer a law but a perversion of law." Quest. 96, art. 4: "Laws framed by man are either just or unjust. If they be just, they have the power of binding in conscience, from the eternal law whence they are derived, according to Proverbs 8:15: 'By Me kings reign, and lawgivers decree just things.' . . . [A]s Augustine says, 'A law that is not just, seems to be no law at all.' Wherefore such laws do not bind in conscience, except perhaps in order to avoid scandal or disturbance. . . . [A]s stated in Acts 5:29, 'we ought to obey God rather than men' " (quoted from *The Political Ideas of St. Thomas Aquinas: Representative Selections*, ed. Dino Bigongiari [New York: Hafner Press, 1969], 13, 58, 71–72).

For a discussion of the "civil rights revolution" that considers the higher law dimensions see Ellis Sandoz, *Conceived in Liberty: American Individual Rights Today* (North Scituate, Mass.: Duxbury Press, 1978), 169–229 at 222–

28; also 28–30, 39, 49, 51, 56–58. Cf. Thomas C. Grey, "Do We Have an Unwritten Constitution?" *Stanford Law Review* 27 (1975): 703, and "Origins of the Unwritten Constitution: Fundamental Law in American Revolutionary Thought," *Stanford Law Review* 30 (1978): 843.

52. Madison attributes the statement to Pierce Butler of South Carolina in his *Debates* as given in *Records of the Federal Convention of 1787*, ed. Max Farrand, 4 vols. (1911; rev. ed. 1937; rpt. New Haven: Yale University Press, 1966), 1:125.

53. McConnell, "Origins of Free Exercise of Religion."

54. The history of this view is concisely sketched from the standpoint of constitutional law and history by Leo Pfeffer, "The Deity in American Constitutional History," in *Religion and the State: Essays in Honor of Leo Pfeffer*, ed. James E. Wood Jr. (Waco: Baylor University Press, 1985), 119–44, and summarized as follows:

> From the initial landing of the Pilgrims on these shores, up to the time of the Declaration of Independence, invocation of the Deity in official governmental acts was a practically universal practice. Thereafter it continued and still continues to be acceptable in state constitutions; indeed it is to be found today in almost all state constitutions. Those who wrote and those who adopted our national Constitution and its Bill of Rights, however, made a deliberate determination not to invoke the Deity therein. The Supreme Court, however, for more than a century and half, showed no reticence in invoking the Deity in its own decisions. In the course of this period, however, it expanded the meaning of the term to encompass the nontrinitarian Deity of the Unitarians and Universalists and by using the term "Judeo-Christian," to include the Deity of the Jews. In its most recent relevant decisions it has employed the amorphous and almost boundaryless term "Supreme Being" as that term is interpreted by each individual for himself. Finally, while it will not exercise its judicial power to inhibit invocation of the Deity outside the arena of public education, it will not sanction denial of privileges such as governmental employment to those who deny the existence of a deity. (141–42)

55. Thomas J. Curry, *The First Freedoms: Church and State in America to the Passage of the First Amendment* (New York: Oxford University Press, 1986), 219.

56. May, *Heart Divided*, 177.

57. For civil theology see *God's New Israel*, ed. Cherry; Joshua Mitchell, *Not by Reason Alone: Religion, History, and Identity in Early Modern Political Thought* (Chicago: University of Chicago Press, 1993); Jürgen Gebhardt, *Americanism: Revolutionary Order and Societal Self-Interpretation in the American Republic*, trans. Ruth Hein (Baton Rouge: Louisiana State University Press, 1993); Sandoz, *A Government of Laws*, 51–162; and Charles W. Calhoon, "Civil Religion and the Gilded Age Presidency: The Case of Benjamin Harrison," *Presidential Studies Quarterly* 23 (fall 1993): 651–67, and the literature cited therein.

Political messianism generally and soteriological nationalism specifically also have a large literature, including Ernest Lee Tuveson, *Redeemer Nation: The Idea of America's Millennial Role* (1968; Chicago: University of Chicago Press, 1980); Jacob L. Talmon, *The Origins of Totalitarian Democracy* (New York: Frederick A. Praeger, 1960), *Political Messianism: The Romantic Phase* (1960; New York: Frederick A. Praeger, 1968), and *The Myth of the Nation and Vision of Revolution: Ideological Polarization in the Twentieth Century*, intro. Irving Louis Horowitz (1981; rpt. New Brunswick, N.J.: Transaction, 1991); Norman Cohn, *The Pursuit of the Millennium: Revolutionary Millenarians and Mystical Anarchists of the Middle Ages*, rev. enl. ed. (1970; rpt. New York: Oxford University Press, 1981); Ernst Gellner, *Nations and Nationalism* (Oxford: Blackwell, 1983); and E. J. Hobsbawm, *Nation and Nationalism Since 1780* (Cambridge: Cambridge University Press, 1990); K. R. Minogue, *Nationalism* (New York: Basic Books, 1967); Paul Gilbert, *The Philosophy of Nationalism* (Boulder: Westview Press, 1998); Karl Löwith, *Meaning in History* (Chicago: University of Chicago Press, 1949); Voegelin, *New Science of Politics*, 107–61, and *Die politischen Religionen* (1938; rpt. Stockholm: Bermann-Fischer Verlag, 1939); and Hannah Arendt, *Origins of Totalitarianism* (New York: Harcourt Brace, 1951). The discussion herein is indebted to Jürgen Gebhardt, "Religion and National Identity" (unpublished ms., 1994). For a general analysis of political nationalism see John Bruilly, *Nationalism and the State*, 2d ed. (Chicago and Manchester: Manchester University Press, 1993), esp. 34–72, 382–403.

58. For the distinctions between the city of the world and the city of God see Saint Augustine, *City of God*, esp. bks. XI–XIV; trans. Marcus Dods, intro. Thomas Merton (New York: Modern Library, 1950), 345–478. The distinction is commonplace in American sermons at the time of the Revolution. It can be glimpsed in John Witherspoon, *The Dominion of Providence over the Passions of Men* (May 17, 1776), in *Political Sermons of the American Founding*, ed. Sandoz, 530–58, which "was the most widely read Calvinist justification of the Revolution" (Robert M. Calhoon, *Dominion and Liberty: Ideology in the Anglo-American World, 1660–1801* [Arlington Heights, Ill.: Harlan Davidson, 1994], 93).

59. As Dumas Malone explains Jefferson's use of the famous phrase:

> His answer to the Danbury Baptist Association of Connecticut [dated October 7, 1801, printed January 1, 1802] was to be quoted long thereafter. In it he declared that by means of the prohibition in the first amendment to the Constitution, a "wall of separation" had been built between church and state. He was seeking to encourage the dissenting minority in Connecticut and to rebuke the politico-religious rulers of the commonwealth. . . . Others besides the Danbury Baptists, seeing in [Jefferson's] past services "a glow of philanthropy and good will shining forth in a course of more than thirty years," believed that God had raised him up to fill the chair of state. His enemies might castigate him as an unbeliever, but the devotion of his followers had a religious fervor. (*Jefferson the President: First Term*, 108–9)

The phrase *wall of separation* made its way into constitutional law in *Reynolds v. United States*, 98 U.S. 145, 164 (1878) and became famous through *Everson v. Board of Education*, 330 U.S. 1 (1947), when Justice Hugo Black wrote for the majority:

> The "establishment of religion" clause of the First Amendment means at least this: Neither a state nor the Federal Government can set up a church. Neither can pass laws which aid one religion, aid all religions, or prefer one religion over another. Neither can force nor influence a person to go to or remain away from church against his will or force him to profess a belief or disbelief in any religion. No person can be punished for entertaining or professing religious beliefs or disbeliefs, for church attendance or non-attendance. No tax in any amount, large or small, can be levied to support any religious activities or institutions, whatever they may be called, or whatever form they may adopt to teach or practice religion. Neither a state nor the Federal Government can, openly or secretly, participate in the affairs of any religious organizations or groups and *vice versa*. In the words of Jefferson, the clause against establishment of religion by law was intended to erect "a wall of separation between church and State." (*Everson v. Board of Education*, 15–16)

The court nevertheless upheld the challenged New Jersey statute, which had for its purpose helping schoolchildren get safely to and from school, whether public or private. Justice Black added that the First Amendment "requires the state to be a neutral in its relations with groups of religious believers and non-believers; *it does not require the state to be their adversary*" (ibid., 18; emphasis added.) See the analysis in A. E. Dick Howard, "The Wall of Separation: The Supreme Court as Uncertain Stonemason," in *Religion and the State*, ed. Wood, 85–118. See also the symposium devoted to the question "Does Religious Freedom Have a Future?: The First Amendment After *Boerne [v. Flores]*," in *Nexus: A Journal of Opinion* 2 (fall 1997): 1–175.

60. See Dwight David Eisenhower, *Crusade in Europe* (Garden City, N.Y.: Doubleday, 1948); Rev. 16:14–16; James Burnham, *The War We Are In: The Last Decade and the Next* (New Rochelle, N.Y.: Arlington House, 1967); Barbara Kellerman and Ryan J. Barilleaux, *The President as World Leader* (New York: St. Martin's Press, 1991), esp. "Ronald Reagan's Campaign for Military Superiority," 174–96; President Ronald Reagan, "Remarks at the Annual Convention of the National Association of Evangelicals," Orlando, Florida, March 8, 1983, *Weekly Compilation of Presidential Papers* 19, no. 10 (1983): 364–70 at 369: "I urge you to beware of the temptation of pride—the temptation of blithely declaring yourselves above it all and label both sides equally at fault, to ignore the facts of history and the aggressive impulses of an *evil empire*, to simply call the arms race a giant misunderstanding and thereby remove yourself from the struggle between right and wrong and good and evil" (emphasis added). Reagan's entire address is a good specimen of contemporary American civil theology. For an overview of the period of

the Cold War from the perspective of foreign affairs, see Amos Yoder, *The Conduct of American Foreign Policy since World War II* (New York: Pergamon Press, 1986).

61. Quoted from Sandoz, *A Government of Laws*, 121.

62. "The 'death of God' in the eighteenth century sent many people in search of focuses for collective identity, quite dissociated from the church and the confraternity of Christian believers. Such a substitute was found in the nation." By the mid-nineteenth century,

> [what] did those salvationist hopes not promise: the coming of eternal peace, the total unfolding of a self-knowing and self-willing Spirit (or Reason) incarnate, the triumph at last of a genuinely spiritual and authentically social New Christianity, the emancipation of the most numerous and poorest class in a classless society, and . . . the liberation of all peoples, and the emergence of a brotherhood of regenerated nations. (Talmon, *Myth of the Nation and Vision of Revolution*, 1, 542)

For a philosophical analysis see Eric Voegelin, *Science, Politics, and Gnosticism: Two Essays*, trans. William J. Fitzpatrick, intro. Ellis Sandoz, Gateway Edition (1968; rpt. Washington, D.C.: Regnery Publishing Co., 1997): "The death of God is the cardinal issue of gnosis, both ancient and modern. From Hegel to Nietzsche it is the great theme of gnostic speculation, and Protestant theology has been plagued by it ever since Hegel's time. In recent years, it has been taken up by American theologians who are faced with the pressing phenomena of urbanization and alienation. . . . The struggle against the consequences of gnosticism is being conducted in the very language of gnosticism" (xx); cf. Voegelin, *New Science of Politics*, 107–32.

63. *How Are We to Structure Russia?—A Modest Contribution*, English trans. quoted from *Foreign Broadcast Information Service FBIS-SOV-90–187*, September 26, 1990, 37–58 at 47.

64. T. S. Eliot's symbol of oblivion and modern man's deformation: "We are the hollow men / We are the stuffed men / Leaning together / Headpiece filled with straw. Alas!" *The Hollow Men* (1925), in Eliot, *The Complete Poems and Plays, 1909–1950* (New York: Harcourt, Brace and World, 1971), 56–59 at 56.

65. *Everson v. Board of Education*, 330 U.S. 1, 18. Cf. Stephen L. Carter, *The Culture of Disbelief: How American Law and Politics Trivialize Religious Devotion* (New York: Basic Books, 1993).

66. For this analysis see Voegelin, "*Ersatz* Religion: The Gnostic Mass Movements of Our Time," in *Science, Politics, and Gnosticism*, 55–78 (in 1997 ed.):

> The term "gnostic mass movements" is not in common use. . . . By gnostic movements we mean such [ideological] movements as progressivism, positivism, Marxism, psychoanalysis, communism, fascism, and national socialism. We are not dealing, therefore, in all of these cases with political mass

movements. Some of them would more accurately be characterized as intellectual movements—for example, positivism, neo-positivism, and the variants of psychoanalysis. This draws attention to the fact that mass movements do not represent an autonomous phenomenon and that the difference between masses and intellectual elites is perhaps not so great as is conventionally assumed, if indeed it exists at all. At any rate, in social reality the two types merge. (57)

67. See Daniel J. Elazar, *American Federalism: A View from the States,* 2d ed. (New York: Crowell, 1972), 50, and *Exploring Federalism* (Tuscaloosa: University of Alabama Press, 1987), 201, 223–24, 264. Justice Robert H. Jackson pointed up one aspect of the problem: "The rise of administrative bodies probably has been the most significant legal trend of the last century. . . . They have become a veritable fourth branch of Government, which has deranged our three-branch legal theories" (*Federal Trade Commission v. Ruberoid Co.,* 343 U.S. 470, 487 [1952], Jackson, J. dissenting; cited in *Immigration and Naturalization Service v. Chadha,* 462 U. S.919, 985 [1983], White, J. dissenting).

68. Cf. Henri de Lubac, *The Drama of Atheist Humanism,* trans. Edith M. Riley (London: Sheed and Ward, 1949). This affirmation of higher Reality, and rejection of the notion of the Autonomous Self or Autonomous Man emblematic of egophanic revolt of which Nietzsche's is a variety, is common to Václav Havel, Aleksandr Solzhenitsyn, and Eric Voegelin alike.

69. "The advanced totalitarian system depends on manipulatory devices so refined, complex, and powerful that it no longer needs murderers and victims. Even less does it need fiery Utopia builders spreading discontent with dreams of a better future. The epithet 'Real Socialism,' which this era has coined to describe itself, points a finger at those for whom it has no room: the dreamers" (Václav Havel, "Stories and Totalitarianism" [April 1987], in Havel, *Open Letters: Selected Writings 1965–1990,* ed. Paul Wilson [New York: Vintage Books, 1992], 328–50 at 332). Cf. Jan Patočka, "The Obligation to Resist Injustice," in Patočka, *Philosophy and Selected Writings,* ed. Erazin Kohák (Chicago: University of Chicago Press, 1989), 341. Cf. also the discussion of "really existing socialism" in the incisive study by Sir Ralf Dahrendorf, *Reflections on the Revolution in Europe* (New York: Times Books, 1990), 44, 49, 67: "the point has to be made unequivocally that socialism is dead, and that none of its variants can be revived for a world awakening from the double nightmare of Stalinism and Brezhnevism" (42); "Socialism was an intellectual invention, from Saint-Simon to Lassalle, from Marx to Gramsci, and through the hundreds of byways of Marxism that are now all ending in the sewers of discarded history" (73).

70. McConnell, " 'God Is Dead and We Have Killed Him!' " 163, 188.

71. *The Federalist,* ed. Rossiter, xvi; in 1789, David Ramsay wrote: "Remember that there can be no political happiness without liberty; that there can be no liberty without morality; and that there can be no morality without religion" (*History of the American Revolution,* 2:667). The conviction of the

nation's dependence upon divine Providence for its happiness is symbolically expressed on the reverse of the Great Seal of the United States (which
dates from June 1782 and now is most readily seen printed on the back of
the U.S. one-dollar bill): "The pyramid signifies Strength and Duration: The
Eye over it and the motto [*Annuit Coeptis:* It (Providence) is Favorable to
Our Undertakings] allude to the many signal interpositions of providence
in favour of the American cause. The date underneath [MDCCLXXVI] is that
of the Declaration of Independence and the words [*Novus Ordo Seclorum:* A
New Order of Centuries/Ages] under it signify the beginning of the New
American Era, which commences from that date" (Gaillard Hunt's 1892
paper on the seal as quoted from Eugene Zieber, *Heraldry in America*, 2d ed.
[Philadelphia: Dept. of Heraldry of the Bailey, Banks and Biddle Co., 1909],
103; see 101–2 for the history and authoritative translations of the mottoes
and their likely sources in Virgil).

72. George Washington, "Farewell Address," September 19, 1796, in
George Washington: A Collection, ed. William B. Allen (Indianapolis: Liberty
Fund, 1988), 512–27 at 521–22; emphasis and capitalization as in original.
James Madison, Alexander Hamilton, and John Jay assisted in the prepara-
tion of this famous speech (ibid., 444.)

73. Harold J. Berman, "Law and Logos," *DePaul Law Review* 44 (1994):
143–65 at 158–59.

74. *Federalist No. 55,* in *The Federalist,* ed. Cooke, 374; cf. *Federalist No. 51,*
in ibid., 349; further in *Federalist No. 55:* "As there is a degree of depravity in
mankind which requires a certain degree of circumspection and distrust: So
there are other qualities in human nature, which justify a certain portion of
esteem and confidence. Republican government presupposes the existence
of these qualities in a higher degree than any other form. Were the pictures
which have been drawn by the political jealousy of some among us, faithful
likenesses of the human character, the inference would be that there is not
sufficient virtue among men for self-government; and that nothing less than
the chains of despotism can restrain them from destroying and devouring
one another" (ibid., 378).

Essay 6. Sir John Fortescue as Political Philosopher

1. References to Fortescue's writings primarily will be to the edition
published privately in two large quarto volumes by Lord Clermont under
the title *Sir John Fortescue, Knight: His Life, Works, and Family History,* ed.
Lord Clermont (London, 1869). Only 120 copies were printed, and it is rare.
It principally includes: (1) *On the Nature of the Law of Nature,* translated
from the Latin original by Chichester Fortescue, later Lord Carlingford,
pp. 187–333 (the first publication of both the Latin original and the English
translation) with the translator's Table of Quotations, pp. 347*-353*; (2) *In*

Praise of the Laws of England, translated from the Latin original by Francis Gregor, pp. 385–442 (a version first published in 1737); (3) *A Dialogue Between Understanding and Faith*, pp. 479–90; and (4) *Declaration Upon Certain Writings Sent out of Scotland*, pp. 519–41. Citation will be by the following abbreviations:

Nature   *A Treatise Concerning the Nature of the Law of Nature, and Its Judgment Upon the Succession to Sovereign Kingdoms*
Praise   *In Praise of the Laws of England*
Governance *The Governance of England; otherwise called The difference Between an Absolute and a Limited Monarchy*

A recent student edition is *On the Laws and Governance of England*, ed. Shelley Lockwood, Cambridge Texts in the History of Political Thought (Cambridge: Cambridge University Press, 1997).

2. Richard Hooker, *Of the Laws of Ecclesiastical Polity: Preface, Book I, Book VIII*, ed. Arthur Stephen McGrade (Cambridge: Cambridge University Press, 1989), 93 (I.10.8).

3. Sir John Fortescue, *De Laudibus Legum Anglie*, ed. and trans. S. B. Chrimes (1942; Cambridge: Cambridge University Press, 1949), xlvii; as Chrimes writes: "the limitation on the king of England is a *parliamentary* limitation; in saying that [Fortescue] was saying something that nobody, so far as we know, had said before, certainly not with such distinctness and insistence. Fortescue was the first writer to abandon merely feudal and pre-feudal notions of the monarchy, and to affirm boldly that it was not only limited, but parliamentary in character. In doing so, he not only reflected the constitutional development that had been taking place since Bracton, but also illumines for us the path that was likely to be followed in the ensuing generations" (cii; emphasis as in original).

4. *The Eighth Part of the Reports of Sir Edward Coke* (1609; rpt. London: E. and R. Nutt and R. Gosling, 1727), [12].

5. Chrimes, editor's introduction, in Fortescue, *De Laudibus*, cvii–viii.

6. I have briefly considered the political and constitutional aspects of Fortescue's writings in *The Roots of Liberty: Magna Carta, Ancient Constitution, and the Anglo-American Tradition of Rule of Law*, ed. Ellis Sandoz (Columbia: University of Missouri Press, 1993), 5–18, 268–72.

7. Aristotle, *Nicomachean Ethics* 1.4, 1095a15–17; *Nature* I.44.

8. *Nature* I.34. Cf. Aristotle, *Politics*, I.1.8–11, 1252b28–1253a18.

9. *Nature* I.31.

10. *Nature* I.16; *Praise* c. 14.

11. *Praise* c. 37; *Nature* I.26; Augustine, *Confessions* 7.12.18–15.21. Cf. Étienne Gilson, *The Christian Philosophy of Saint Augustine*, trans. L. E. M. Lynch (New York: Vintage Books, 1960), chap. 3.

12. Proeemium (¶ 3) of the *Proslogion*, text and translation in Gregory Schufreider, *Confessions of a Rational Mystic: Anselm's Early Writings* (West Lafayette, Ind.: Purdue University Press, 1994), 312.

13. 1 Cor. 12, a favorite of Fortescue's; Eph. 4:4–13; Col. 1:18.

14. *Praise* c. 13; *Governance* c. 2.

15. *Nature* I.37, II.17, c. 63. On the amplitude of memory *(memoria)* in Augustine see Gilson, *Christian Philosophy of Saint Augustine,* 299n110 and texts cited therein, esp. *Confessions* bk. 10 and *On the Trinity* bks. 10 and 14. Fortescue frequently quotes Boethius (480?-524?), whose anthropology may be taken as a key ingredient in his own Neo-Platonic-Augustinian conception of human nature and personality; it is set forth in Boethius, *Consolation of Philosophy,* ed. Irwin Edman (New York: Modern Library, 1943), esp. 108–20. It also should be noted that Fortescue was acquainted with and relied upon the translations and work of the pivotal fifteenth-century Florentine Renaissance scholar Leonardo Bruni (1377–1444), himself a humanistic Thomist, including the new Latin translations of Aristotle's *Ethics* and *Politics* (commissioned by Humphrey, duke of Gloucester), translations of Plato's dialogues, and, most directly, Bruni's introduction to philosophy entitled *An Isagogue of Moral Philosophy.* See *The Humanism of Leonardus Bruni: Selected Texts,* ed. Gordon Griffiths et al. (Binghamton, N.Y.: Medieval and Renaissance Texts and Studies, Renaissance Society of America, 1987), esp. chaps. 4 and 6 by James Hankins. Bruni was not only a conduit of Greek and Latin classicism, including Platonism, into Italy and to some degree also into England but also "the best-selling author of the fifteenth century" *(Humanism,* 45). See the discussion of Fortescue's sources for *Praise* in Chrimes, *De Laudibus,* lxxxix–xcv.

16. *Nature* II.35.

17. Summarizing Thomas Aquinas (admittedly Fortescue's master), *Summa theologiae* I–II, quest. 94, art. 2; for further discussion of this conception of natural law see Essay 7 herein.

18. *Nature* I.42, II.63.

19. The literature on Fortescue neglects these matters. The best study is Norman Doe, *Fundamental Authority in Late Medieval English Law* (Cambridge: Cambridge University Press, 1990); also Stephen A. Siegel, "The Aristotelian Basis of English Law, 1450–1800," *New York University Law Review* 56 (April 1981): 18–59. Fortescue's theories are resumed by Christopher St. Germain a half century later; cf. *St. German's Doctor and Student* (First Dialogue 1523, Second 1530), ed. T. F. T. Plucknett and J. L. Barton, Selden Society vol. 91 (London: Selden Society, 1974), 13–15, 81–90.

20. *Nature* I.29, II.71.

21. Fortescue is of two minds on this important subject, and only a hint can be given here. Cf. Doe, *Fundamental Authority,* 78–80, 83, 179: "The will of the community, in its creation of customary law, is subordinate to the authority of reason. And it is from the presence of this general natural law outlook that the basic tension in late medieval law arises. It is clearest in Fortescue, for, at the same time as saying 'law is that which is consented to by king and people,' and 'bad rules are still laws,' he also says 'law is that

which is authorized by divinely created natural law,' and 'bad rules, if they offend natural law, are not laws at all' " (83).

22. Matt. 7:12; Gratian, *Decretum* I.1; *Nature* I.10 and c. 12. Aquinas writes: "Wherefore Gratian, after saying that 'the natural law is what is contained in the Law and the Gospel,' adds at once, by way of example, 'by which everyone is commanded to do to others as he would be done by' " (*The Political Ideas of St. Thomas Aquinas: Representative Selections*, ed. Dino Bigongiari [New York: Hafner Press, 1969], 50 [text of Aquinas, *Summa theologiae I–II*, quest. 94, art. 4, reply obj. 1]). For detailed discussion of this subject see Harold J. Berman, *Law and Revolution: The Formation of the Western Legal Tradition* (Cambridge: Harvard University Press, 1983), 143–98; Brian Tierney, *The Idea of Natural Rights: Studies on Natural Rights, Natural Law, and Church Law, 1150–1625* (Atlanta: Scholars Press, 1997), chap. 2. For "Reason" as the synonym of "natural law" in English jurisprudence see the citation of Saint Germain in Essay 7, Note 25, and the accompanying text.

23. *Nature* I.25; *Praise* c. 37; *Governance* c. 8.

24. That is, *servus servorum Dei: Nature*, II.4; *Governance* c. 8.

25. *Nature* I.7 and c. 9; *Praise* cc. 9 and 12. Cf. Gen. 10:8–9.

26. *Nature* I.1.

27. *Nature* I.57.

28. *Praise* c. 42. "Where the spirit of the Lord *is*, there *is* liberty" (2 Cor. 3:17); "Stand fast in the liberty wherewith Christ hath made us free, and be not entangled again with the yoke of bondage" (Gal. 5:1).

29. *Praise* cc. 32, 36.

Essay 7. American Religion and Higher Law

1. Edward S. Corwin, *The "Higher Law" Background of American Constitutional Law* (1928, 1929; rpt. Ithaca: Cornell University Press, 1955). The present essay originated as a talk to the Philadelphia Society during its annual meeting, held in Philadelphia, Pennsylvania, in April 1997, and is previously unpublished.

2. Arthur L. Harding et al., eds., *Origins of the Natural Law Tradition* (Port Washington, N.Y.: Kennikat Press, 1954), vi.

3. George C. Christie and Patrick H. Martin, eds., *Jurisprudence: Text and Readings on the Philosophy of Law*, 2d ed. (St. Paul: West Pub. Co., 1995), 119. Cf. Heinrich A. Rommen, *The Natural Law: A Study in Legal and Social History and Philosophy*, trans. Thomas R. Hanley, intro. Russell Hittinger (German, 1936; English, 1947; rpt. Indianapolis: Liberty Fund, 1998).

4. *Calder v. Bull*, 3 Dall. (3 U.S.) 386 (1798). For discussion see Ellis Sandoz, *Conceived in Liberty: American Individual Rights Today* (North Scituate, Mass.: Duxbury Press, 1978), 8, 28–30, 33, 39, 49, 51, 56–61, 222–28, and

A Government of Laws: Political Theory, Religion, and the American Founding (Baton Rouge: Louisiana State University Press, 1990), 157–60, 192–96, 209–11; also Robert Lowery Clinton, *God and Man in the Law: The Foundations of Anglo-American Constitutionalism* (Lawrence: University Press of Kansas, 1997), esp. 129–70.

5. Quoted to the present effect by the editor in Algernon Sidney, *Discourses Concerning Government*, ed. Thomas G. West (Indianapolis: Liberty Fund, 1996), xxiii.

6. "Rebellion to tyrants is obedience to God" is the "supposititious epitaph" of John Bradshaw, president of the court that condemned King Charles I to death in 1649, and is inscribed on a cannon near his tomb in Martha Bay, Jamaica. Benjamin Franklin seems to have had a hand in communicating the epitaph to Jefferson. John Bartlett, *Familiar Quotations . . .* , 11th ed. (Garden City, N.Y.: Garden City Pub. Co., 1944), 939–40, and the sources cited therein. The complete inscription was published in Franklin's *Pennsylvania Evening Post*, December 14, 1775, and is reproduced in Benjamin Franklin, *Writings*, ed. J. A. Leo Lemay (New York: Library of America, 1987), 743–44. For full discussion see Dumas Malone, *Jefferson and His Time*, vol. 1, *Jefferson the Virginian* (Boston: Little, Brown and Co., 1948), 242n14, and the sources cited therein.

7. James Madison, "Memorial and Remonstrance," in *The Papers of James Madison*, ed. William T. Hutchinson et al., 17 vols. to date (Chicago: University of Chicago Press; Charlottesville: University Press of Virginia, 1962–), 8:298–302 (for analysis see Essay 5 herein); Christian de Cherge, "Last Testament," *First Things* 65 (August/September 1996): 21.

8. Quoted from Corinne Weston, "Epilogue: Diverse Viewpoints on Ancient Constitutionalism," in *Roots of Liberty: Magna Carta, Ancient Constitution, and the Anglo-American Tradition of Rule of Law*, ed. Ellis Sandoz (Columbia: University of Missouri Press, 1993), 232–51 at 234–35.

9. See Bernard Schwartz, ed., *The Great Rights of Mankind: A History of the American Bill of Rights*, 2 vols. (New York: Chelsea House, 1971), 1:8–14 and passim; also Stephen D. White, *Sir Edward Coke and "The Grievances of the Commonwealth," 1621–1628* (Chapel Hill: University of North Carolina Press, 1979).

10. Sir Edward Coke, *Second Part of the Institutes of the Laws of England . . .* (1641; London: M. Flesher and R. Young, 1642), 3, 47.

11. John Phillip Reid, *The Concept of Liberty in the Age of the American Revolution* (Chicago: University of Chicago Press, 1988), 120. In the manner of Edmund Burke, Reid argues prescription rather than theory. But it is worthwhile to recall Montesquieu's formulation: "liberty can consist only in having the power of doing what one should want to do and in no way being constrained to do what one should not want to do. . . . Liberty is the right to do everything the laws permit; and if one citizen could do what they forbid, he would no longer have liberty because the others would likewise have this same power" (Charles de Secondat, baron de Montesquieu, *The*

Spirit of Laws [1748; bk. XI, chap. 3], trans. Anne M. Cohler et al. [Cambridge: Cambridge University Press, 1989], 155).

12. *The Federalist,* ed. Jacob E. Cooke (Middletown, Conn.: Wesleyan University Press, 1961), 247 (No. 38), 250–58 (Nos. 39–40) for compound mixed republic, 327–28 (No. 47), 349–53 (No. 51). Publius quotes the Constitution of Massachusetts—1780, part the first, art. XXX; see Francis N. Thorpe, ed., *The Federal and State Constitutions, Colonial Charters, and Other Organic Laws of the United States,* part I, ed. Ben Perley Poore (Washington, D.C.: Government Printing Office, 1907), 960; cf. Montesquieu, *Spirit of Laws,* bk. 11, chap. 6. Prepared under the watchful eye of John Adams, this was "the great document that contemporaries eventually recognized as joining the American need for government to the British principle of ordered liberty through law" (Reid, *Concept of Liberty,* 121). On the transition from English to American constitutionalism more generally see Donald S. Lutz, *Popular Consent and Popular Control: Whig Political Theory in the Early State Constitutions* (Baton Rouge: Louisiana State University Press, 1980), esp. 238. For a revisionist (and interesting, although ultimately unpersuasive) account of American liberty see Barry Alan Shain, *The Myth of American Individualism: The Protestant Origins of American Political Thought* (Princeton: Princeton University Press, 1994).

13. *The Federalist,* ed. Cooke, 578, 580 (No. 84).

14. John 8:32; cf. Plato, *Republic* 435ff; *Laws* 698f.; Cicero: "Est quidem vera lex recta ratio naturae congruens, diffusa in omnes, constans, sempiterna, quae vocet ad officium iubendo, vetando a fraude deterreat" (*Republic* III.22.33, recovered from Lactantius, *Institutes* VI.8.6–9; quoted from Cicero, *De re publica, de legibus,* Loeb Edition no. 213, trans. and ed. Clinton W. Keyes [Cambridge: Harvard University Press, 1928], 210–11); cf. Cicero, *Laws* I.7.23, in ibid., 320–23.

15. Cf. Plato, *Republic,* VIII.14–19, 562a–569c, which concludes: "this is at last tyranny open and avowed . . . the *demos* trying to escape the smoke of submission to the free would have plunged into the fire of enslavement to slaves, and in exchange for that excessive and unseasonable liberty has clothed itself in the garb of the most cruel and bitter servile servitude" (quoted from Plato, *The Republic,* 2 vols., Loeb Edition no. 276, trans. and ed. Paul Shorey [Cambridge: Harvard University Press, 1935], 2:333); cf. Aristotle, *Politics* 1287a20–37, where the rule of law is commended—on the basis of the frailty of reason and virtue when confronted with the passions present in every man. This theory of human nature and its implications is shared by *Publius:* "In all very numerous assemblies, of whatever characters composed, passion never fails to wrest the scepter from reason. Had every Athenian citizen been a Socrates; every Athenian assembly would still have been a mob" (*The Federalist,* ed. Cooke, 374 [No. 55]).

16. Coke, *Second Institutes,* 47.

17. Quoted and abstracted from Camden's speech as given in J. W. Gough, *Fundamental Law in English Constitutional History* (1955; corrected

ed., Oxford: Clarendon Press, 1961), 193–94, citing and summarizing *Parliamentary History* 16:168, 178. For James Otis, see *Pamphlets of the American Revolution, 1750–1776*, ed. Bernard Bailyn (Cambridge: Harvard University Press, 1965), 1:409–17.

18. Nimrod (Gen. 10:8–9) as the emblem of tyranny par excellence is invoked by Sir John Fortescue, *In Praise of the Laws of England* (chap. 12) and elsewhere; see Fortescue, *On the Laws and Governance of England*, ed. Shelley Lockwood (Cambridge: Cambridge University Press, 1997), 19; cf. Essay 6 herein. Natural law as teaching unappealable rule of an absolute king is set forth in James I's *The Trewe Law of Free Monarchies . . .* [1598], reprinted in King James VI and I, *Political Writings*, ed. Johan P. Sommerville (Cambridge: Cambridge University Press, 1994), 62–84, and defended in the writings of Sir Robert Filmer and Thomas Hobbes—not to mention more recent authors.

19. Thomas Aquinas, *Summa theologiae* I–II, quest. 91, art. 6, quoted from *The Political Ideas of St. Thomas Aquinas: Representative Selections*, ed. Dino Bigongiari (New York: Hafner Press, 1953), 21–22; also Saint Thomas Aquinas, *Summa theologiae, 1a2ae, Questio 94*, Latin text and English translation, introductions, notes, appendixes, and glossaries, Blackfriars Edition, vol. 13 (London: Eyre and Spottiswoode, 1963), 74–97. For the pertinence of the classical and medieval theory of natural law to the American context, see Sandoz, *A Government of Laws*, esp. 189–200; also James Tully, *A Discourse on Property: John Locke and His Adversaries* (Cambridge: Cambridge University Press, 1980) and *An Approach to Political Philosophy: Locke in Contexts* (Cambridge: Cambridge University Press, 1993). For a clarification of the often ill understood terms of the debate over positivism (legal and otherwise) and its deficiencies, see Leszek Kolakowski, *The Alienation of Reason: A History of Positivist Thought*, trans. Norbert Guterman (Garden City, N.Y.: Doubleday, 1969), esp. chap. 1; for a concise critique of positivism in political and legal studies see Eric Voegelin, *The New Science of Politics: An Introduction* (Chicago: University of Chicago Press, 1952), 1–26; also Ellis Sandoz, "The Philosophical Science of Politics beyond Behavioralism," in *The Post-Behavioral Era: Perspectives on Political Science*, ed. George J. Graham and George W. Carey (New York: David McKay Co., 1972), 285–305; and Ellis Sandoz, *The Voegelinian Revolution: A Biographical Introduction* (Baton Rouge: Louisiana State University Press, 1981), 188–216. Also see Eric Voegelin, *The Collected Works of Eric Voegelin*, vol. 27, *The Nature of the Law and Related Legal Writings*, ed. John William Corrington, Robert A. Pascal, and James L. Babin (1991; available Columbia: University of Missouri Press, 1999).

As has been observed, "The positivist rationalist [i.e., most contemporary American and British intellectuals who may at the same time also be Marxists] has grounds for concern . . . about a renascent 'irrationalist' barbarism. What he does not appreciate . . . is that his own impoverished philosophy is a major cause of what he fears" (Thomas A. Spragens Jr., *The Irony of Liberal Reason* [Chicago: University of Chicago Press, 1981], 310; cf. chap. 8 passim.)

20. Cf. Verna May Hall, ed., *The Christian History of the American Revolution* (San Francisco: Foundation for American Christian Education, 1976), esp. xxiii–xxxvi; more generally, J. C. D. Clark, *The Language of Liberty, 1660–1832: Political Discourse and Social Dynamics in the Anglo-American World* (Cambridge: Cambridge University Press, 1994), 56–57, 382–91.

21. Quoted from *Records of the Federal Convention of 1787*, ed. Max Farrand, 4 vols. (1911; rev. ed. 1937; rpt. New Haven: Yale University Press, 1966), 1:450–52.

22. Adams to Jefferson, June 28, 1813, quoted from *The Adams-Jefferson Letters: The Complete Correspondence between Thomas Jefferson and Abigail and John Adams*, ed. Lester J. Cappon, 2 vols. in 1 (1959; rpt. New York: Simon and Schuster, 1971), 2:339–40.

23. Meyer Reinhold, *Classica Americana: The Greek and Roman Heritage in the United States* (Detroit: Wayne State University Press, 1984), esp. 23–49.

24. Quoted from Corwin, *"Higher Law" Background*, 10. See note 14, above.

25. T. F. T. Plucknett and J. L. Barton, eds., *St. German's Doctor and Student* ([1523]; London: Selden Society, 1974), 13–15.

26. Ralph Barton Perry, *Puritanism and Democracy* (New York: Vanguard Press, 1944), 82–83.

27. *Works of the Reverend John Witherspoon*, 4 vols. (Philadelphia: William Woodward, 1800–1801), 4:21. "Witherspoon was probably the most influential teacher in the entire history of American education. . . . There were times when the Constitutional Convention must have looked like a reunion of Princetonians" (Garry Wills, *Explaining America: The Federalist* [1981; rpt. Harmondsworth: Penguin Books, 1982], 18–19). Cf. M. E. Bradford, *A Worthy Company: Brief Lives of the Framers of the United States Constitution* (Marlborough, N.H.: Plymouth Rock Foundation, 1982).

28. Brian Tierney, *The Idea of Natural Rights: Studies on Natural Rights, Natural Law, and Church Law, 1150–1650* (Atlanta: Scholars Press, 1997), 35— quoting and rejecting as untenable the views of Leo Strauss and Walter Berns.

29. Sidney, *Discourses*, ed. West, 49.

30. Ibid., 357n, 432.

31. Ibid., 403, 416, 405–6; emphasis added.

32. Ibid., 510.

33. Ibid., 519.

34. Ibid., 210, 359, 436.

35. Ibid., 380, 355.

36. Ibid., 372–73.

37. Quotations and summarizing paraphrase from *Summa theologiae I–II*, quest. 94, arts. 2, 4, substantially as given in *Political Ideas of St. Thomas Aquinas*, ed. Bigongiari, 42–54; augmented from Aquinas, *Summa theologiae*, Blackfriars Edition, 77–83, 86–91; citing Gratian, *Decretum* 1.1.

38. Cf. Friedrich A. Hayek, *The Constitution of Liberty*, Gateway Edition

(Chicago: Henry Regnery Co., 1960), chap. 11 and 457n4; on Locke and Hooker see Locke, *Two Treatises of Government: A Critical Edition with an Introduction and Apparatus Criticus,* ed. Peter Laslett (1963; student ed., Cambridge: Cambridge University Press, 1988), 56–58 and passim (with a bibliography). While we say little about him here, the stature and importance of Richard Hooker are hard to exaggerate, as J. W. Allen rightly insists: "Not merely as a controversialist but as a political thinker, he was incomparably the greatest Englishman of the sixteenth century and on the Continent had few compeers" (*A History of Political Thought in the Sixteenth Century* [1928; rpt. London: Methuen, 1967], 184).

39. See *Political Sermons of the American Founding Era, 1730–1805,* ed. Ellis Sandoz (Indianapolis: Liberty Fund, 1991), for a sampling of this rich literature with bibliography. A separate index to *Political Sermons* was published in 1997 by Liberty Fund, and a second edition in two volumes was published in 1998.

Essay 8. The Crisis of Civic Consciousness: Nihilism and Resistance

1. George Washington before Congress, December 7, 1796, and Thomas Jefferson to James Madison, February 17, 1826, both quoted from Bernard Crick, *The American Science of Politics: Its Origins and Conditions* (Berkeley and Los Angeles: University of California Press, 1967), 3.

2. Leszek Kolakowski, "The Idolatry of Politics," in *Modernity on Endless Trial* (Chicago: University of Chicago Press, 1990), 146–61 at 149. Delivered as the Fifteenth Jefferson Lecture in the Humanities on May 7, 1986; emphasis added.

3. Diagnosis of the modern crisis in terms of social amnesia was explicit in Eric Voegelin's *Order and History* from its beginning; see vol. 1, *Israel and Revelation* (1956; available Columbia: University of Missouri Press, 1999), ix (first page of preface). It continued as a principal theme in his later work, as the title of his 1966 *Anamnesis* (Munich: Piper Verlag, 1966) intimates; and the introduction he wrote in 1977 for its English translation is entitled, with a bow to Marcel Proust, "Remembrance of Things Past" (*Anamnesis,* trans. and ed. Gerhart Niemeyer [1978; Columbia: University of Missouri Press, 1989], 3–13). See Essay 10 herein for further discussion. The theme is powerfully taken up from a related perspective by Jaroslav Pelikan in "Pernicious Amnesia: Combating the Epidemic," Response to the Conferral of the Inaugural Jacques Barzun Award, American Academy for Liberal Education (Washington, D.C., November 8, 1997), who classifies himself as "an 'amnesiologist' in the department of epidemiology of the school of public health, because I have spent a scholarly lifetime trying to combat an epidemic of pernicious amnesia" (MS, p. 2). Last, we may also notice that

Michael Oakeshott's critique of gnostic rationalism and appeal to tradition and the *continuity* principle share much with the perspective we have here adopted and that is reflected in the writings of Kolakowski, Voegelin, and Pelikan. See his *Rationalism in Politics and Other Essays,* new and expanded ed., ed. Timothy Fuller (1962; Indianapolis: Liberty Fund, 1991), esp. 6, 20, 60–62, 88, 396, 398.

4. David Ramsay, *The History of the American Revolution,* ed. Lester H. Cohen, 2 vols. (Indianapolis: Liberty Fund, 1990), 2:667.

5. Ellis Sandoz, *A Government of Laws: Political Theory, Religion, and the American Founding* (Baton Rouge: Louisiana State University Press, 1990), 239.

6. The "crisis" of our civilization is an old theme, of course, one associated most readily with Oswald Spengler. Perhaps it has only become more crassly evident of late. Cf. John H. Hallowell, *The Moral Foundation of Democracy* (Chicago: University of Chicago Press, 1954); Ronald William Dworkin, *The Rise of the Imperial Self: America's Culture Wars in Augustinian Perspective* (Lanham, Md.: Rowman and Littlefield, 1996); Samuel P. Huntington, *The Clash of Civilizations and the Remaking of World Order* (New York: Simon and Schuster, 1996); William Ophuls, *Requiem for Modern Politics: The Political Tragedy of the Enlightenment* (Boulder: Westview Press, 1998).

7. Quotations from Eric Voegelin, *Science, Politics, and Gnosticism: Two Essays,* trans. William J. Fitzpatrick, intro. Ellis Sandoz, Gateway Edition (1968; Washington, D.C.: Regnery Publishing Co., 1997), 24–25.

8. See Essay 4 and the literature cited therein; M. Stanton Evans, *The Theme Is Freedom: Religion, Politics, and the American Revolution* (Washington, D.C.: Regnery Publishing Co., 1994), esp. 131–48; Forrest McDonald, *Novus Ordo Seclorum: The Intellectual Origins of the Constitution* (Lawrence: University Press of Kansas, 1985), esp. 42–46, 159–62; also Kolakowski, "The Idolatry of Politics."

9. The classic statement of the consensus at the time of the framing of the Constitution is *Federalist No. 2.* For a standard presentation of the constitutional aspects of the Civil War and Reconstruction see Alfred H. Kelley and Winfred A. Harbison, *The American Constitution: Its Origins and Development,* 5th ed. (New York: W. W. Norton, 1976), 354–467; for a recent analysis see Marshall L. DeRosa, *The Confederate Constitution of 1861: An Inquiry into American Constitutionalism* (Columbia: University of Missouri Press, 1991).

10. Edmund Burke, *Letters on a Regicide Peace (I),* in *The Writings and Speeches of Edmund Burke,* 12 vols. (Boston: Little, Brown, 1901), 5:308–10. For a broader analysis, one encompassing recent European history, of the impact of the "death of God" see Jacob L. Talmon, *The Myth of the Nation and Vision of Revolution: Ideological Polarization in the Twentieth Century,* intro. Irving Louis Horowitz (New Brunswick, N.J.: Transaction, 1991), esp. 3, 542–54.

11. Translated as "Yet Another Effort, Frenchmen, if You Would Become Republicans," in *The Marquis de Sade: The Complete Justine, Philosophy in the Bedroom, and other Writings,* ed. Richard Seaver and Austryn Wainhouse, intro. Jean Paulhan and Maurice Blanchot (New York: Grove Press, 1965), 296–339. It apparently was first published as a digression in the "Fifth Dialogue" of *La Philosophie dans le boudoir in 1795.* See *Oeuvres complètes,* ed. Gilbert Lely, 16 vols. in 8, Tête de Feuilles edition (Paris: P. Seglers, 1973), 3:478–524; cf. Pierre Klossowski, "Sade et la Révolution," in *Oeuvres complètes,* 4:349–65.

12. Friedrich Nietzsche, *The Will to Power,* trans. W. Kaufmann and R. J. Hollindale, ed. W. Kaufmann (New York: Vintage Books, 1968), 7, 14; hereafter cited in the text as *WP.* Cf. Friedrich Nietzsche, *Der Wille zur Macht: Versucht einer umwertung aller Werte,* ed. Alfred Baeumler (Stuttgart: Alfred Kröner Verlag, 1930), 7, 16.

13. *The Portable Nietzsche,* ed. and trans. Walter Kaufmann (1954; rpt. Harmondsworth: Penguin Books, 1976), 95–96 (sec. 125), 447–48 (sec. 343); hereafter cited in the text as *PN.*

14. Nietzsche, *Morgenroethe,* sec. 79, as given in Eric Voegelin, *The New Science of Politics: An Introduction* (Chicago: University of Chicago Press, 1952), 129.

15. There is ample literature; particularly recommended are Henri de Lubac, *The Drama of Atheist Humanism,* trans. Edith M. Riley (London: Sheed and Ward, 1949), 1–73; Karl Löwith, *From Hegel to Nietzsche,* trans. David E. Green (New York: Holt, Rinehart and Winston, 1964), esp. 175–200, and *Nietzsches Philosophie der ewigen Widerkehr des Gleichen* (Stuttgart: Kohlhammer, 1956); Karl Jaspers, *Nietzsche: An Introduction to the Understanding of His Philosophical Activity* (Chicago: University of Chicago Press, 1965); Eric Voegelin, "Wisdom and the Magic of the Extreme," in *The Collected Works of Eric Voegelin,* vol. 12, *Published Essays, 1966–1985,* ed. Ellis Sandoz (1990; available Columbia: University of Missouri Press, 1999), 315–75; and David Walsh, *After Ideology: Recovering the Spiritual Foundations of Freedom* (1990; rpt. Washington, D.C.: Catholic University of America Press, 1995), esp. 9–41.

16. Stanley Rosen, *Nihilism: A Philosophical Essay* (New Haven: Yale University Press, 1969), 73. For a perspective on such destruction in the realm of constitutional law see Michael W. McConnell, " 'God Is Dead and We have Killed Him!': Freedom of Religion in the Post-Modern Age," *Brigham Young University Law Review,* 1993, no. 1, 163–88. See Essay 5 herein for discussion.

17. The subject is most readily studied in Voegelin, *Science, Politics, and Gnosticism,* 35–50; cf. Ellis Sandoz, *The Voegelinian Revolution: A Biographical Introduction* (Baton Rouge: Louisiana State University Press, 1981), chap. 4 and passim, esp. 239–43, and *Political Apocalypse: A Study of Dostoevsky's "Grand Inquisitor"* (Baton Rouge: Louisiana State University Press, 1971), esp. 221–54 (2d ed. Wilmington, Del.: Intercollegiate Studies Institute,

forthcoming). Closely related is the important new analysis of antiphilosophy in David Hume's distinction between "true" and "false" philosophy presented by Donald W. Livingston in *Philosophical Melancholy and Delirium: Hume's Pathology of Philosophy* (Chicago: University of Chicago Press, 1998).

18. Lionel Trilling, *Beyond Culture: Essays on Literature and Learning* (New York: Viking Press, 1965), 26; quoted from Gertrude Himmelfarb, *On Looking into the Abyss: Untimely Thoughts on Culture and Society* (New York: A. A. Knopf, 1994), 4.

19. Voegelin, *Science, Politics, and Gnosticism*, 75.

20. George Orwell, *1984* (1949; New York: New American Library, 1961), "Appendix: The Principles of Newspeak," 246. Especially opposition to radical secularization has generated a substantial literature from many perspectives, including John Davison Hunter, *Culture Wars: The Struggle to Define America* (New York: Basic Books, 1991); Stephen Bates, *Battleground: One Mother's Crusade, the Religious Right, and the Struggle for Control of Our Classrooms* (New York: Poseidon, 1993); Stephen L. Carter, *The Culture of Disbelief: How American Law and Politics Trivialize Religious Devotion* (New York: Basic Books, 1993); Richard John Neuhaus, *The Naked Public Square: Religion and Democracy in America* (Grand Rapids, Mich.: W. B. Eerdmans, 1984); John W. Whitehead, *Religious Apartheid: The Separation of Religion from American Public Life* (Chicago: Moody Press, 1994) and *The Second American Revolution* (Elgin, Ill.: Crossway Books, 1982); Daniel L. Dreisbach, ed., *Religion and Politics in the Early Republic: Jasper Adams and the Church-State Debate* (Lexington: University of Kentucky Press, 1996); and Noel B. Reynolds and Cole Durham, eds., *Religious Liberty in Western Thought* (Atlanta: Scholars Press, 1996).

21. Huntington, *Clash of Civilizations*, 306–7. The Theodore Roosevelt quotation is taken by Huntington from Arthur M. Schlesinger Jr., *The Disuniting of America: Reflections on a Multicultural Society* (New York: W. W. Norton, 1992), 118. Cf. Arnold J. Toynbee, "The Prospects of Western Civilization," in *A Study of History*, 12 vols. (London: Oxford University Press, 1934–1961), 9:406–644.

22. Crick, *American Science of Politics*, 247–48.

23. Gal. 5:3; cf. Matt. 13:33.

Essay 9. Eric Voegelin a Conservative?

1. This previously unpublished essay was written in spring 1997.

2. Eric Voegelin, *The Collected Works of Eric Voegelin*, vol. 1, *On the Form of the American Mind*, trans. Ruth Hein, ed. Jürgen Gebhardt and Barry Cooper (1995; available Columbia: University of Missouri Press, 1999).

3. *Conversations with Eric Voegelin*, ed. R. Eric O'Connor (Montreal: Thomas More Institute, 1980), 65–66.

Essay 10. Voegelin's Philosophy of History and Human Affairs

1. Voegelin's works will be cited using the following abbreviations:

CW *The Collected Works of Eric Voegelin,* projected 34 vols. These volumes will be available Columbia: University of Missouri Press as of 1999: Vol. 1, *On the Form of the American Mind,* trans. Ruth Hein, ed. Jürgen Gebhardt and Barry Cooper (1995). Vol. 2, *Race and State,* trans. Ruth Hein, ed. Klaus Vondung (1997). Vol. 3, *History of the Race Idea,* trans. Ruth Hein, ed. Klaus Vondung (1998). Vol. 4, *The Authoritarian State: An Essay on the Problem of the Austrian State,* ed. Gilbert Weiss (1999). Vol. 12, *Published Essays, 1966–1985,* ed. Ellis Sandoz (1990). Vol. 19, *History of Political Ideas,* vol. I, *Hellenism, Rome, and Early Christianity,* ed. Athanasios Moulakis, general introduction to the series Thomas A. Hollweck and Ellis Sandoz (1997). Vol. 20, *History of Political Ideas,* vol. II, *The Middle Ages to Aquinas,* ed. Peter von Sivers (1997). Vol. 21, *History of Political Ideas,* vol. III, *The Later Middle Ages,* ed. David Walsh (1998). Vol. 22, *History of Political Ideas,* vol. IV, *Renaissance and Reformation,* ed. David L. Morse and William M. Thompson (1998). Vol. 23, *History of Political Ideas,* vol. V, *Religion and the Rise of Modernity,* ed. James L. Wiser (1998). Vol. 24, *History of Political Ideas,* vol. VI, *Revolution and the New Science,* ed. Barry Cooper (1998). Vol. 25, *History of Political Ideas,* vol. VII, *The New Order and Last Orientation,* ed. Jürgen Gebhardt and Thomas A. Hollweck (1999). Vol. 26, *History of Political Ideas,* Vol. VIII, *Crisis and the Apocalypse of Man,* ed. David Walsh (1999). Vol. 27, *The Nature of the Law and Related Legal Writings,* ed. Robert A. Pascal, James L. Babin, and John W. Corrington (1991). Vol. 28, *What Is History? And Other Late Unpublished Writings,* ed. Thomas A. Hollweck and Paul Caringella (1990). Vol. 31, *Hitler and the Germans,* ed. Detlev Clemens and Brendan Purcell (1999).

NSP *The New Science of Politics: An Introduction.* Chicago: University of Chicago Press, 1952; rpt. 1987 with a foreword by Dante Germino.

OH *Order and History,* 5 vols. Available Columbia: University of Missouri Press, 1999. Vol. 1, *Israel and Revelation* (1956); vol. 2, *The World of the Polis* (1957); vol. 3, *Plato and Aristotle* (1957); vol. 4, *The Ecumenic Age* (1974); vol. 5, *In Search of Order* (1987). *Israel and Revelation* is cited herein as *OH1.*

2. The present essay—apart from the epilogue—concentrates on Voegelin's writings themselves with little direct reference to the burgeoning secondary literature or to the work of other writers addressing related issues. The primary intent is to examine an extensive body of work still surprisingly unfamiliar to many political theorists almost a half century after *The New Science of Politics* first saw the light. There exists, indeed, a substantial secondary literature, and those interested in it can consult for guidance the excellent compilation of Geoffrey L. Price, ed., *Eric Voegelin:*

A Classified Bibliography, Bulletin of the John Rylands University Library of Manchester 76 (1994): 1–180. This extensive bibliography is periodically updated electronically in the *Voegelin—Research News,* archive address: http://vax2.concordia.ca/vorenews. Another help for readers new to Voegelin's writings is the glossary in Eugene Webb's *Eric Voegelin: Philosopher of History* (Seattle: University of Washington Press, 1981), 277–89. Since 1986, the Eric Voegelin Society has conducted programs of up to nine panels in conjunction with the American Political Science Association's annual meetings; for the thirteenth annual meeting in 1997 see *PS: Political Science and Politics* 30 (1997): esp. 311, 355, and the Eric Voegelin Institute website at http://www2.artsci.lsu.edu/ voegelin/voegelin.html for additional program, conference, and bibliographic information.

3. *Time Magazine,* March 9, 1953, pp. 57–60.

4. For a detailed account of these matters see Thomas A. Hollweck and Ellis Sandoz, "General Introduction to the Series," *CW19 (History of Political Ideas* I), 1–48.

5. Ibid., 10. Letter to Henry B. McCurdy, July 5, 1954, Eric Voegelin Papers, Hoover Institution Archives, box 24, file 8.

6. *CW12,* 265–91; *CW28,* 173–231; *OH5,* passim.

7. Cf. Eric Voegelin, *Autobiographical Reflections,* ed. Ellis Sandoz (1989; available Columbia: University of Missouri Press, 1999), 93–107.

8. Eric Voegelin, *Wissenschaft, Politik und Gnosis,* inaugural lecture at the University of Munich (Munich: Kösel Verlag, 1959), 33. English edition: *Science, Politics and Gnosticism: Two Essays,* trans. William J. Fitzpatrick, intro. Ellis Sandoz, Gateway Edition (1968; rpt. Washington, D.C.: Regnery Publishing Co., 1997), 15. The 1997 ed. is repaginated and indexed.)

9. Cf. *OH4,* 11–30, 227–38.

10. On the last see Essay 8 herein.

11. Summarizing the appendix to "Reason: The Classic Experience," reproduced in Ellis Sandoz, *The Voegelinian Revolution: A Biographical Introduction* (Baton Rouge: Louisiana State University Press, 1981), 214–17; also *CW12,* 265–91.

12. *OH5,* chap. 1.

13. *Laws* 644d-645b, 903b–d; *OH3,* 231–36.

14. That is, the King James Version (or Authorized Version) of the Bible, first translated into English and published in 1611, by authorization of King James I.

15. *Conversations with Eric Voegelin,* ed. R. Eric O'Connor (Montreal: Thomas More Institute, 1980), 138. For this substantive and extended meaning of reason see the listing from Voegelin's 1967 Candler Lectures given in Ellis Sandoz, "The Philosophical Science of Politics beyond Behavioralism," in *The Post-Behavioral Era: Perspectives on Political Science,* ed. George J. Graham and George W. Carey (New York: David McKay Co., 1972), 285–305 at

301–2; also Ellis Sandoz, "Medieval Rationalism or Mystic Philosophy? Reflections on the Strauss-Voegelin Correspondence," in *Faith and Political Philosophy: The Correspondence between Leo Strauss and Eric Voegelin, 1934–1964*, trans. and ed. Peter Emberley and Barry Cooper (University Park: Pennsylvania State University Press, 1993), 297–319 at 308–10; Dante Germino, "Leo Strauss *versus* Eric Voegelin on Faith and Political Philosophy," *Revista internazionale di filosofia del diritto* 4th series, 72 (1995): 527–48. The detailed analysis underlying the summary given in the text is presented in "Reason: the Classic Experience," in *CW12*, 265–91; it is related to a comparative analysis of key philosophical and New Testament texts given in "The Gospel and Culture," in *CW12*, 172–212; also Voegelin's deathbed meditation entitled "Quod Deus Dicitur?" in *CW12*, 376–94. Rejection of the distinctions traditionally separating faith and reason as empirically insupportable is argued by Voegelin in "The Beginning and the Beyond: A Meditation on Truth," in *CW28*, 173–232: "We can no longer ignore that the symbols of 'Faith' express the responsive quest of man just as much as the revelatory appeal, and that the symbols of 'Philosophy' express the revelatory appeal just as much as the responsive quest. We must further acknowledge that the medieval tension between Faith and Reason derives from the origins of these symbols in the two different ethnic cultures of Israel and Hellas, that in the consciousness of Israelite prophets and Hellenic philosophers the differentiating experience of the divine Beyond was respectively focused on the revelatory appeal and the human quest" (211). See also Paul Caringella, "Voegelin: Philosopher of Divine Presence," in *Eric Voegelin's Significance for the Modern Mind*, ed. Ellis Sandoz (Baton Rouge: Louisiana State University Press, 1991), 174–205. The Thomas Altizer and Voegelin exchange in *Eric Voegelin's Thought: A Critical Appraisal*, ed. Ellis Sandoz (Durham: Duke University Press, 1982), 179–98, is particularly relevant, along with other essays included and Voegelin's own epilogue to the volume; see also *CW12*, 292–303.

16. "Immortality: Experience and Symbol," in *CW12*, 52–94 at 78.

17. See the analysis in Sandoz, *The Voegelinian Revolution*, 243–51.

18. William C. Havard, *The Recovery of Political Theory: Limits and Possibilities* (Baton Rouge: Louisiana State University Press, 1984), 97; internal quotes of Gregor Sebba are taken from his "The Present State of Political Theory," *Polity* 1 (1968): 259–70.

19. *The Collected Essays of Gregor Sebba: Truth, History and the Imagination*, ed. Helen Sebba, Aníbal A. Bueno, and Hendrikus Boers (Baton Rouge: Louisiana State University Press, 1991), 198.

20. See Sandoz, *The Voegelinian Revolution*, chap. 7, "*Principia Noetica:* The Voegelinian Revolution . . . ," 188–216. Good presentations of Voegelin's political science are given in Barry Cooper, *The Political Theory of Eric Voegelin* (Lewiston/Queenston: Edwin Mellen Press, 1986), *The Restoration of Political Science and the Crisis of Modernity* (Toronto: Edwin Mellen Press, 1989), and *Eric Voegelin and the Foundations of Modern Political Science* (Columbia:

University of Missouri Press, 1999). See also Dante Germino, *Beyond Ideology: The Revival of Political Theory* (1967; rpt. Chicago: University of Chicago Press, 1972), and John Ranieri, *Eric Voegelin and the Good Society* (Columbia: University of Missouri Press, 1995). Voegelin's work considered as a "new science" under the aspects of epistemology and ontology has been studied in the following three political science Ph.D. dissertations at Louisiana State University: Seung-Hyun Baek, "Reality and Knowledge in Voegelin's Political Philosophy" (1989); Charles Warren Burchfield, "Eric Voegelin's Mystical Epistemology and Its Influence on His Theories of Ethics and Politics" (1994); and Todd Eric Myers, "Nature and the Divine: Classical Greek Philosophy and the Political in the Thought of Leo Strauss and Eric Voegelin" (1997). Background in terms of the "German Context" of *Geisteswissenschaft* and *Staatslehre* is concisely given in the "Editors' Introduction" to *CW1*, ix–xxxv, where Jürgen Gebhardt outlines some of the key connections of Voegelin's work to Edmund Husserl, Max Scheler, and Karl Jaspers and discusses his exodus from the neo-Kantianism of his mentor, Hans Kelsen, and the "pure theory of law" *(Reine Rechtslehre)*. Voegelin's intentions are directly suggested by his early article "Zur Lehre von der Staatsform," *Zeitschrift für öffentliches Recht* 64 (1927): 572–608, and more fully in the manuscript fragment entitled "Herrschaftslehre und Rechtslehre," which dates from ca. 1931, and runs some 125 pages in typescript (Hoover Institution, Voegelin Archives, box 53, file 5). The developments of the early period in Voegelin's thought have been carefully studied by Sandro Chignola in "Fetischismus der Normen: Tra normativismo e sociologia; Eric Voegelin e la dottrina dello stato (1924–1938)," *Rivista Internazionale di Filosofia del Diritto*, ser. IV, 70 (1993): 515–65.

21. Cf. *NSP,* 31, 52, 117, 133. "Unoriginal thinking" is formulated in the essay "Equivalences of Experience and Symbolization" as follows: "The validating question will have to be: Do we have to ignore and eclipse a major part of the historical field in order to maintain the truth of the propositions, as the fundamentalist adherents of this or that ideological doctrine must do; or are the propositions recognizably *equivalent* with the symbols created by our predecessors in the search of truth about human existence? The test of truth, to put it pointedly, will be the *lack of originality in the propositions*" (*CW12,* 122; emphasis added).

22. Bernhard W. Anderson, "Politics and the Transcendent: Eric Voegelin's Philosophical and Theological Analysis of the Old Testament in the Context of the Ancient Near East," *Political Science Reviewer* 1 (1971): 3, and "Revisiting Voegelin's *Israel and Revelation* after Twenty-five Years" (conference paper, University of Manchester, July 1997), 1–2; cf. Bernhard W. Anderson, *"Israel and Revelation," Bible Review,* October 1997, pp. 17, 46–47. For detailed analysis of Voegelin's writings from the perspective of theology and religion see Michael P. Morrissey, *Consciousness and Transcendence: The Theology of Eric Voegelin* (Notre Dame: University of Notre Dame Press,

1994), esp. the comparison with Bernard Lonergan, 171–226; also John Kirby and William M. Thompson, eds., *Voegelin and the Theologian: Ten Studies in Interpretation*, Toronto Studies in Theology 10 (New York: Edwin Mellen Press, 1983); and William M. Thompson, *Christology and Spirituality* (New York: Crossroad Pub. Co., 1991), esp. chap. 2. Of particular interest for this dimension of Voegelin's work is *CW19*, esp. 30–47 and "Part Two: Christianity and Rome," 149–224. See also Glenn Hughes, *Mystery and Myth in the Philosophy of Eric Voegelin* (Columbia: University of Missouri Press, 1993).

23. The Weberian aspect of Voegelin's political science is discussed in *Autobiographical Reflections*, esp. 11–14, 16, 33, 45–46. It is the subject of a lively debate between Jürgen Gebhardt and Frederick G. Lawrence, who favors Voegelin the mystic-philosopher, in *International and Interdisciplinary Perspectives on Eric Voegelin*, ed. Stephen A. McKnight and Geoffrey L. Price (Columbia: University of Missouri Press, 1997), 10–58. This volume also includes a valuable topical bibliography by Price. That the imagined two Voegelins—scientist and mystic—are not mutually exclusive but complementary also can be seen from Voegelin's lecture "On the Greatness of Max Weber [1964]," which concludes by suggesting that Weber considered himself to be a mystic. See Eric Voegelin, *Ordnung, Bewusstsein, Geschichte: Späte Schriften—eine Auswahl*, ed. Peter J. Opitz (Stuttgart: Klett-Cotta, 1988), 78–98.

24. *Autobiographical Reflections*, 44.

25. See David J. Levy, *The Measure of Man: Incursions in Philosophical and Political Anthropology* (Columbia: University of Missouri Press, 1993), chap. 2; *Realism: An Essay in Interpretation and Social Reality* (Manchester: Carcanet New Press, 1981); and *Political Order: Philosophical Anthropology, Modernity, and the Challenge of Ideology* (Baton Rouge: Louisiana State University Press, 1987).

26. Eric Voegelin, "The Oxford Political Philosophers," *Philosophical Quarterly* 3 (1953): 97–114 at 114. The persons and works considered are indicated on p. 100.

27. David Levy explores this subject in the works cited in n. 25, above. The starting point for Voegelin, in his work of the 1930s, was the Platonic-Aristotelian and Christian anthropology of Max Scheler and of one of his mentors at Vienna, Othmar Spann. See Max Scheler, *Die Stellung des Menschen im Kosmos* (1928) as well as *Der Formalismus in der Ethik und die materiale Wertethik* (1913–1916), *Vom Umsturz der Werte* (1915), *Vom Ewigen im Menschen* (1921), and *Vom Wesen der Sympathie* (2d ed. 1923), all published in *Gesammelte Werke*, 9 vols. (Zurich and Munich: Francke Verlag, 1954–1976); Othmar Spann, *Gesellschaftslehre* (Leipzig: Quelle und Meyer, 1923). For discussion and analysis see William Petropoulos, "The Person as *Imago Dei*: Augustine and Max Scheler in Eric Voegelin's *Herrschaftslehre* and *The Political Religions*" (conference paper, 1993, 1997). Petropoulos concludes: "Meditation as the basic form of philosophizing, and the person as *imago Dei*,

remain of fundamental importance throughout Voegelin's philosophical career" (36). See also Udo Kessler, *Die Wiederentdeckung der Transzendenz: Ordnung von Mensch und Gesellschaft im Denken Eric Voegelins* (Würzburg: Königshausen and Neumann Verlag, 1995); Mendo Castro Henriques, "A Filosofia Civil de Eric Voegelin" (Ph.D. diss., Catholic University of Portugal, 1992).

28. Much of the secondary literature is taken up with these aspects of Voegelin's writings. To be mentioned here are only a few select items: Webb, *Eric Voegelin: Philosopher of History* and *Philosophers of Consciousness: Polanyi, Lonergan, Voegelin, Ricoeur, Girard, Kierkegaard* (Seattle: University of Washington Press, 1988); *L'Histoire et ses interprétations; Entretiens autour de Arnold Toynbee sous la direction de Raymond Aron* (Paris: Mouton, 1961); *Eric Voegelin's Search for Order in History*, ed. Stephen A. McKnight, expanded ed. (Lanham, Md.: University Press of America, 1987). The issues of modernity and gnosticism within Voegelin's theories of politics and history are addressed in Ellis Sandoz, *Political Apocalypse: A Study of Dostoevsky's "Grand Inquisitor"* (Baton Rouge: Louisiana State University Press, 1971); James V. Schall, *Reason, Revelation, and the Foundations of Political Philosophy* (Baton Rouge: Louisiana State University Press, 1987); Peter J. Opitz, ed., *Eric Voegelin, Alfred Schütz, Leo Strauss, Aron Gurwitsch: Briefwechsel über Die Neue Wissenschaft der Politik* (Freiburg/Munich: Karl Alber Verlag, 1993); Ted V. McAllister, *Revolt against Modernity: Leo Strauss, Eric Voegelin, and the Search for a Postliberal Order* (Lawrence: University Press of Kansas, 1996); Thomas Langan, *Being and Truth* (Columbia: University of Missouri Press, 1996); Stephen A. McKnight, *The Modern Age and the Recovery of Ancient Wisdom: A Reconsideration of Historical Consciousness, 1450–1650* (Columbia: University of Missouri Press, 1991); Stephen A. McKnight, ed., *Science, Pseudo-Science, and Utopianism in Early Modern Thought* (Columbia: University of Missouri Press, 1992), which examines the Hans Blumenberg, Karl Löwith, Voegelin debate over modernity; Dante Germino, *Political Philosophy and the Open Society* (Baton Rouge: Louisiana State University Press, 1982); Norman Cohn, *The Pursuit of the Millennium: Revolutionary Millenarians and Mystical Anarchists of the Middle Ages*, rev. enl. ed. (1970; rpt. New York: Oxford University Press, 1981); Klaus Vondung, *Die Apokalypse in Deutschland* (Munich: Deutscher Taschenbuch Verlag, 1988); David Walsh, *The Mysticism of Inner-Worldly Fulfillment: A Study of Jacob Boehme* (Gainesville: University Press of Florida, 1983); Gianfrancesco Zanetti, *La trascendenza e l'ordine saggio su Eric Voegelin* (Bologna: Cooperative Libraria Universitaria, 1989); Michael Franz, *Eric Voegelin and the Politics of Spiritual Revolt: The Roots of Modern Ideology* (Baton Rouge: Louisiana State University Press, 1992); Kenneth Keulman, *The Balance of Consciousness: Eric Voegelin's Political Theory* (University Park: Pennsylvania State University Press, 1990). On various aspects of liberalism: Karl Forster, ed., *Christentum und Liberalismus: Eric Voegelin, Erich Mende, Paul Mikat, Gustav Gundlach, Alexander Rüstow, Paul Luchtenberg, Wilhelm*

Geiger (Munich: Karl Zink Verlag, 1960); Ellis Sandoz, *A Government of Laws: Political Theory, Religion, and the American Founding* (Baton Rouge: Louisiana State University, 1990); David Walsh, *After Ideology: Recovering the Spiritual Foundations of Freedom* (1990; rpt. Washington, D.C.: Catholic University of America Press, 1995) and *The Growth of the Liberal Soul* (Columbia: University of Missouri Press, 1997); Sandoz, "The Crisis of Civic Consciousness" (Essay 8 herein); Henrik Syse, "Natural Law, Religion, and Rights: An Exploration of the Relationship between Natural Law and Natural Rights, with Special Emphasis on the Teachings of Thomas Hobbes and John Locke" (Ph.D. diss., University of Oslo, 1996).

29. "Die Person, sagten wir, sei der Schnittpunkt von göttlicher Ewigkeit und menschlicher Zeitlichkeit; in ihr offenbart sich die Endlichkeit also das Wesen der Welt. Person ist die Erfahrung der Grenze, an der ein Diesseitig-Endliches sich gegen ein Jenseitig-Unendliches absetzt" ("Herrschaftslehre," MS, 7).

30. In *Race and State* (*CW2*, see esp. 8–16, 19–36, 128–53) the author begins with a condemnation of the race "theorists'" "system of dogmas . . . that, in short, I will call the system of scientific superstition" (9). Voegelin's two race books are analyzed in Thomas W. Heilke, *Voegelin on the Idea of Race: An Analysis of Modern European Racism* (Baton Rouge: Louisiana State University Press, 1990); also Nils Winkler, "Philosophische Aspekte der Rassismus-Kritik Voegelins von 1933," Wissenschaftliche Hausarbeit zur Erlangung des akademischen Grades eines Magister Artium der Universität Hamburg (1997).

31. See Peter J. Opitz and Gregor Sebba, eds., *The Philosophy of Order: Essays on History, Consciousness, and Politics* (Stuttgart: Klett-Cotta, 1981), 74–90, 431–65.

32. Eric Voegelin, *Anamnesis*, trans. and ed. Gerhart Niemeyer (1978; rpt. Columbia: University of Missouri Press, 1990), 4–5; *CW12*, 306.

33. See "Introduction," *OH4*.

34. *CW21*, 76–77. This line of analysis is palpably continued and elaborated, with attention to what is here termed the intellectualist fallacy as a major defect, in the philosophies of history of Hegel and Jaspers, in Voegelin's late work; see esp. *OH4*, chap. 7, "Universal Humanity," 300–335.

35. *CW21*, 261–62; emphasis added. The critical updating of Aristotle's philosophical anthropology is a prominent subject of "What Is Political Reality?" (1966) in *Anamnesis*, 143–214; see the summary at 172–74.

36. *Science, Politics and Gnosticism*, 75.

37. Other contemporary authors whose work in some significant way is comparable to Voegelin's and/or influential upon it, and who are not otherwise cited or mentioned herein, include: Michael Oakeshott, Martin Heidegger, Alfred North Whitehead, Emmanuel Levinas, Talcott Parsons, Harry A. Wolfson, Martin Buber, Leszek Kolakowski, Albert Camus, Friedrich A. von Hayek, Carl Schmitt, Petirim Sorokin, Wolfhart Pannenberg, Étienne Gilson,

Hans Jonas, John Hallowell, Jacob Taubes, Gottfried von Haberler, Gerhart Niemeyer, Jacob L. Talmon, Hermann Broch, Thomas Mann, Robert Musil, Heimito von Doderer, Mircea Eliade, Karl Kraus, Albert Paris Gütersloh, Flannery O'Connor, Hans Urs von Balthasar, Geoffrey Barraclough, Maurice Natanson, Paul G. Kuntz, Arnold J. Toynbee—among many others, but the list already is too long. It can be filled out and supplemented from *Autobiographical Reflections*. See also Voegelin's two Festschriften: Alois Dempf, Hannah Arendt, and Friedrich Engel-Janosi, eds., *Politische Ordnung und Menschliche Existenz: Festgabe für Eric Voegelin zum 60. Geburtstag* (Munich: C. H. Beck, 1962), and Opitz and Sebba, eds., *Philosophy of Order*.

Index

Abolitionist movement, 90
Abraham, 137, 150, 159
Acton, Lord, 119
Acts, book of, 113, 117
Adams, John: and Backus, 193*n*41; on Christianity and founding of U.S., 67–68, 111, 184–85*n*9, 189*n*23; importance of, for U.S. society, 14, 137; influences on, 96; as lawyer, 107; on liberty, 67–68, 72, 184–85*n*9; on Massachusetts Constitution of 1780, 205*n*12; on religious liberty, 74
Aeschylus, 127
Afghanistan, 5
Agnoia (ignorance), 156
Allegory of the Cave, 166
Allen, Ethan, 49, 65
Allen, J. W., 208*n*38
Als ob, 26
America. *See* United States
America—My Country 'Tis of Thee, 105
American Bar Association, 16
American Revolution, 6, 7, 52, 57–64, 75, 111, 115, 126, 128, 184*n*7
Amor Dei (love of God), 72, 177*n*17
Amor sui (love of self), 177*n*17
Amos, 158
Amnesia. *See* Social amnesia
Anamnesis (Voegelin), 168, 208*n*3, 218*n*35
Anaximander, 44
Anderson, Bernhard, 165

Anglican Church and Anglicans, 77, 183*n*2
Anglican-Methodists, 54
Anselm of Canterbury, 100, 143, 145, 169
Anthropocentrism, 10
Antichrist (Nietzsche), 131
Anti-Federalists, 11, 19
Antigone, 38
Apeiron, 44, 148
Apocalypticism, 142
Aporein (question), 156
Aquinas. *See* Thomas Aquinas
Arendt, Hannah, 8
Aristotle: on *bios theoretikos* and civic life, 39; and Bruni, 202*n*15; and Fortescue, 98, 99, 101; on good, 120; on great chain of being, 44, 189*n*22; on *homonoia,* 177*n*17; on human nature, 107, 205*n*15; importance of, for U.S. society, 137; on law, 112; on natural and divine law, 110; on *nous* (Reason), 155; on *phronesis* (prudence), 176*n*7; on *politeia* (mixed regime), 21–22; and Sidney, 115; and Socrates, 29; and Solzhenitsyn, 10–11; on truth, 127; and Voegelin, 145, 168, 218*n*35
—Works: *Ethics,* 202*n*15; *Nicomachean Ethics,* 22, 118, 123; *Politics,* 22, 112, 123, 202*n*15, 205*n*15
Arminianism, 50
Aron, Raymond, 5

Phronimos (prudential virtuoso), 39, 176*n*7
Pietism, 77, 81
"Pink Coalition," 25–26
"Pink tank" episode, 25–26
Plato: on *bios theoretikos* and civic life, 39; and Bruni, 202*n*15; on disease *(nosos)* of soul and polity, 124; on divine Puppet Master, 149; on great chain of being, 44; on human nature, 107; importance of, for U.S. society, 137; on *mache athanatos,* 143; on *metaxy,* 133, 146, 148; Nietzsche on, 130; on *nosos* (disease), 124; on *nous* (Reason), 155; opposition of, to sophists, 142; relationship with Socrates, 165; and Sidney, 115; and Solzhenitsyn, 10–11; on truth, 127; on tyrannical man, 72; and Voegelin, 168
—Works: *Laws,* 18; *Republic,* 9, 134, 189*n*22, 205*n*15
Plato and Aristotle (Voegelin), 144, 145–46
Pneumatic apperception, 38, 146–49
Poetry. *See* Politics: of poetry
Poland, 5, 7–8, 27, 32, 33, 34
Politeia (mixed regime), 22
Political correctness, 36–37, 91, 128
"Political messianism," 22
Political science, teaching of, 122–23
Political sermons, 48–49, 56–62, 191*n*28, 196*n*58
Political Testament (Patočka), 10
Politics: as art as well as science, 40; of civility, 26–27; Fortescue as political philosopher, 14, 16, 95–103, 106, 110, 201*n*3, 206*n*18; and human beings as ungovernable, 39; of imperfection, 22–24; limitations on political power, 40–41; of moderation, 41; and paradigm of new politics, 10–12; of poetry, 1–12; and private property and security, 39, 40; of resistance, 134–38, 142–43, 147–49; of truth, 35–42. *See also* Government; Liberty; and specific countries

Politics (Aristotle), 22, 112, 123, 202*n*15, 205*n*15
Pope, Alexander, 44–45
Positivism, 104, 110, 128, 137, 165, 206*n*19
Pratt, Lord, 107, 109
Presbyterians, 54, 59, 62, 79, 82, 88, 114, 183*n*2
Press, freedom of, 20
Private property, 28–29, 39, 40
Prometheus, 127
Prometheus Bound (Aeschylus), 127
Property. *See* Private property
Prophets, 147, 154–55, 157–60
Protestantism. *See* Christianity; and specific Protestant groups
Proust, Marcel, 208*n*3
Proverbs, 1
Psalms, 11, 54, 58, 59, 113, 153–54, 180*n*32
Pseudo-Dionysius, 180*n*27
Psyche, 158
Puritanism, 50–51, 114
Purvey, John, 181*n*37

Quakers, 50, 54, 79, 88, 183*n*2

Race and State (Voegelin), 168, 218*n*30
Radical feminism, 128
Radio Act of 1926, 20
Ramsay, David, 124, 184*n*7, 199*n*71
Ratio, 102
Reagan, Ronald, 3, 197*n*60
Reason, 72, 112–13, 115–16, 140, 155–56, 214*n*15
Red Army, 2
Reid, John Phillip, 107, 204*n*11
Reinhold, Meyer, 112
Religion. *See* Bible; Christianity; God; Religious liberty
Religious Freedom Restoration Act (RFRA), 91, 187*n*12
Religious liberty: in American founding, 65–94; concluding comments on, 89–94; constitutionalism, higher law, and, 86–89, 194*nn*50–51; developmental phases of, 78–79; and Jefferson, 60, 74, 79, 84, 106; and Madison, 60, 68–74, 79–86,